Blood, Sweat, and Tears for 46 Years

Blood, Sweat, and Tears for 46 Years

THE SCIBLE "BIBLE" OF A HIGH SCHOOL FOOTBALL COACH

Jim Scible

ISBN: 1537556649
ISBN 13: 9781537556642
Library of Congress Control Number: 2016914968
CreateSpace Independent Publishing Platform
North Charleston, South Carolina

Contents

Preface

I knew when I was in the ninth grade that I wanted to be a football coach. Not many people are fortunate to be absolutely positive about how they want to live life at such a young age, but I believe I was born to be a football coach. That's why my life has been one of passion, exhilaration, despair, and most of all, hard work. My career has pretty much ruled my world, and being a coach means that I've also been a teacher. In 11 jobs in seven states, I've taught thousands of kids hundreds of lessons. Along the way—during 46 years of "blood, sweat, and tears," I've learned a lot of lessons myself, oftentimes through the school of hard knocks, including some I must say, that were caused by my own occasional stupidity or downright stubbornness!

Now after all that pain and gain, what coach worth his salt wouldn't want to share those lessons with the young, old, and anyone in between. You see, even when off the field and out of the classroom, it's in the blood: coaches coach and teachers teach. But you don't have to love high school football, or any kind of sports really, to appreciate my Coaching Points in *The Scible "Bible."* Why? Because this isn't a sports story. It's a life story. Full of adventures, and yes, a few regrets. But not many regrets, except that I didn't learn some of these lessons sooner. That's why I'm writing my story for you. *The Scible "Bible"* isn't holy, that's for sure. But it's wholly true. I mean, who'd make this up?

CHAPTER 1

You Might Have to Start as a First-grade P.E. Teacher

May as well start at the beginning. I was born 16 days after Pearl Harbor, on December 23, 1941, in beautiful Annapolis, Maryland, located on the Chesapeake Bay. It was a small, friendly, yet cosmopolitan, town. My dad served in the Army during the war and didn't meet his firstborn until I was two. Even though I was mischievous as a kid and was often punished for getting in trouble, I recall a happy childhood. I didn't do so well in school, as evidenced by my early report cards which my mom kept as memorabilia. When my children were teenagers, they found them in a box in the attic at her house, and oh boy! One of the kinder reports from my second grade teacher read, *"This is the worse child I've had in twenty years."* My mom's reply to that teacher: *"Everybody knows you're not a good judge of character."* But for years, my children teased me good-naturedly about that teacher's comment. And I teased my mother, "Hey Mom, you didn't need to save *everything!*" One thing that she did save I treasure still: a letter from my dad which he wrote to me from Japan when I was four-years-old. It reflects his great love and pride for his son, how much he missed me, and how he could hardly wait to come back home so we could play.

Junior high school is often a very difficult time for many kids, but having nothing to do with school, it was especially traumatic for me. My grandmother had been living with us for several years, and one day, while the rest of us

1

were gone, the second floor of our house caught fire. By the time my mother got back home and tried to climb the stairs to rescue her mother from her bedroom, the smoke was too heavy, and my grandmother perished. I'll never forget a neighbor picking me up from school, taking me to her house, with no explanation. I was so scared. Then when my parents arrived to tell me what had happened, I was in shock. Many times during the six months afterwards, my parents, our neighbors, and I tried to clean the upstairs with Clorox and paint to eliminate that terrible smell. But the smell—which I recall to this day—would not go away.

After we moved to a new house, and I wasn't having to relive the trauma of my grandmother's death, life gradually began to feel normal again. Then, what a blessing it was to meet a man, Coach Dick Perette, who set the course for the rest of my life. Until I moved away to go to college, he was a perfect role model, with his toughness, coupled with compassion, when I did not meet his high expectations. He inspired me to want to be like him, which led to my decision to spend my life as a teacher and a football coach.

Coaching Point:Approach life looking to find your passion. Whether this discovery happens at an early age or later in life, do what you love to do, and if possible, make a living at it.

When I got to high school where for the first time, football was offered, I couldn't wait to start playing. I loved everything about the sport—including the attention. Back in the "day"—as is still true—if you were an athlete, it seemed that girls were attracted to you, and that was cool, especially for this short, not athletically gifted young man, who was as fond of the girls as they were of me. A couple of my teammates and I were nicknamed "The Three Musketeers" because we were always getting involved in pranks. Nothing serious, but I guess I never outgrew my tendency as a kid to be mischievous and always trying to bend rules that I didn't agree with.

Even though I have to say I was just average in most areas—including athletics and especially academics—I did possess the quality of working hard in everything I did. This served me well and I became the football captain my senior year. But in that role, a super embarrassing thing happened. As the football captain, it was the tradition—and my honor—to crown the homecoming queen at halftime. That night was cold and so rainy, the field was a sea of mud. On the 50-yard line, in front of a stadium filled to standing room only, just as I was placing the crown on the queen's head, it slipped from my fingers and fell into the mud! Of course, the only thing to do was pick it up and put it on her head, which I did—mud and all. I'll never forget the specks of mud on her white dress, and when I hugged her, as was customary, no wonder her hug was not as enthusiastic as mine. And no wonder that moment made me the brunt of jokes for the rest of the season, and later was immortalized in the yearbook. A bit audaciously, I tried to date the homecoming queen, but that wasn't going to happen.

> *Coaching Point:* **No matter what—through disasters or embarrassments—it's not your APTITUDE that determines your altitude in life, but your ATTITUDE.**

During my junior and senior football seasons, my dad volunteered as a trainer to help with the players' injuries. I cherished this time—as I do even more in hindsight—because it deepened our bond and love for each other. Growing up, I just assumed that all families were like mine with a wonderful mom and dad who loved each other and their children so much. In fact, I never once saw my parents fight or be ugly to one another. Like my parents, my younger sister, Janet, also loved and supported me through thick and thin, as she does to this day. My family helped build my self-confidence, which certainly shaped my character and personality. Having seen over the years during my career how not all kids are nearly so fortunate, I've come to appreciate even more how blessed I was to be a member of this family.

———————

I finished high school with a high C average. In addition to football, I also played lacrosse. Both sports would have an impact on my future. My heart was set on attending Springfield College in Massachusetts because that's where my influential ninth-grade coach had graduated. Unfortunately, my application was rejected for insufficient grades and test scores, but I was accepted to the University of Maryland on provisional status.

I didn't get to play football my freshman year, but I did play lacrosse. I also discovered the "party" part of college. To save money, I rented a room in what had been a shut-down fraternity house, where most of the other renters were 25-year-olds who had served in Vietnam. So as an under-age 18-year-old, I was soon involved every other weekend in the Thursday afternoon–to–Sunday night drinking parties, which of course, obliterated Fridays for attending class. Even so, I did okay in most of my subjects, except chemistry and ROTC. I definitely respect the military, but I had a problem with taking orders from a college ROTC student pretending to be a general in the Army. As a result of my rebellious attitude, I never passed the course—in four semesters. I didn't pass chemistry either. Not the second time or the third. By the beginning of my junior year, three things were about to change my life: ROTC, chemistry, and a girl!

By now, I was a 20-year-old, and I had to make some decisions. Here I was in college basically because I wanted to be a teacher and a football coach, so I had to get my degree. But I couldn't pass the required chemistry course, and since my attitude towards ROTC hadn't changed, I couldn't get that done either. Plus, I was involved in my first serious romance with a girl who hadn't gone to college but worked back in my hometown. One weekend when I went to see her, I arrived early. She wasn't there, but when I let myself in, I discovered some love letters she had received from another guy. When I later asked her about them, she admitted that he was "the new love of my life." I was devastated. Not only had I kept flunking two required courses, now my heart was broken. So I called my mentor, that ninth-grade coach who had been such an inspiration to me, and with my life at rock bottom, I asked in desperation, "Now what?"

He said, "Jim, you need a change. Why don't you transfer to a small school called Shepherd College in West Virginia? I know some people there. Let me see what I can do." Well, it worked out. Neither chemistry nor ROTC was required for admission and all my credits transferred, so I was able to enter Shepherd College as a second-semester junior, in January of 1962. During the admission process, I had discussed my new direction with Mom and Dad, and true to form, they said, "If that's what you want to do, we support you 100 per cent." They agreed to continue paying my tuition and room and board, and I planned to continue earning money for incidentals during spring breaks and summer vacations.

Soon I was off to a new college where I didn't know a soul. But the next year-and-a-half got real interesting, as it involved a Marine, a girl, and new hope.

***Coaching Point:* An attitude that began to shape my life for the next 40 years: Sometimes change is not only necessary, but also good in the long run.**

Arriving at Shepherd College at the beginning of the school year's second semester, I was immediately struck by the culture shock. Coming from the University of Maryland with an enrollment of more than 20,000 and only eight miles from Washington, D.C., to a school of only 1,500 in the middle of rural West Virginia, I was in another world. Even so, life was looking up, with just three semesters away to the start of my coaching career.

Now living in a dorm instead of "Animal House," it was ironic that the first guy I met was a former Marine, although as they say, "Once a Marine, always a Marine." We hit it off immediately and became best buds for the duration of my college life. I hate to admit this, but we did some crazy things like wondering, "If we each drank a bottle of wine, could we run non-stop to Martinsburg?" That was a trek of about ten miles, and yes, we could!

Then a few weeks after my arrival, I spotted a girl in the cafeteria. What first caught my eye was her bright yellow umbrella. We started dating and everything kept getting better. I loved her, I loved this school, my grades went way up, and I even made the Dean's List, which made Mom and Dad proud. I was taking several coaching classes, I was eagerly awaiting graduation and the start of my football coaching career, but I couldn't wait to make Joan my bride. We were married during our senior year, in April of 1963.

Like most college kids, we had no money. So to support us, I worked at a horse racing track parking cars. There were about ten of us doing the job, and whoever called out the make and model first, got to park the car. It was very competitive. We worked solely for tips, and in those days, tips were pocket change, usually 25 or 50 cents, sometimes even a dollar bill, if the car owner had hit a big race.

After work I would scurry home where Joan had a hot bath waiting for me. While I was in the bathtub, she would count the change, and life went on. We ate liver and onions about five days a week because it was cheap. About a month after we got married and Joan started getting sick, I thought it must be the flu. Nope. She was pregnant. Wow! By now, it was June and being short a couple of credits, I had to go to summer school in order to graduate.

Coaching Point: **Always expect the unexpected.**

About a week before school started, I landed my first job as an elementary P.E. teacher near my hometown, and after school, traveled 45 minutes to volunteer as an assistant football coach at my alma mater, Annapolis High School. My yearly teaching salary was $4,400. That's no typo folks. It was 44-*hundred*. Rent for our new apartment, though, was $75 a month back in the day when gasoline was just 18 cents a gallon. Compared to my loose change earnings from the race track, this $4,400 felt like we'd hit the lottery. I was thrilled to be coaching finally, even as a volunteer, and for liver and onions to be on the menu only once a week. Little did we know that this job would be my first of 11 in seven states.

Coaching Point: **As another old saying goes: A lifetime journey begins with the first step.**

On my first day of teaching, facing a class of 30 first-graders, I was scared to death. None of my training had anything to do with elementary school, much less first-graders. When another teacher brought the kids out to me on the playground, they were all lined up in a row. I introduced myself, and after the teacher went back to the building, I said, "Let's line up in groups of five." At that moment, the kids scattered like quail over the entire one-acre playground. I started blowing my whistle and running all over the field trying to corral them back to me. Finally, the other teacher came outside, lined up the kids again, grabbed me by the arm, and scolded me, saying, "Hey, these are first-graders, not your football team!"

Fortunately, things got better each week. I became active in the PTA and even did some fundraising. We put on a gymnastics show for the entire school, and then did an evening show for the parents, all to raise money for gymnastics equipment.

Football coaching was going well and everything was as I'd hoped it would be.

———

During the third month of the school year, on Friday, November 22, 1963, at 3:00 PM, the world changed. When I walked into the office to sign out for the day, I saw that everybody was crying. I asked, "What's going on?" Somebody said, "Haven't you heard? President Kennedy was shot and killed in Dallas." Like everyone else around the country, I was shocked beyond belief. For the next 48 hours, Joan and I watched TV and cried. As with all of us who lived through that terrible time, this is a memory that will stay with me forever.

———

While coaching at Annapolis High School, I discovered an interesting fact. A boy who was ten years younger than me lived up the street seven houses from where I grew up. His dad was a coach at the U.S. Naval Academy by the name of Belichick, and his son—that young boy who had lived nearby—would go on to become one of the greatest NFL coaches of all times. We both started by playing football and lacrosse at Annapolis High, and we both became football coaches, but worlds apart. Many years later,

I introduced myself to Coach Bill Belichick while we both were visiting the University of Florida. He spouted off the names of many plays that we both had run as players, ten years apart, at the same high school. I found myself wishing we at least had played marbles together in the neighborhood when he was a young boy.

Coaching Point: **Be friendly and kind to EVERYONE because you never know....**

CHAPTER 2

My First Job as Head Football Coach

Well, I made it through the first semester of my first year in my chosen profession. It was Christmastime, and Joan and I were anxiously awaiting the birth of our first child. It being1963, science was not yet able to tell us whether our child would be a boy or a girl, but secretly, I was hoping for a boy.

Of much greater importance than our child's gender, was our first major financial hurdle: insurance would not cover the costs of childbirth because my wife became pregnant before I signed my first teaching contract. In Maryland, medical expenses were very high. Because Joan was originally from Delaware where costs were much less, we decided to have the baby there. In preparation for that, we made the trek throughout her pregnancy—about an hour-and-a-half drive—to her parents' home in Georgetown to see Joan's doctor there.

It was the first week in January of 1964, and from what the doctor had told us, we were expecting the baby to be born in about two weeks. I had taken Joan to her mother's house, and after making my way through a snowstorm, I finally arrived back home around five o'clock in the evening. I was in bed at 11 o'clock when I got a phone call from her mom who told me, "Get here quick! Her water just broke."

I immediately headed out in the worsening snowstorm in our *very* used Vauxhall, which was all we could afford at the time. About halfway over the seven-mile Chesapeake Bay Bridge, the driver's side windshield wiper blew off and that part of the windshield began to freeze over. So for about an hour until I arrived at the hospital, I was driving with my right hand on the steering wheel, my head out the window, and my left hand trying to keep the windshield clear.

Just after I arrived at the hospital and said a brief hello to Joan's mom, a nurse brought me my newborn son, Gregory, wrapped in a blanket. I had missed his birth by mere minutes. He hadn't even been cleaned up yet and I thought, *"Oh my God, he looks terrible!"* Later, when they brought him back to me, he looked beautiful and I was as happy as I'd ever been. His birth cost us a whopping $75, and a week later, we headed back home to Maryland.

Coaching Points: **Know that at all times—whether before your first job or between jobs, or without a job, you need health insurance. AND before a road trip—snowstorm or not—always check your windshield wipers.**

Later that spring, with mom and baby doing fine, I was at my dad's house when I decided to try to install a radio in our Vauxhall. The car was on a hill, I was lying on the front floorboard, and I guess I somehow accidentally hot-wired the car because it started lurching up the hill with me hanging out of it. I hung on for dear life and about ten feet later, it sputtered and stopped.

It cost a small fortune to have all those wires replaced, the first of many botched fix-it jobs for which I became notorious.

Coaching Point: **If you're not a handyman, pay somebody to fix things. It's cheaper.**

Another big event that spring: I coached lacrosse, and little did I know how important that would become in future years.

As the first year of my teaching and coaching career was coming to a close, I thought about how full it had been and with such opposite emotional events: the sadness of President Kennedy's assassination, then the joy of our first child's birth.

I was looking forward to the summer and to my second year of teaching and coaching, and also eager to move on to teaching in high school, but there were no openings at the time. With an annual salary of only $4,400, I certainly couldn't lounge around and enjoy the summer. So I got a good-paying construction job at the Naval Academy where they were rebuilding one of the big dorm buildings. During my first two weeks, I ran a jackhammer that busted up concrete floors on four stories. After that, I spent ten hours a day wheeling out liquid concrete to build the new floors. Needless to say, it was such hard physical work that I could hardly wait for school to start. Teaching and coaching were a piece of cake compared to that construction work.

The upside of that grueling summer was the extra money I earned which enabled Joan and me to make a down payment on our first brand new car. It was a green Volkswagen Beetle that cost $1,800, almost half of my regular annual salary. But going from an old Vauxhall to a new Volkswagen was a real treat. Maybe I loved German vehicles, or maybe I just liked the "V's" which stand for victory!

My wife's mom, Fannie Bell, called one evening in early August to tell us that she saw an ad for a teaching/coaching position at a school in Bethany Beach, Delaware. She said that she knew someone on the school board there and that maybe I should apply. Well, I did apply, and the next week they called and asked me to come in for an interview. Man, I was on fire! The position was at a very small K-12 school, Lord Baltimore High. The position involved being the school's athletic director and head football coach, and head basketball coach, and head track coach, and physical education teacher, *and* summer recreation director. What? Talk about wearing many hats! The interview went well I thought, and sure enough, a week later I was offered the job. I accepted, quit my construction job, and we started planning our move.

So I went from being an elementary teacher and an assistant high school football coach to basically being in charge of everything. It was a very small school with only about 300 kids from kindergarten to twelfth grade. But I was proud to have my first head coaching job at the ripe old age of 22.

We rented a house with three bedrooms in a great location about half a mile from the school and about two miles from Bethany Beach, which was on the Atlantic Ocean. Thus began my second passion in life: my love for the ocean and the beach. But my first passion would become a challenge. I knew I was lucky to have secured this job at such a young age, but once school started, I was about to learn some big lessons about kids, teaching, and coaching.

Coaching Point: **Sometimes when jumping into a new job, it's "better to be lucky than good"—until your experience catches up with your enthusiasm.**

CHAPTER 3

A Two-man Coaching Staff Wears Many Hats

That August of 1964, after accepting my new job and moving from Annapolis, Maryland to Bethany Beach, Delaware, was a joy. We loved going to the beach almost every day, and every weekend we visited Joan's mom and dad, who lived only 18 miles away. We got our first dog, a boxer we named Michael after our son's middle name, and at seven months old, Gregory had finally moved out of his 20-hour a day colic phase. For the first time since he was born, Joan and I weren't having to take turns walking or rocking him almost 24/7. I was eagerly preparing to be a head football coach, among my other duties at Lord Baltimore High, but mainly I loved where we lived, so close to the ocean.

Located in Sussex County, Bethany Beach's main industries were farming and raising chickens. We had to travel miles to the nearest grocery store or for any kind of shopping—the place was so small, except in the summer when it was bustling with tourists who'd come to the beach. These days, 50 years later, this part of the country is the playground of the Washington, D.C. crowd, and I'm sure that many homes in Bethany Beach are now priced in the million-dollar range. But back then, with my annual salary of $4,900—a $500 increase from Annapolis—we could afford only to rent, because even when property values in 1964 were pennies on the dollar of today's valuations, being a homeowner was out of my range.

Lord Baltimore High and I began the school year in September. Until the last week before then, I wasn't counting on any coaching help at all. Zilch. None. But lucky for me, just a few days before school started, they hired a new teacher from somewhere named Pete DeSimone. His duties were to be a teacher, assistant football coach, head girls' basketball coach, and head baseball coach. He was a first-year teacher with even less coaching experience than I had—he had *no* coaching experience. Quite a staff, right?

At our first football practice, 15 boys showed up to be on the team. Our goals were modest: that no one get injured and that we'd have a respectable year. Our offense consisted of the "I" formation with a few basic plays. And on defense, we used the tried-and-true 5-2 (now called the 3-4). The kids were great and played hard, but basically, we had limited talent and finished the year with only three wins. At least we had no serious injuries. Our stadium consisted of one baseball bleacher that held 100 people, maybe. Sometimes we got a standing room crowd of a few more than 100, but usually not.

I learned a lot about being a coach that year because Pete and I had to do everything—including chalk the field, cut the grass, wash the uniforms, and drive the bus.

I enjoyed the teaching because my classes were small, and most days the superintendent would stop by my office and we'd chat about anything. Outside, the kids would be playing a game of touch football or basketball and just having fun, totally unsupervised. No way would that happen today.

Coaching Point: **When you are young, be eager to learn and willing to do more than what is asked of you. In fact, that's a great philosophy at any age.**

The football season ended on a Friday, and the following Monday, we started basketball practice. Up to now, the full extent of my experience in basketball had been as a spectator at some of my high school games. So right after I was hired for this job back in August, I ordered a coaching basketball handbook that included the essential 1-3-1 defense. Toward the end of our school's football season, between watching college football on Saturdays and pro games on Sundays, I glanced at it a few times

On that first day of basketball practice, we made an announcement that boys' and girls' tryouts would begin at three o'clock for the girls' team, and six o'clock for the boys'. As the only coaches for everything, we decided to split our duties so that Pete coached the girls and I coached the boys. When six o'clock rolled around, I was sitting in the gym when the candidates for my team arrived. Turns out, 15 boys showed up—my entire football team! I'd said I planned to keep only 12, but I just couldn't cut three of my football players, so I told them that maybe 15 would be okay as long as they all came to practice every day.

Little did I know that ten of those boys had played basketball the previous two years. I wasn't a good judge of basketball talent, but as the pre-season began, I thought they looked pretty good. They didn't know about my lack of basketball knowledge. They just accepted what we did during practice and worked hard.

———◆———

If you are a young person now, it's hard to relate to the sports world of 1964. ESPN didn't exist and even the pro athletes got different jobs in their off-season. Kids got to be kids: they weren't pigeonholed into one specific sport by overzealous coaches or parents. There was no off-season conditioning such as lifting weights, and kids played every sport they wanted throughout the school year. Then, during the summer, they worked a job. Looking back, I think this was the best of times for kids, coaches—and parents!

———◆———

To augment my meager basketball knowledge, I kept that little basketball coaching handbook hidden in my file cabinet, and read some of it each day to expand on what we had done the day before. I did know about hard work and conditioning, and during our three-hour practices, we covered drills, ball handling, dribbling, shooting, and full scrimmages. Each practice also included half an hour of "suicide" conditioning—dozens of all-out sprints up and down the basketball court. Coaches used to say back then—and many still do—"We're gonna run ya' 'til ya' puke." We didn't mean that literally, but a bucket was always handy for those who needed it. And this conditioning started developing a pretty darn good-looking team.

Because at heart I was still their football coach, I'd add a little something different when practice was over. After the players took about a five-minute water break, I brought out the footballs and ran plays in the gym for about 15 minutes. Imagine doing something like that today—when rules limit practices with balls for each sport to certain well-defined dates. It'd be probation here we come!

In our basketball program, we had a boys' varsity team and a girls' varsity team. The girls played at six o'clock and the boys played at 7:30. After expecting only about 100 spectators—if that—during football season, I was shocked when for the first home game for girls' basketball, the gym was packed. Standing room only. Altogether, about 300 or 400. *What is this?*, I thought. That's when I discovered that Lord Baltimore was a basketball school, and that the crowds loved watching both the girls' and the boys' teams equally. Even though Pete had a coaching handbook like I did, he later told me that he never knew girls' basketball had six players and not five, until he read the book. These girls were talented too, and he coached them as tough as I coached the boys.

We won our district hands-down and were headed to the playoffs. Football is all I had ever known, but I began to think maybe I was destined to be a basketball coach. More on that when next year's story rolls around.

During the latter part of this season, we played in four playoff games. The first three were all overtime games. Toward the end of the third game, during the second consecutive overtime, I told the team during a timeout, "Let's win this game before I have a heart attack." Well, we did win it, and I didn't have a heart attack. But something weird happened the following week. I started feeling sick, so sick that I had to go to the doctor. I asked him, "Do I have the flu?" He said, "No, but you have something much more serious. You have mumps, and you have *got* to stay in bed because if this gets worse, you could become sterile." When I told him I had a big playoff game Friday and that I *had* to be there, he replied, "I'm sorry about that, but I'm *telling* you: Go home and go to bed."

I called Pete and told him he would have to take the team this week because of the mumps. Joan and I agreed that this was best, so I stayed home all week. But late on game day, I couldn't help myself. I said to Joan, "I'm going to the game, and I'm going to coach my team, to hell with the mumps!" She retorted, "You're gonna sacrifice our future family for the sake of a basketball game?" "Hell, yeah!" I fired back, as I stormed out the door. When I walked in to the locker room about an hour before the start of the game, the kids jumped up when they saw me and started cheering. I was taken aback and tears sprang to my eyes. But I quickly gathered myself and said, "Enough of this crap. We've got a ball game to win."

It was close, but we lost that game, and our season came to an end. But, thank goodness, not my ability to reproduce! Life went on as normal, although I often wondered how I would have felt if that doctor's prediction had turned out to be true. It's one thing to lose a game but looking back, I can't imagine never having had our other child.

Coaching Point: **If you're going be a coach—or in any career—and make a decision based on your passion and impulses, saying "to hell with the consequences," you sure as heck better be lucky.**

CHAPTER 4

Frank Glazier and the Beach

After basketball season, I began looking into football coaching clinics. A football clinic is a one-to-three-day seminar, held at an out-of-town hotel, where you go and listen to various topics all about football. Even though it was difficult to get away, I had attended several football clinics earlier in basketball season, and now it was time to get serious.

I had become friends with one of my main competitor coaches in the district, Frank Glazier. With basketball season over, we were able to go to two of the biggest football clinics in the East. The first was in Atlantic City, New Jersey. It began on a Friday night and ended the following Sunday at noon. That's when I started to learn a lot from Coach Glazier, even though he was one of our biggest opponents. He took about five legal pads and plenty of pencils into each session, and we sat together for three days through every session. We'd talk football for what must have been 20 hours a day. That clinic turned out to be the beginning of my true "football coaching education" which would carry me through the next 40 years.

At night after these sessions were over, we'd go to someone's room and talk more football, and drink beer. That's when the stories began to fly. The second most exciting time of the year, beyond the season itself, was the gossip about who was getting fired and what jobs were going to be opening up. This talk was exciting and I loved it. But I learned from Frank that the real purpose of these clinics was to learn, learn, learn—not to network and drink. We certainly did enjoy the latter, but not until after the work was done.

Our second big trip was the Kodak Coach of the Year Clinic in Washington, D.C. I met Frank at his house at noon on Friday, and we arrived at the fancy D.C. hotel around five o'clock that evening. We checked in, and the first thing I remember seeing as I walked toward my room were two guys, half-naked, chasing a third guy down the hall while shouting and shooting a fire extinguisher. Obviously, these coaches had started drinking already, even before the first session. This football clinic was owned by Michigan coach Duffy Daugherty and the legendary Bud Wilkinson of Oklahoma. We listened to some fantastic speakers and learned many innovative ideas that would help us be more competitive and successful in our own coaching.

On Saturday evening at five o'clock, after the last speaker, all the coaches were told to leave the ballroom so that the D.C. beer distributors could set up for the free Beer Blast to be held between eight and ten. Oh boy, did this young coach get an education as to how crazy some of these coaches could get. But that's not the only reason the Beer Blast was such an memorable experience. Suddenly the noise of 2,000 coaches drinking and talking just ceased. I looked around to see what was happening, and that's when I saw, coming down the short steps not five feet from me—THE coach, Vince Lombardi. WOW! Nervously and in awe, I managed to say, "Hello, Coach Lombardi," and I was thrilled when he nodded his head.

Another highlight of that clinic happened on Sunday morning. I was waiting for an elevator when the door opened and there stood Alabama coach Bear Bryant with his wife. I had no choice but to gather my wits and say respectfully, "Good morning, Coach Bryant." He replied in his gruff voice, "Hello, young man." So in less than 24 hours, I had seen and spoken to two legends. And they had acknowledged me!

Later that morning, coaches Daugherty and Wilkinson addressed the crowd pointedly. "Boys," said Coach Daugherty, "If you can't show a little restraint in your behavior on Saturday nights, we're not having the Beer Blast anymore." That ultimatum was followed by Coach Wilkinson's blast to the heart. "Coaches," he said, "I have one question. If your players had been with you last night, would they have been proud of you?" Many heads lowered.

Coaching Point: **To excel in your career, be a lifelong learner while, at the same time, remember that moderation in (most) everything is better than excess.**

During the spring, I coached track. But because we didn't have a track, we trained by having the boys run to the beach where I met them in my Volkswagen Beetle. I was able to drive on the beach because the sand was hard-packed, and with no spring breakers around—it was 1965—we pretty much had the beach to ourselves. I would drive behind them, giving my coaching instructions on a bullhorn as to how I wanted them to run: fast, slow, sideways. Then after about an hour, they'd have to turn around and run back to the school. We had built a modified high-jump and long-jump pit, so several on the team practiced those events. We also had purchased a shot put and discus, so other team members practiced with those in an end zone. No doubt we had an unsophisticated program, but we were proud to win two of the five track meets that season.

Also during that spring, Coach Glazier and I talked two or three times a week, comparing notes about what we'd learned at the football clinics. This was unusual because after all, we knew we would be opponents in the fall. Our conversations may have been good for both of us, but I'm sure they were good for me because he was so much older and wiser. My football knowledge expanded greatly, thanks to Frank Glazier.

During the summer, I was in charge of the recreational programs for the first through twelfth graders. Because these programs ran only from 9AM to noon, I was able to get a great temporary job from midnight to 8AM at a local hotel as a night desk clerk and auditor for the previous day's receipts.

Lots of interesting things happen at a hotel after midnight. I even learned that some people just want to rent a room for a few hours. I guess they just needed a cat nap! Hmmm. After I was replaced near the end of the summer by someone able to work permanently, a friend of mine called and said he heard of a part-time night job as a "chicken catcher." I said, "A what?"

Seems there were lots of chicken-growing farms in the area. Chicken catchers would go in for a five-hour shift beginning at 10PM, enter the chicken coop, get on their hands and knees in the dark, grab the chickens by their legs, and then crate the chickens for shipment. It was a dirty, smelly, nasty job, but I made good money, even better than the hotel job. We were paid by the number of chickens we caught and I was fast. What a relief that this job lasted for only two weeks before school started. I couldn't wait.

Coaching Point: **Early in your career, you may have to work at many different, sometimes unpleasant, jobs to earn extra money. But don't be afraid to get your hands dirty. Hard work is good for you. It makes you appreciate other hard workers, and also your "real job."**

CHAPTER 5

Integration and the Jersey Job

In early August of 1965, some important things were about to happen around the country and in southern Delaware. We got word that when school started, we would accept black students for the first time ever and none of us knew what to expect.

That first day of school, several of my players came to me and said, "Coach, there are some black boys asking around about who is the Phys Ed coach?" My players said they thought the other boys meant who's the football coach, so my players said they were going to send them to me.

Back when I was in high school, there was another school, Bates High, where all the black kids went, so this was my first experience in dealing with young black kids. People have often said they thought Northern schools were *always* integrated. Nope, not so.

Later that same morning, seven or eight young black men came to my office and introduced themselves. They wanted to know if they could play football. I asked them if they had ever played organized football before, and they said no. I sent them to a local doctor and soon they all came back with results of good physicals in hand. Pete and I outfitted them with pants, helmets, shoulder pads, and cleats. I told them to show up immediately after school, ready to go to work.

The biggest of these young men was "Big Dog Holden." Later that day, we were having our first full contact scrimmage, and I asked "Big Dog" if he wanted to play defensive tackle. He responded, "Yup." So I walked him into the defensive huddle and told him to line up on the tackle. He wasn't sure what to do, so I said, "Just hit him with your forearm and go tackle the guy with the ball." And, tackle he did, play after play after play. He was so dominant that we finally had to temporarily remove him from the scrimmage so that it would be more equal for the other players.

Several other new players were nearly as talented, and it looked like the fortune of our team was about to improve dramatically.

The next day we were working on special teams which involved all phases of the kicking game: kickoffs, extra points, punts, and field goals. The players looked pitiful, particularly on kickoffs when nobody who had tried was able to kick the ball more than 25 yards. Finally, "Big Dog" asked if he could try the kick-off, and of course we said yes. He took two or three steps and then kicked it out of the end zone. WOW! We'd just found our kick-off man.

At the end of practices, our kids would usually just catch a ride home, or their parents would come pick them up. There was no activity bus. When I asked my new players how they were going to get home, they said, "We'll just walk." When I asked how far away they lived, they said, "About seven or eight miles." By then I had a station wagon, so I told them to jump in back. They were all pretty happy as off we went. About an hour later, after dropping them off, I got back to school and then headed home. This became my daily routine for the rest of the season. But at first, after about a week of this, I started getting phone calls from some of the parents and townspeople complaining about my "showing favorites." "Well," I answered, "If *your* son lived eight miles from school and had no ride, I would do the same for him."

Late one Friday afternoon, as we were loading equipment onto the bus that would take us to our away game, we noticed that one of our new key players was missing. I asked if anybody had seen him, and nobody had. About five minutes before the bus was scheduled to leave, the missing player showed up out of breath. He looked stricken. Huffing and puffing, he said, "I'm sorry I'm late, but we had an accident at our house—my mother shot and killed my father and I had to stay with the police and help clean up before I could leave." Stopping for a moment to catch his breath, he pleaded, "I can still play, can't I?" Stunned, I gave him a hug, and said, "Of course you can." He burst into tears as he said, "Thank you, Coach," and jumped on the bus.

———

We all learned some valuable lessons that year. Without regard to black or white, the boys meshed and got along very well, focused more on the team and winning games, than on the racial differences that sometimes preoccupied their parents.

———

Coaching Point: **Not just in football, but also in life, be ready for change because it's inevitable. Embrace it!**

———

Happily, that football season was a reversal of my first year. We ended up winning seven games, instead of only three, and we even beat my buddy Frank Glazier's team. This was a huge moment for me. Against my mentor, I had won!

Unlike our good fortune in football, my second season of basketball was not nearly as successful. This time, some of the strategies that I had used during the first season just didn't work. One night after a couple of losses, I realized a very important fact: In coaching, as in life, it's not "always the X's and O's that matter, it's the Jimmie's and the Joe's."

Coaching Point: **Even more important to success than your strategy or game plan, are the people who will execute that plan.**

In simple terms, what happened was that most of our winning team had graduated the previous year, and now that expert basketball coaching was needed, my lack of experience was painfully evident. Coaching is important, but a team's talent is equally if not more important. That's why in college athletics, the best coaches know the significance of recruiting.

In any event, I guess I was really meant to be a football coach after all. With no remorse whatsoever, it turned out that would be my last encounter coaching basketball. My days of faking it as a basketball coach were over.

Coaching Point: If you're going to fake it, you can fake it only for so long. But when the jig is up, good can come out of change.

Meantime, Frank and I continued learning and sharing ideas about football. We steadily increased our attendance at clinics, and from the end of January through February, we traveled to a clinic nearly every weekend. Many nights my phone would ring at one or two in the morning, and Frank would say, "Get your pad out. I have some more ideas on this 'new offense.'" He would explain what he was thinking, and then we might talk for another hour or so.

One day, Frank called me and said, "I'm taking a new job in New Jersey and I wonder if you want to go along as my top assistant." Over the next several days, Joan and I talked about it, and plans were set for me to go interview. The interview went well, and a week later I was hired.

So now, I was leaving a rural Delaware school of 300 students in twelve grades, to go to Bergenfield, New Jersey, a bedroom community of New York City, to a high school of 2,000 students. Another culture shock. Little did I know the impact *this* move would have on my entire coaching career. I was all of 24-years-old.

For the next several months before making the move, Frank and I looked at every football film from Bergenfield High School's last football season. We compiled a book of over 100 pages that would serve as our blueprint for the new football program, including our offense and defense.

Coaching Point: **If you're going to be a career coach, consider buying stock in U-Haul. Seriously.**

The U-Haul was packed and we moved to our new garage apartment in Bergenfield in late May. Although it seemed like we were moving to another world, it was really just 210 miles north. Driving up the New Jersey Turnpike didn't sit too well with our three-year-old son, Gregory. The smell of the chemical plants along the way made him so nauseous, he kept vomiting. But we arrived, settled in, and on Monday, I went to work.

About ten days later, my world was rocked.

Frank Glazier, my boss and mentor, had a massive heart attack. The doctor absolutely insisted that Frank could not coach for at least a year.

The school board met and asked me to take his job. I was certainly ill-equipped to assume this position, but I was young and self-assured enough to give it my best shot.

The first thing I did was to spout off to the press about the book Frank and I had put together as a blueprint of every opponent, and audaciously guaranteed an opening night victory. My second big move was to demand that the school change its nickname from the Mighty Mites to the Bears.

Both moves would come back to haunt my short stay at BHS. In the fourth quarter of that opening game, as we were losing badly, spectators in the visitor stands were on their feet shaking their newspapers, mocking my prediction of a guaranteed win. We went on to lose just about every game after that, and yet I was eager to start my second year with renewed enthusiasm.

Coaching Point: **If you're going to be arrogant, be prepared to eat crow, but don't let it choke your passion.**

I was still so excited about being head football coach that we decided to buy a house and settle in. We found a great home about 20 miles from the school. Houses were expensive even then in North Jersey, and I had to borrow

$3,000—about 30 per cent of my $9,500 annual salary—from my parents for the down payment. All this was happening in late February of 1967.

In late March, I heard about a job opening at Lehigh University in Bethlehem, Pennsylvania for a head freshman football coach and a head lacrosse coach. Even though we were due to close on our new house in early April, I sent my application to Lehigh, and they called me to come in for an interview. A week later, Coach Dunlap, the head football coach there, called and offered me the job.

I felt both total excitement and total fear after calling the real estate company and being told, "Your $3,000 deposit is non-refundable." What now?

My lifetime dream of coaching in college was on the brink of becoming a reality. If I turned this opportunity down, would I ever get another chance? Joan and I had a huge decision to make.

Here's what we did. We bought the Bergenfield, New Jersey house the next week from the real estate company, and then sold it back to them 30 minutes later, having never slept a single night there. They kept the $3,000, and I took the job at Lehigh University in Bethlehem, Pennsylvania. Although it was a very expensive decision, it was one I never regretted.

We paid my mom and dad in installments over the next four years, until the $3,000 debt was paid in full.

And I was off to be a college coach!

Coaching Point: If you're going to borrow money from your parents, one way or another you have to pay it back.

CHAPTER 6

College Coaching or Bust

For the fourth time in my young career, time to pack up the U-Haul. We were on our way to Bethlehem, Pennsylvania and Lehigh University.

After losing $3,000 on a house we never lived in, we opted this time to rent a house. The university was located on one side of the mountain and our rental was on the opposite side, in Saucon Valley in the town of Coopersburg. With lots of trees and small farms everywhere, the openness felt totally different from North Jersey. It was so peaceful, it was like we had moved to another new world.

Lehigh University is a prominent engineering school, and in 1967, its nickname was the Engineers. Admission requirements were very high and our athletes were obviously very smart and very motivated. This was my entrance to college coaching.

Our offices were located over the mountain at the university. I remember making this one-mile drive back and forth over the mountain several times a day—in sunshine, rain, or snow. Our practice facilities were located near the area where our house was, and most days, I left for work in the dark and returned after dark.

College coaching is much different from high school coaching mainly because of the recruiting. Recruiting is the lifeblood of a football program and it never stops. No "Jimmies 'n Joes," no job!

I began work almost immediately upon my arrival in June. My duties were head freshman football coach, physical education instructor (three classes a week), head lacrosse coach, and the coach in charge of recruiting, which meant I organized all the weekend visits, professors' meetings with recruits, weekend meals, and transportation for recruits. My recruiting areas included some local schools in the Bethlehem area, South New Jersey, Philadelphia and a few of its surrounding counties, Delaware, and Washington, D.C.

Most people think college football recruitment works this way: if a school wants a player, the school offers that athlete a scholarship, which the athlete then either accepts or not. But that's not how it works in the Ivy League and at schools like Lehigh. We'd evaluate a young man on three key factors. First, he had to be a good football player who we wanted, and with good character. Secondly, he had to be an outstanding student with high test scores. Lastly, we hoped he came from a family with limited finances because our scholarships were based on something called the PCS, the Parents' Confidential Statement. This calculated a family's income with the cost of the Lehigh University tuition, and then produced a figure we could offer the student. But if a student came from a wealthy family, we could offer him no money, regardless of his athletic ability. We competed with the Ivy League for players and our recruiting was ongoing for 12 months a year. Traveling for these recruiting efforts usually meant I drove my own car, leaving on Sunday afternoon and returning Friday afternoon, and then getting ready for the recruits' visits over the weekend.

Coaching Point: **As I realized very quickly, you can work a lot harder than you think you can.**

When I arrived in June, the other coaches were enjoying a two-week vacation. But that didn't mean they could be gone for two weeks straight. Coaches were expected to come into the office periodically to follow up on our incoming recruits and to see whatever else was going on.

When everybody got back from vacation, we started getting ready for full-speed coaching. At first, we didn't have to be at work until around eight in the morning, and we usually left around six in the evening, but this would change once the players reported for fall practice. At that point, our daily schedule started at 6AM and lasted until we were done, which was usually around 9 or 10PM.

As the head freshman football coach, I had two part-time assistants working with me. Except when I was teaching my classes, I attended all staff meetings, which I was happy to do because being a full-time college coach meant I no longer had to attend faculty meetings like I did while teaching in high school. So not only was I learning new offenses, defenses, and strategies for college football, I also had no more worries related to the typical high school problems, such as players skipping practice. These players were all there, every day.

Keeping a college coaching job depends almost exclusively on a season's wins and losses. So it was very important for all of us to get off to a fast start and win our first game. I was assigned to do something that, although was prevalent at the time, I realized later wasn't exactly playing by the rules. Because I was young and looked like a graduate student, I went to the practice sessions of our first opponent and was able to blend in while I hung around to become familiar with their game plan. My subsequent reports on what I observed were very valuable as we prepared for this first game, and during the game itself, I made sure I was nowhere near the sideline or press box so that no one on the opposing side would recognize me. I was ecstatic that we won that opening game and that my inside knowledge proved to be beneficial.

Earlier, each coach had been assigned to study two or three opponents, and we spent the summer breaking down their films and compiling preliminary game plans. This way, before we played each team, we knew some of their tendencies on offense and defense. Then the week right before we were to play that opponent, I was assigned to scout their game against *their* opponent that week, and present a detailed report to our staff.

In addition, all teams swapped films from their three previous games, which we all spent many hours studying to get our opponents' tendencies on offense and defense. It still works the same way today, but no one scouts a team in person anymore. Because of today's technology, everyone now has the ability to get every game film exchanged digitally on the internet.

Several weeks into the season, I was scouting Army at West Point, while Lehigh was playing in South Carolina at The Citadel. That Saturday night when I got home, I received a phone call from the head coach who said, "Get into the office immediately." This was around midnight and I was scared to death that I had done something wrong. When I walked into the staff room, everyone was just looking around at each other with blank looks on their faces like something terrible had happened.

Coaching Point: You never know what tomorrow will bring, so best you can, be prepared. But truthfully, there are times when there's no way to prepare for what life is going to hand you.

Then came the news. Our offensive coordinator, Coach Jim McConalogue, had been on his way out of the press box at halftime during the Citadel game, when he suddenly collapsed and died of a heart attack. Our entire staff was in a state of shock. Head Coach Dunlap explained that funeral arrangements would be announced in a few days, but for now, there would have to be some staff changes. First, he announced that Coach John Whitehead would move to offensive coordinator as well as continuing as offensive line coach. Then, Dunlap floored me when he said, "And Coach Jim Scible will move from freshman head coach to the position of varsity running back coach." He also told me that I would move my office to Coach Whitehead's office and that this would take place on Monday morning.

Driving home, still in shock, it occurred to me, _This is the second time in two years I've been promoted because of a fellow coach's heart attack._ Certainly not the way I would have chosen to advance my career, and again, as before, I felt apprehensive about taking on significantly more responsibility with so little advance preparation.

John Whitehead was a big and physically imposing man in his 40s who had been a legendary high school coach in Pennsylvania before coming to Lehigh the previous year. He loved players from Pennsylvania, but sometimes was not as tolerant of players from other states. I could tell, too, that he was not enamored with this younger 26-year-old sharing his office space and working side-by-side with him every day. Not only that, Coach Whitehead was a very strong personality and definitely not a morning person.

When I arrived for work Monday morning, I noticed that all the furnishings from my office had already been moved in with Coach Whitehead's. It was 6AM—that's when the work week started—and I walked into the office cheerfully saying, "Good Morning, Coach." I got no response. So right away I thought, "*How is* this *going to work out?*"

The three Phys Ed classes I taught met from 7 to 9AM Monday, Tuesday, and Wednesday. So that Monday, I left my new office around 6:45 and headed to my first class, where as usual, the students would participate in their choice of basketball, lifting weights, or volleyball.

Meanwhile, downstairs, each morning at 7:30, a staff meeting with the football coaches was being held which, during the first part of the week, I never attended because as the freshman coach, I had these teaching duties. This Monday, as usual, I was upstairs in the gym with my Phys Ed students when around 7:35, a graduate assistant came running in and whispered to me, "Coach Dunlap says you better get your butt immediately to the staff meeting." I was stunned and confused, thinking, *How can I be in two places at once?* But I rushed downstairs, and when I walked in, Coach blurted out, "You'd better work something out with those classes of yours because you're now on the varsity football staff." I nodded and said, "Yes sir."

I arranged to have my classes covered by a Phys Ed equipment person. He took roll every day, and whoever showed up for roll call at least 90 percent of the time got an "A" in the course. So much for my teaching duties.

From then on, I would walk into our office every morning, sit at my desk next to Coach Whitehead, and work on what I thought I should be doing, until around 10:45, when John would look up and say, "All right let's get to work." He'd then go to the chalkboard and we'd begin game planning and practice preparation.

Our weeks went this way: Monday through Wednesday, arrive at 6AM, have lunch at my desk, and at 3:45, head to the practice field. We finished practice around 6:30 in the evening, and then we went to the training table and ate with the players. At around 7:30, we headed back to the office for a staff meeting, then more film study until around 10PM. Then around 10:30, Coach Dunlap dismissed us to go home. On Thursday, we were allowed to come in at eight in the morning and work on recruiting until about 11AM, and then we headed out on recruitment visits to our assigned high schools which were within a 45-minute drive.

On Friday nights, whether for home or away games, the team and coaches stayed in a hotel. On Saturday mornings, we'd have a light breakfast with the players around 7AM, followed by offensive and defensive walk-throughs in either the hotel or the parking lot. The pre-game meal was at 11AM. Then the players who needed it got physical therapy treatment and all the players got their ankles taped before being ready to play at 1PM.

After the game, if we were on the road, we'd have a post-game meal, then by either bus or plane, travel back to campus. After the players put away their equipment and got treated for any injuries, we all headed home, usually around midnight. The great joy in our week was when we won, and especially when we won our home games because there was no travel involved and we all got home by 5PM. During three months of football season, these five or six Saturdays of home games were the only times we'd get home before dark. On Sundays, we were back in the office at 6AM, grading our players on the previous day's game. We compiled a scouting report for the players and began film study on the next week's opponent. Around 2PM Sunday, after the players arrived, we watched the game film, distributed the scouting reports, and gave the players their grades for yesterday's game. At 4PM, we all went to the practice field and had a short one-hour workout, followed by the team meal at 5:30. After that, the players went home, while the coaches headed back to begin more film breakdown and have a final quick meeting before heading home around 11PM.

Monday morning at 6AM, the same weekly routine started all over again. During these 16-hour days, we saw very little of our families, and 80-to-100-hour work weeks were typical. Let me tell you, it takes a very special woman to be the wife of a college or pro football coach.

Coaching Point: **The choice of a supportive mate and your ability to work long hours if need be, are essential to professional success.**

CHAPTER 7

Could I Be Fired My First Season as a College Coach?

My first year at Lehigh University—my first of college coaching—was so chockful of new experiences and tumultuous events that this young inexperienced coach was nearly overwhelmed. Our staff of nine was organized into specific offensive and defensive coaches, based on what each of us would coach both on and off the field. Each coach also had a non-coaching responsibility which was just as important as our coaching. Among these: scouting, personnel, recruiting, equipment purchases and maintenance, research and development of new strategies, and alumni relations. My assigned area was organizing the recruiting program for the other coaches. In addition to their coaching and other non-coaching responsibilities, each coach was assigned a specific geographic area from which to recruit. As I've said, I was responsible for coordinating all campus weekend visits for the potential recruits, including setting up transportation arrangements for all the incoming players. A big job.

Dealing with on-the-field football coaching, plus recruiting, while also preparing to be a lacrosse coach left my head spinning sometimes. However, the thrill and excitement of actually being a college football coach exceeded my wildest expectations.

Because most of what I learned these first two years set the foundation for how I would coach offense for the rest of my 46-year career, the learning experience was priceless.

Coaching Point: **Taking advantage of every opportunity to learn new skills should be a cornerstone in life.**

I couldn't help but be disappointed, though, that as far as wins and losses were concerned, we weren't having a great year. Going into our last game, against our oldest rival Lafayette College, Coach Dunlap said, "We have to win this one or we'll probably all be fired." To make us feel better about the pressure we were under, he also told us it would be okay to have our sons—if they were ten-years-old or older—join us on the sideline during the game. But it didn't help when he added, "Because this may be the last time your sons get to see you coach." My son, Gregg, because he was only four at the time, missed that experience, although I was able to enjoy his presence on the sideline hundreds of times in years to come when he played and coached for me. Here in 1967, this game against Lafayette was so intense with the scoring and lead going back and forth, we were thrilled to finally pull out a win—and hugely relieved when we all soon received new contracts.

As soon as the football season was over in late November, we hit the re-cruiting trail hard. We each left for our respective locales on Sunday after-noons, and were required to visit five schools a day for four or five days a week. At night, we were usually on the phone following up with our potential recruits. On Friday mornings, I'd head back to campus to complete all the arrangements for our recruiting weekend. We hosted 10 to 15 recruits on our campus every weekend through March. They'd arrive Saturday morning and each was met by his assigned coach. The recruits then proceeded to our offices where they were interviewed by the head coach, before heading off to meet a professor in the area where they might major academically. At noon, we provided a luncheon for them, and then each was met by his student host for the weekend. Saturday afternoon and evening, the recruits attended a bas-ketball game, followed by a fraternity party or some other social event. On Sunday morning, we all met for breakfast and then said our goodbyes before the recruits headed home. Then the coaching staff went back to work, evaluating the players and the weekend. By around one o'clock that afternoon, we'd finally head home to be with our families for just a few hours before heading back out again to recruit.

Coaching Point: **Long days and long nights don't feel so long when you're working in a career you love. So make sure you choose your career wisely, for as the saying goes, "If you work in a profession you love, you'll never work a day in your life."**

Despite the long hours and time away from my family, that first and second year were exciting for me professionally as I got to meet a lot of coaches and visit many schools. By January, my duties included organizing my lacrosse team for practice that would begin on January 15th. The soccer coach, Coach Mike, one of my assistants who handled most of the pre-season conditioning, had a huge influence on me regarding physical fitness. He was a dedicated runner and introduced me to the joy of daily exercise, which I've continued throughout my life to this day.

Coaching Point: **Staying physically fit is important not only for good health, but also for managing professional and personal stress. So make some kind of exercise part of your daily life.**

We had an exciting lacrosse season which included travel to many other campuses such as Penn State, the U.S. Naval Academy, and Rutgers. I loved being head coach of my own team and enjoyed working with the players. But even as the lacrosse season was in progress, my duties as a football coach continued every day. What with recruiting, research and development, plus planning for each practice during spring football, my life was a whirlwind.

By the time spring football practice began, our lacrosse season was almost over. But because football was my primary responsibility, sometimes I had to schedule lacrosse practice afterwards under the lights.

When the school year was finally over and summer was approaching, we looked forward to a break. All coaches were given a two-week vacation, but as I'd already discovered when I first arrived, we were expected to be gone no more than two or three days in a row. During vacation, I usually went into the office for an hour or two each day following up with recruits and checking on the players' summer conditioning program.

My second year at Lehigh was a blur, somewhat a repeat of the first year. I was more comfortable in my dual roles, and I think Coach Whitehead was more comfortable with me. I felt I finally had some say in the formulation of game plans and game-day responsibilities.

But several memories of that season do stand out, although for different reasons.

Each coach was responsible for the study of three opposing teams during the off-season. So during the summer months, we studied those teams' game films, gathering the teams' tendencies on down and distance, hash marks and formations. One of my teams was the University of Delaware, a powerhouse program that ran the wing-T formation. This team was coached by the legendary Tubby Raymond and was a perpetual thorn in our side. They had killed us the previous year with a play called the half-to-half reverse. Now I knew this play very well because I had studied it in detail from their last season's game films.

But when we were getting ready to play Delaware this season, Coach Dunlap said, "Jim, I don't see the half-to-half play in your scouting report." I replied, "Coach, they haven't run this play all year. I suppose it's not in their plan this year." Well, of course, you can predict what happened. The third play of the game they busted that play for an 80-yard touchdown. And they ran it again, several other times, for huge gains. Naturally, I got the evil eye from Coach Dunlap throughout the game, but was relieved I wasn't fired on the spot when he came up to me after our devastating loss and said, "You damn well better study your opponents a little more thoroughly in the future." Even though I had done my homework, I felt personally responsible for us losing that game.

During another big game, another "fun" thing happened. We were backed up inside our eight-yard line when Coach Dunlap asked me on the headset, "Got any suggestions, Jim?" I replied, "I think it's a great time for the quick kick." He called it, and then it got blocked for a touchdown. Another evil eye for me at halftime. I never called that play again for the rest of my career. Fortunately, though, we won that game, and all was well.

One of my recruiting areas was the city of Philadelphia where I got my first exposure to the world of inner city schools. Student populations in these schools were huge in number and racially diverse. I was in search of great players with the ability to win games who also had the great grades required for admittance into Lehigh. Even though this was sometimes a tough combination to find, we were fortunate to land some great recruits who were gifted both athletically and academically.

On one of my trips to Philadelphia, I had a pleasant surprise. I discovered that my former coach and mentor, Frank Glazier, had surfaced at Philly's Widener University as defensive coordinator. Several times after his heart attack two years earlier, we had talked, but somehow during our busy schedules in different locations, we'd lost track of each other. But from then on during my trips to Philly, I usually spent the night with Frank in his dorm room which was furnished with just a bunk bed and a desk. He had no need for chairs or a TV, the so-called "frills" in life. Like the old days, we talked football into the wee hours of the morning. But that's not the reason he was the greatest coach I ever knew. As you will see, he left a legacy like no one before or since.

Coaching Point: If you are fortunate to have a mentor in life, be eternally grateful. Frank Glazier was mine.

———————

Even though Lehigh had a decent football season that year, I was proud that as head coach we had a great lacrosse season. We won almost all of our games.

CHAPTER 8

From Fun at Summer Football Camp to Career Frustration to Freedom

Sometime in the spring 1969, I became friends with our track coach at Lehigh, John Covert, and he talked to me about a summer camp in the Poconos. John was part owner of that camp with Jay Demarest, a coach from New Jersey. They asked me if I was interested in running the football section of the camp, so one weekend, Joan and I went to visit the place, located on one of the most beautiful mountains of Pennsylvania.

John and Jay had developed a camp in the Poconos that was used to host individual camps for basketball, soccer, gymnastics, and cheerleading, among others. The property contained a huge facility that once had been an old country inn, featuring a huge dining area and a big fireplace in the lobby. This facility with four or five floors of bedrooms was able to accommodate hundreds of campers per week.

John, Jay, and I agreed that I would run the football camp for two consecutive weeks in July. This happily coincided with my two-week vacation at Lehigh University. The first week's camp was for kids aged five to nine. The second week was for kids between ten and fourteen.

Because the five-to-nine-year olds were so much younger than the other kids, dorm areas for these football campers were located in a separate facility about 100 yards from the main inn, which was a good thing considering the drama of that first week.

All the coaches who were directors, including myself, stayed in the main inn. My football coaches slept in the separate facility with the youngest campers. So as a director, I was able to bring my wife and son with me for those two weeks as a vacation for Joan and a free camp for Gregg. Joan was able to lounge around the pool every day and do some fun things with the other coaches' wives, which was an extra treat for her because by then, she was four months pregnant with our second child. Next door to our room, stayed a basketball official who was working at the camp as a coach. He later became one of the most famous NBA officials of all times. I can't recall his name, but I do remember seeing him on TV for many years officiating almost every NBA championship. Down the hall from us was a basketball coach—another whose name I don't recall—who later became a major Division One basketball coach.

During that first week with the five-to-nine-year-olds, almost every night after the kids' bedtime, one of the coaches would come knock on my door to ask me to come help in the football facility. They just couldn't get the boys to settle down. The first two nights were really crazy because most of these kids had never been away from home before. Some cried, some played childish pranks, or got into other mischief. So we hugged them, counseled them, and as a last resort, got them outside to run at 2AM, so they could burn off all that energy. Just as their week at camp was about to end, the boys finally settled down when they realized it was better for them if they'd just lie down and go to sleep. And it was better for us coaches too! But the following year, there were a couple of boys who never did make the adjustment. They whined and cried so much all day and all night, we finally had to call their parents in the middle of the week and say "Come get 'em."

One of my young football campers was the owner's son, Chris Demarest. Many years later, when I was coaching high school football in Florida, I got a call from Chris. He asked, "Do you remember me?" I said, "Of course I do." When he told me that he was now a graduate assistant coach at Florida State University, I was proud that he remembered me. He said my name had come up at FSU because they had recruited some of my Kissimmee players who'd turned out to be terrific, and Chris wanted to let me know that he was proud of my reputation. Chris went on to become a well-known assistant football coach at many Division One schools.

During camp, after all the kids were tucked in for the night, the directors would order pizza and beer and sit around swapping stories. One night, the camp's owner, Coach Jay Demarest, was telling a story about a New Jersey coach who was causing quite a stir. The stories had us all laughing so hard until our ribs hurt. I finally asked, "What's this guy's name?" Coach Demarest said, "I'm not sure, but something like Grazier?" I started laughing all over again. "Is it Frank Glazier?", I asked. Jay said, "That's him." Seems like Frank's name just kept popping up. I had no way of knowing back then that Frank and I again would end up working together after he founded the Frank Glazier Football Clinics which would be held in locations all across the country. Every high school football coach in America would come to know his name and tens of thousands would attend his clinics each year. I was honored when he hired me to be one of his national clinic directors, a job I held for 15 years.

Coaching Point: Always network and stay in touch with people in your profession, including your former colleagues. I could have done a better job of that.

With camp and the summer behind us, I was now entering my third year at Lehigh University as an assistant football coach and head lacrosse coach. Life was becoming somewhat easier for me because I now knew the routine and had adjusted to the long work weeks.

My immediate boss, John Whitehead, was still the offensive coordinator and offensive line coach. We still shared an office. He was a fiery coach both with players and with alumni. Many times when he was on the phone with a prominent alum, he would get abrupt. One time after a particularly heated telephone exchange, I asked him, "Who was *that*?" He said, "It was the president of Bethlehem Steel." Coach Whitehead had no problem speaking his mind with anybody. Even so, he was an outstanding line coach and coordina-tor, and the kids loved him. He was rough and tough, but genuine.

Head coach Dunlap was also the defensive line coach. One day in prac-tice, the offensive line was going against the defensive line, and tempers were getting hot. I looked over and heard an angry exchange between Coach Dunlap and Coach Whitehead. A minute later, Coach Whitehead stormed off the field. So I took over the offense and we ran through plays for about ten minutes. No one said a word about the rift. We just carried on running our conditioning drills before the kids left to go to dinner. Not even in the coaches' room did anyone say a word about what had happened. After dinner, all the coaches, except Coach Whitehead, reported for our regular staff meet-ing. Coach Dunlap then asked me, "Jim, have you heard from John?" I said, "No sir." That was the extent of the staff meeting. Soon we were all dismissed.

The next morning, when I walked in the office, John was sitting at his desk as if nothing had happened. I figured he and Coach Dunlap had some-how worked out their differences, but we never talked about it.

Because football is a very tough game played by tough, competitive kids with highly competitive coaches, verbal exchanges and even physical exchang-es between coaches are not uncommon. I've experienced more of these inci-dents in my career than I can count. They just came with the territory.

Coaching Point: **If you fight fair without saying words you'll ultimately regret, disagreements will soon pass and be forgotten.**

———

Our family lived over the mountain in a little yellow house that overlooked a beautiful farm with mountains in the distance. It was in this idyllic community that our son, Gregg, entered first grade, but not without some trauma. That first day, as Joan walked him to school, Gregg didn't want to go and Joan was in tears. I suppose this has been going on for ages—moms and dads seeing their kids go off to school for the first time—but that doesn't make it any easier when it's your family. It was a tough time for us. The fact that Joan was pregnant—now in her seventh month—no doubt added to her emotional stress.

Several weeks later, Joan called me, really upset and crying. Some violent rainstorms had suddenly flooded our basement with three feet of water. I went home right away, concerned that the gas heater down in the basement would explode. But the water quickly receded, there was no explosion, and everything worked out fine.

Coaching Point: **To paraphrase Mark Twain: I've worried about many things in my life. Fortunately, most of them never happened.**

Football season went fairly well, and we were excited about the birth of our second child, a daughter, Jennifer, born in Allentown, Pennsylvania, on November 25, 1969. We were so proud even as we knew I wouldn't be home much to help Joan out when she would need me. Coaches' wives have a tougher time than a lot of wives because of their husbands' work schedules, and it's true that during those years, I was gone most of the time. But I did the best I could. No excuses, just a fact. Fortunately, Joan was supportive of my career and understood the challenges.

By the end of my third season at Lehigh, I wanted to become a head college football coach. I was just 28-years-old and full of myself, but I also felt I was ready. I applied at three small colleges and before Christmas, interviewed at all three. One school was in Kenyon, Ohio. The other two were in Philadelphia and the Boston area. Fortunately—or unfortunately—I've never quite figured which, I was rejected for all three jobs, although I think I came in second for the Ohio job. Obviously in *their* minds, I wasn't ready, probably due to my young age.

Anyway, during December and January, I was flying to various cities speaking to alumni groups on behalf of our head coach, who delegated me for the task. These groups were interested mostly in how the team was looking for next season and how recruiting was going. Of course, these speeches required more time away from my young family, even as my ongoing duties of coaching and recruiting continued. By now in my third year at Lehigh, I was feeling much less enamored with the pressures of recruiting. What had once been exciting—visiting five schools a day and organizing weekend recruiting visits—was now becoming a royal pain. Ironically, as I traveled around on those high schools visits, I began to realize that maybe going back to coaching in high school was where I really belonged. Besides, in the late 1960s and early 70s, the financial rewards of coaching college football were non-existent. In fact, our salaries at Lehigh barely matched those of most high school coaches. On top of that, with all the extra time and travel required that kept me from my family, I was seriously wondering if college coaching was worth it.

Meantime, our lacrosse season was going extremely well. We had upset a couple of powerhouse teams, and I was gaining a reputation in this sport. But I was not interested in making a career in lacrosse. I was a football coach, following my dream I'd had since ninth grade.

Just before football practice began in the spring of 1970, I encountered some friends who were prominent Lehigh alumni now living in Harrisburg. We were enjoying a couple of drinks, and I must have revealed my burnout with recruiting, because they asked if I would be interested in going back to coaching high school. I casually replied, "Maybe." Then they told me that I would be a good fit for a job they knew about, where they were personal friends with several school board members. A week later, I interviewed at East Pennsboro High School in Enola, Pennsylvania, and soon after, was offered the job.

After meeting with Coach Dunlap and telling him I felt I was ready for a change, he indicated he had sensed that, considering all the other college job interviewing I had done. A few days later, I was relieved and excited—as was Joan—when I accepted the head football coaching job at East Pennsboro High.

Our next step was a familiar one: find a house in our new location, then call the trusty folks at U-Haul.

> *Coaching Point:* **Sometimes what looks like a step down in life is really a step up. I think I was always meant to coach high school, not college after all. Don't ever let "appearances" of status, prestige, or other people's perceptions of where your career path should lead keep you from following your dream. After all, it's *your* dream, not theirs.**

CHAPTER 9

Back to High School Coaching

Our family—now including our six-month-old daughter, Jennifer—left Lehigh University in May of 1970. This was my fifth move since I began coaching in 1963, and I was seeing the pattern. I remember before Joan and I got married telling her parents, Norman and Fannie Bell Abbott, that I would always take care of my family and that to provide for us, I would never be without a job. I would have gotten a job digging ditches if necessary. I also told them how hard I would try to be a good husband and father. I loved my wife and our two children, but as I've said, my jobs created an environment where, far more than many men, I was at work more hours every day than I was at home. As an ambitious climber, I also was always in search of the new and better job. Looking back, I know that in addition to my long work hours, moving around a lot to take on that next opportunity put a tremendous strain on our family.

It helped that my relationship with Joan's parents was fantastic and I loved being around them. Many weekends when I wasn't recruiting, plus several weeks each summer, we spent time with them at their home in Georgetown, Delaware. Georgetown was very small with just one short main street and a little coffee shop by the name of Henry's. From their house, you could walk down the alley and be at Henry's in five minutes. Another fun fact: they lived about 18 miles from the ocean and the town of Rehobeth Beach, which is now the playground for many of Washington, D.C.'s rich and famous.

During our visits, we all would sit on the front porch, drinking coffee in the morning and again after dinner. We'd help Fannie crank out gallons of her homemade ice cream, and in the evenings, I'd smoke cigars with Norman in his back office where we talked about commodity investing. Many days, we'd all head to the beach and just have fun. These times began my absolute love of the ocean and great desire to be around water.

But it wasn't all fun and games because Fannie usually had some daily chores for me as a way to help pay for our room and board. For several years, their side yard was covered with pine trees and she wanted them gone. After Fannie finally hired a company to cut them down, my job was to dig up the stumps. It took me plenty of years and many blisters to get rid of those stumps.

I recall several old chicken houses out back that had been converted to storage areas. Norman kept his cigars in one of those houses, and every time we were getting ready to leave, Fannie would sneak me five or ten good cigars saying, "He'll never miss them."

My parents, as was I, were born and raised in Annapolis, Maryland, where on weekends and holidays, Joan and I also enjoyed spending time. Like her parents, mine were fun to be around, but where they lived—in a subdivision—just wasn't as much fun as Georgetown.

Coaching Point: **Remember you're also choosing your in-laws when you're choosing a mate. Hopefully you'll be as lucky as Joan and I both were in that department.**

———

Before beginning my new job, we made several trips to the Harrisburg and Enola areas to find a place to live. The house we selected to rent was located about ten miles from East Pennsboro High. This old two-story house, with a circular drive in front on about an acre of land, was huge. Our previous house was so tiny, we didn't have much furniture, but now we needed a lot more to fill this place. Thank goodness for friends, families, and garage sales. Joan was always a great decorator and before we knew it, she had made this house feel like home.

East Pennsboro High School is located in the quiet little town of Enola, Pennsylvania, on the Susquehanna River, which would prove to be both a blessing and a curse. Even though Enola was home to several small businesses, it was mainly known as the world's biggest "railroad re-classification yard," meaning that as trains came in on a specific track, they were rerouted onto another track going in another direction.

With few, if any, black families in town, Enola couldn't boast of much ethnic diversity, so my players were all white, many of whom came from poor families who lived down by the river in a section they proudly called "rat town." Seems like everywhere I would coach in my career, there was a section of town that produced many good players, but their neighborhoods' nicknames were not always so kind.

Enola is not far from what is known as the "coal regions," comprised of many towns with people who were passionate about their football teams some *very* passionate. Folks in these towns—with a bar and church on every corner—were quite provincial and not too friendly to outsiders. But they did expect their coaches to make the rounds at the local bars after each game to say hello and share a shot of whisky and a beer with the fans. I knew of several coaches with winning records who got fired because they didn't go along with that tradition. I never got the opportunity to schmooze with those fans because during my last year at Lehigh, after I interviewed at one of these "coal region" schools, the superintendent called to tell me, "Jim, you have great credentials and would be a good coach for us, but because you're not from around here, I would recommend you take your hat out of the ring." So I did, and thanked him for his honest advice. My job at Enola, even though only 50 miles away, was a different world. It was welcoming to outsiders.

———

Pennsylvania is a great state with great people, but I found out pretty quickly a few things that were quite unexpected from my previous experience. One example happened during my first summer at the Booster Club kick-off function held at the local VFW where several hundred townspeople had gathered to meet and greet the coaches and their wives. After they met all of us at the door and directed us to our table, the president of the club came up to me and said, "Coach, here's your bottle of Jack Daniels for the night. Have fun." This was just as accepted as the coaching staff dropping by the VFW, only three blocks from the school, to have a couple of "brewskis" at the end of the day on their way home.

Coaching Point: **When in Rome, you do what the Romans do.**

I spent that first summer getting our coaching staff lined up while the kids were working out. As time went on, I met and became friends with other faculty members. In my experience until then, and even later, it was unusual for a football coach and P.E. teacher to consider a shop teacher, a history teacher, a choir director, and many others to become some of their best friends. Coaches typically just run around with other coaches. But EPHS was different, and I sensed that I was really going to enjoy this job. Our school superintendent, John Gross, was very supportive of our football program, and in the wintertime, the townspeople also liked their wrestling and basketball teams. The gym was usually packed for these events, often standing room only. Our basketball program had been very good and was directed by an outstanding coach, Dave Lebo. I would not say that he and I were friends, but we did peacefully co-exist, at least for a while. We were both strong personalities, each wanting our own way so much that we were like "oil and water." I was a hard-core football coach, and basketball coach Lebo was equally passionate about his sport. But Dave wanted his kids to specialize only in basketball and forego football altogether. I believed, on the other hand, that kids should play multiple sports. We had so many heated discussions over this that it got to the point where the principal intervened one day and told us to stay away from each other and "don't even walk down the same hallway." This belief is an argument I've had with many other coaches in many other schools: don't coerce a kid into making a decision to play just one sport. High school athletes need to participate in as many sports as they want to, without coaches directing them at this stage in their lives where to specialize.

Coaching Point: **Don't be afraid to defend a principle you deeply believe in—even if it gets you into hot water with those who disagree.**

———

I was thrilled with our football coaching staff and we loved working together. Crazy Dave ran the defensive backs. Coach Bernie, who taught special education, was the defensive line coach. Coach Statler, who had played in high school for Coach Whitehead, my boss at Lehigh, entertained us with stories from his days of playing for John. Bill Downs, a bright and upcoming coach, was our offensive coordinator. We also had a JV (junior varsity) staff and a freshman staff, both headed up by Coach Stains.

For our offense, we installed the same one that we had used at Lehigh University, but a scaled-down version for our high school team with fewer plays. These kids were tough and we coached them tough. Our game schedule consisted of playing teams such as Hershey High School, home of Hershey chocolate; Milton Hershey High School, a school for orphans with a roster of boys who came from all over the country; Middletown High School; Palmyra, and many others.

Our practice sessions were long—sometimes lasting three hours or more. We put our emphasis on the fundamentals such as blocking and tackling. Our practice field was not lighted, so as the season changed from fall to winter and daylight got shorter, I would tell our manager to climb the ladder on the tennis courts and adjust the lights in our direction so that we could get in another hour or two of practice. Usually we practiced the varsity and junior varsity teams together. Basically, we used the younger JV kids to run the opponents' plays against the varsity. This is known as the scout team and is used throughout football, up to and including the pro level. These young kids got beat on by the older kids every day, but they got tougher and tougher as the season progressed. I was a young, aggressive coach and I just wanted our kids to be in shape and be able to out-tough our opponents. Even though we didn't have great team speed, our kids were definitely tough.

I certainly didn't do this later in my career when we avoided daily full-contact practice due to the greater knowledge about safety issues, but at East Pennsboro in the early 70s, we were in full pads every day we practiced. On Thursday afternoons, we had a junior varsity game at four o'clock and the entire varsity sat in the stands while the JV kids played their game. Then, at the conclusion of that game, both the JV and the varsity team went to the locker room where the varsity got dressed for practice in full equipment. We had full-contact scrimmage lasting about two hours. And again, the manager had to climb the ladder on the tennis courts and adjust the lights so we could see after dark. If a coach did that today, he would be fired pretty quick, but parents in those days accepted whatever a coach did. My, how things changed when parents started questioning coaches about everything.

———

In the beginning at EPHS, we didn't pass the ball much, as we were a power running football team with great defense. However, we were fortunate to have on our team a young man by the name of Mickey Shuler. His dad was Bob Shuler, my shop teacher friend. Mickey had the best set of hands of any kid I ever coached in my 46 years. He was about six-foot-three and had glue for hands. Mickey started out playing tight end for us, but we eventually moved him everywhere in order to get him the ball. He was also a great basketball player, and one year he told his dad he was going to quit football to concentrate on basketball. Bob said, "Okay, son, but you are not going to be allowed out of the house. You'll just come home after school every day and do your homework, that's it." The next afternoon, Mickey was back at football practice and finished high school by breaking every school pass-receiving record. Mickey Shuler went on to Penn State, where he started and played for Joe Paterno. After graduating from Penn State, Mickey signed with the New York Jets and played in the NFL for 17 years. Turns out his dad's ultimatum about basketball resulted in Mickey's earning millions of dollars during his professional football career.

Coaching Point: Just like in the old TV show, "Father (usually) Knows Best," even though it may not seem so at the time.

CHAPTER 10

Would You Sell Your Blood for Football?

A s our first season at East Pennsboro was moving along, I began to notice something interesting going on at our home games. Before every play, the kids would glance over at the sideline at the chain crew. Now for many years, this chain crew was comprised of the same men who had positioned someone close to the opponent's signal caller who would then signal to our kids whether the upcoming play was going to be a run or pass. None of our opponents had ever picked up on this, and it took me a couple of games before I noticed it myself. Stealing opponents' signals—or at least the effort—still goes on today. If you watch a college game and see players holding a towel in front of the signal caller, this is to prevent the opponent from stealing the signal. A pro football signal caller will often hold the play sheet in front of his mouth so no one can read his lips as he calls the plays. As the saying goes, "All is fair in love and war"—and football!

The town of Enola was located just across the river from the state capital of Harrisburg. A friend of one of our coaches told him how he could make some extra money—and it wasn't illegal or immoral. That coach then passed the word onto us: we could donate our blood plasma and make good money for doing it. Coach Dave asked me if I wanted to donate, and I said, "Heck no, I'm scared of needles." But one afternoon after school—on a dare—four or five football coaches, myself included, went to the blood plasma center and we each donated a pint of plasma. Afterward, the center's staff fed us cookies and orange juice, and each of us received a small check. We were told that we could do this as often as twice a week because only plasma was extracted, not whole blood cells.

You know by now that I was—and have remained for four decades—a football junkie. I love studying the game and attending clinics. But I never expected that my passion for football would lead to my "Eureka" moment as a solution for our team's tight budget. In the face of extremely limited funds to attend football clinics and for research and development, I asked the coaches if they would be willing to go with me to Harrisburg to give blood plasma twice a week so we could pool our money for visits to clinics and college spring practices. Everyone agreed that, yes indeed, this was the answer to our financial problems. So when we'd walk in, we'd be greeted like celebrities before the center's staff guided us to our regular chairs. Our twice-weekly blood donations—with free snacks—were easy money and continued for several years, enabling us to afford the cost of a visit to at least one major college spring practice every March, as well as to several football clinics.

When one of our coaches, Crazy Dave, discovered he had a rare blood type and would be paid double, I think he became obsessed because one day he asked me, "Can you cover my class? I'm going over to pump out a pint." Soon, all the kids knew what we were doing and asked us if they, too, could contribute. "Nice offer, young man, but no way. You have to be 18." On many days when the kids were griping about a tough practice, I would tell them, "Hey, quit your complaining. We BLEED for you!"

In the fall of 1969, the University of Texas won the football National Championship using a new offense called the Wishbone. It was invented by Coach Emory Bellard and watching the team be unstoppable on offense, I became obsessed with learning this offense so I could bring it to EPHS. During Christmas vacation, my mind raced with ideas of how we could learn everything there was to know about the Wishbone offense. By the time school resumed in January, I had the plan. Now all I had to do was sell the superintendent and school board on it. I met with them and presented our need to take our staff to Austin, Texas, for a week so we could study this winning offense. Later, they told me the trip was approved, but for only one other coach to go with me, and only the expenses for our airplane tickets would be paid. I thanked them and began planning our trip for a week in March.

We would need extra money for food, lodging, and a cheap rental car after we arrived in Austin, so we needed a fund raiser. What better choice than to involve the plasma center? We asked friends and faculty if they would throw in a few bucks to help us, or if their money was tight, we'd be glad to set them up for a blood donation appointment. We got 10 or 15 enthusiastic takers on our offer, and later hosted a beer blast party for them as a way of saying thanks.

———◆———

Getting to that one week of football training at the University of Texas really paid off. What I learned there about coaching offense resulted in hundreds of victories that benefitted thousands of kids over the next 35 years.

———◆———

Coaching Point: **Give blood for any good cause, including just to help folks in your community who need it. Blood is something we all have, and at some point you may be the one who needs more.**

CHAPTER 11

Two Coaches and Longhorn Football Films

With the Texas trip approved, I decided to take our offensive coordinator Bill Downs along. Only when we made our plane reservations, did it finally hit me that this was really going to happen. We continued to raise money and got just enough for the trip.

We arrived in Austin, Texas, the last week of March of 1971. When we'd left Pennsylvania, the weather was in the 20s with snow in the forecast. I had never been to the Lone Star State, but immediately I loved Texas weather—the temperature was in the low 70s. Due to our limited funds, we rented a small room in what was known as a trailer court, and our rental car was—what else?—an old Volkswagen Beetle. Our food for the week consisted basically of peanut butter and jelly on white bread.

Of course, after 12-hour days at the UT football offices and then practice, we needed some adult beverages to relax. I remember that Lone Star and Jax beer were our two top choices. On several nights, we splurged and treated ourselves to pizza.

Dozens of high school coaches were there doing the same thing we were: studying the new Wishbone offense. However, most of these coaches were from Texas. Some came from Oklahoma. We were the only ones from anywhere else.

Every day at 8AM, we would go to the football office and try to get an "audience" with one of UT's assistant coaches. We were very fortunate because we were able to tag along with several Texas high school coaches who already had good relationships with the UT staff. The offensive coordinator for the Longhorns, Emory Bellard, the inventor of this triple-option offense—in the shape of a wishbone—was very guarded about what he would share with us. He didn't want to give away all of his secrets. The most important thing he kept to himself was a technique called the load-blocking scheme. We did everything we could to uncover this secret, and it helped that on a daily basis, we usually got to talk with an assistant UT coach for an hour or so. Hanging around the Texas high school coaches helped, too. Sometimes the UT coaches would tell us, "You boys can get some sandwiches in the break room if you want." Man, was that a treat compared to the PB&Js we'd been eating. A ham sandwich never tasted so good.

After lunch, we looked at hours of what is known as film cut-ups, repetitions of just one play against opponents from all their games. But still no film on the load-blocking scheme. Around 3PM, we went outside and observed the players practicing until around 5:30. Even though we were contained in a certain area and allowed only limited access, we still were able to see most everything and learned a lot.

I remember a couple of risky things from that week. One night, after a really long day, Bill and I decided to go to a bar. The moment we walked in, we decided to get out of there fast, as we could tell immediately the regulars knew we weren't from around there and didn't take too kindly to strangers. I guess our lack of boots, hats, buckles, and Wrangler jeans gave us away, and we weren't about to mix it up with this crowd who had us greatly outnumbered. Another night, on a whim, we decided to drive down to Mexico. After all, it was so close and we wanted to visit one of those little border towns where we imagined many beautiful children begging for money and a few not-so-beautiful ladies begging for our company.

Two hours into the trip, with no Mexico in sight, we came to our senses and realized that we'd better turn around *el pronto*. Who knows what kind of trouble we might have gotten into down there? Eight o'clock came early the next morning, but we were right on time, with no one the wiser about our Mexican fantasy.

On our next-to-last day in Austin, after all our badgering, Coach Bellard finally decided to crack the code for us into his top-secret load-blocking scheme. Man, were we excited about it all coming together! Our last day at UT, we were in the film room with several other high school coaches, and after everybody had left, there Bill and I were, alone, with all those film cut-ups. We did something that I'm embarrassed to admit, but I'm glad we did it. We took three of the highlight cut-up films and stashed them in my briefcase. With so many copies of each play, it's not like they were left with no back-ups. As a matter of fact, I doubt if they ever missed them. But to us, this was a windfall. We quickly left the facility, put my briefcase in the trunk of the car, went to practice, and watched from the fringes, trying to be as inconspicuous as possible. Back in the room, I was scared to death the cops would come and arrest us, and it didn't help that Bill kept knocking on the wall in the middle of the night, screaming, "Open up! Austin Police Department!"

The morning of our departure back to Pennsylvania couldn't come fast enough. And once back home, we never shared those films with anybody except when training our staff. They knew where we got them, but never blew our cover. Fortunately, the law never came calling, and these films benefited the many coaches I worked with throughout my career, so everything turned out okay.

Coaching Point: *Never take something that doesn't belong to you. We just "borrowed" those films and anytime UT wants them back, I'll be glad to oblige!*

Can't leave the story of our Texas trip without confessing one more incident that could have kept us there much longer—uncomfortable and confined against our will. After that restless night of Bill's pranks and my own guilt pangs, our flight was scheduled to leave around nine. We had already paid the car rental company a good-sized deposit when we arrived in Austin, but now, more money was owed which we could not pay. By then, we were flat broke, except for some loose change in our pockets, which we left along with the keys on the floorboard, and hustled away just in time to catch the plane. As we took off, we were hugely relieved to have escaped Texas unscathed and we landed back in Pennsylvania feeling: "Mission Accomplished."

CHAPTER 12

Battleball and Sarge

The kids at East Pennsboro were a tough bunch. They loved football and they loved other rough and tumble sports. In P.E. class, they wanted to play either a game called battleball or go outside and play what *they* called rugby, really a modified version that still involved tackling. Battleball, played in the gym, was a lot like dodgeball, but instead of using kickballs, these kids insisted on using volleyballs, which were much harder and would sting on impact. Bloody injuries were not uncommon, yet whenever given the option of playing another game, the kids would start chanting, "We want battleball! We want battleball!" So much for teaching lifetime sports, such as tennis, golf, or archery during my tenure. Battleball was a brutal game, but the kids loved it.

In those days, students were divided into sections such as 12P, 12C, and so on. Twelve P was comprised mainly of my football players. They were respectful, but they were a handful. These kids had so much energy it wasn't easy keeping them in line. Almost every week, the principal, Mr. Walters, would have a conference with me about one or more of their behaviors that wasn't acceptable. For example, one day, 12P had a substitute teacher for a history class, and when the substitute walked in the room, they told him, "Just take us to the gym so we can play battleball." When he said no, they kept insisting, until finally, they somehow managed to get him downstairs, where they locked him in the gym closet, holding the two doorknobs closed with a broomstick handle while they played their beloved game. The next period, when Sarge, our female P.E. teacher, came into the gym, and heard the sub yelling and banging on the locked doors, she let him out. The guy left East Pennsboro High School that day and never came back. Fortunately, Mr. Walters never found out about what happened, but as their punishment, I ran those kids hard for a week, up and down the big hill behind our practice field.

More about Sarge. I loved this woman. She was "old school," kind of like me at the time. One day during lunch duty, she barged up to me and ordered me to follow her down the hall. Not knowing what was up, I said "Okay," and at the end of the hall, she went into a janitor's closet and got a big bucket of water. Right next to this closet was a girl's bathroom where it was rumored some of the girls went to smoke. Sarge instructed me, "When I say 'NOW,' you throw open the bathroom door." I did exactly as I was told—this was Sarge, after all—as she charged into the bathroom, yelling "FIRE," at which time she threw the water all over the girls who were in there smoking. Then she said, "Oh, I'm sorry, I thought there was a fire in here!" The girls never went in there to smoke again.

In the gym, Sarge would usually sit on a chair as the girls played volley-ball, and sometimes, she would nod off. One day, she actually fell fast asleep and I was told later that when the period ended, the next class came in and just started playing. When she woke up about ten minutes later, she looked around, and asked, "Where did *you* girls come from?"

Times were great in the 1970s, although a lot that happened in those days would definitely get you fired today. Such as, once during lunch, the principal asked Sarge, "Where's Jim?" When she told him that I had taken a professional day and was at a football clinic, and when he then asked, "Who's covering his classes?", it was apparent that somebody had forgotten to get a substitute. Turns out that when the students in my first class saw I wasn't there, they asked the janitor to open the equipment closet so they could get out the balls for battleball, which they played for the hour. When the bell rang, the kids handed the balls to the next class, and they proceeded the same way. Same with the third class. Everything went smoothly, no problems. But today, that would be a lawsuit, leaving kids unsupervised.

In the spring, I got a call from the town's recreation director, asking if I wanted to make some extra money. Since donating blood wasn't cutting it for all the extra money we needed for attending clinics, I became the women's physical fitness director for the town of East Pennsboro. We met twice weekly at night and would often have 50 to 100 women scattered around the gym, exercising, doing the equivalent of modern-day aerobics. Big or small, I trained them all. That experience ultimately benefited me as well, since I was able to establish a good rapport with these ladies who got to know me in a different light other than as just the high school's Friday night football coach, which helped my personal PR in the community.

> *Coaching Point:* **Creating a good rapport and getting along with women both at work and in the community can save guys a lot of trouble in the long haul. After all, we all know it's the women who rule the roost!**

During my second year at EPHS, my mom and dad retired and moved to a little town near Fredericksburg in northeast Virginia. Dad had always wanted to be a gentleman farmer. So, along with another couple, they built two big log cabins on five acres each. It took them about two years to complete this project because they did the majority of the work themselves. Many weekends, Joan, the kids, and I would go down there to help them out on some project that was in progress. I think our kids enjoyed these trips, sort of like mini-vacations.

We bought a big, brand new stripped-down green van which carried us back and forth to Mom and Dad's house. As time went on, we customized the interior with insulated wood paneling, as well as with a built-in bed and couch. That van became one of the best, most practical vehicles I ever owned because now when we traveled, the kids could sleep along the way, or just be more comfortable having more room to move around instead of being cooped up in a car. Looking back, these trips and later escapades in the van were some of our family's most treasured times.

Coaching Point: To encourage reflection and gratitude of the past, consider writing a book. Otherwise, your story with its humor, treasured moments, and ups and downs may go untold, largely unremembered by you, your children, and subsequent generations. Even if you never publish your book, it will be a great experience for you to write it, and also will endure as an enriching chronicle for your kids and their kids to appreciate not only your personal life's story, but also the way things were in the "good old days."

CHAPTER 13

How to Motivate Your Players with Hijinks

A great part of coaching is trying to figure out how to motivate your kids to practice hard and then give their full effort on Friday nights. We would have competitive drills daily with the winning player or group getting a reward. Rewards included sitting out conditioning that day, getting an ice cold coke after practice, receiving a star on their helmet, that sort of thing. But before big games, we decided the motivation needed to get a little more radical. So we'd meet, usually at a coach's house, to brainstorm various ideas. One of these turned out really well.

One of our coaches wrote a letter to the captain of our football team as if the letter came from that week's opponent. The coach even drove to the opponent's town so it would have that postmark. The letter was a bit inflammatory—with remarks about what they would do to us on Friday at the game. I actually thought the letter was pretty lame and would just cause our kids to chuckle a bit. But that's not what happened. The letter arrived at our school on Friday morning and when the captain brought it to me, I said, "So what are you going to do about this?" He replied, "You'll see." That afternoon the team walked in to the pep rally, holding up the letter. With wild looks on their faces, in front of the entire student body, the boys tore the letter into 40 pieces and each of our 40 players put a piece of that letter inside their helmet. Come game time, our team hit the field with fire in their eyes and played "lights out" for four quarters. The score was a resounding win—by ironically enough, 40 points. Later I said to the other coaches, "Well, looks like it worked!"

Each week, we'd come up with some little things to motivate the kids, but two more pranks in particular made an impact. A big game was coming up, so we decided we needed something really big. Someone brought an old bedsheet and some spray paint. We painted some derogatory sayings on the sheet and decided we would hang it from the school roof late on Thursday night, before the next night's game. Our coaches met at a parking lot about a mile from the school at midnight. It was freezing cold with snow on the ground. Down at the practice field were some old tires that we used for practice drills. Each coach grabbed two of the tires and headed to the back of the school. We found a six-foot ladder and used it to get to the first-floor landing. We passed our tires up to a coach who then threw them up to the second-floor roof. Then we climbed the ladder to the second floor and proceeded to hang the sign over the front of the school using the tires as anchors. Just as we were about finished, we heard sirens and looked up to see in the distance police cars headed our way. "Oh crap!" somebody yelled. "Here come the cops!" We took off running and jumped from the second floor to the first floor before sprinting to a bank of trees just before the cops pulled up. Several of us twisted an ankle on that jump, myself included. For about 30 minutes, we all laid on the ground in the snow, barely breathing, scared to death. When the police finally left, we got to our cars and went home.

The next morning, the school was in an uproar over this sign which read, "East Penn, don't even show up!!!" The students and faculty were so outraged, it's a good thing no one ever suspected their own coaches. Later we found out that it was the school's night janitor who'd called the law after he heard footsteps on the roof. Bottom line though: ANOTHER BIG WIN!

Off and on throughout my four years at EPHS, we continued pulling off successful stunts in order to motivate our team. The last stunt was against Milton Hershey High School. Because we needed Milton Hershey to win against Cumberland Valley in order for us to go to the play-offs, Crazy Dave wrote a highly-offensive letter to the MH coach, who was a personal friend of his, as if the letter came from CV. From seats up in the stadium, the other coaches and I observed them talking over the fence down below during pre-game warm-ups. Suddenly a letter was pulled out of the MH coach's pocket, and handed to Dave. Our hearts were in our throats as we watched Dave read the letter without letting on to his friend that he was the one who had written it. They talked for a minute or two, and suddenly the MH coach sprinted to the field and rushed his team to the locker room. Dave bounded up the stadium where we were eager to find out what the heck had happened, and he explained that the Milton Hershey coach told him that he had not yet shown the letter to his players, and had asked him what he thought he should do. Without hesitation, Dave had replied, "Read it to them NOW!" Back in the locker room, the MH coach must have read the letter aloud because it looked like a different team rushing back onto the field. Suffice it to say, Milton Hershey slaughtered Cumberland Valley, and we at East Penn were off to the playoffs.

Later, when both of the other teams were talking about the letter, the prevailing belief was that a disgruntled Cumberland Valley player had written it. None of them ever found out the real culprit. These sorts of antics may appear now to reflect poor sportsmanship, but in the context of those times, it was fun and exciting to win so many games, especially with players who were less talented than most of their opponents.

Coaching Point: **In the game of life, it's important to identify what motivates you. Is it money? Prestige? Fame? Our kids at East Pennsboro were motivated by competition—and so was their head coach! To be successful, it helps greatly when your type of motivation matches your type of career.**

The following year, our district built a new aquatic center at the middle school. All coaches were required to become certified in advanced lifesaving techniques, so we had to attend a two-hour training session every Wednesday night. Now I love the water, but I am not a good swimmer. The class instructors were from outside our district, and put us through two hours of torture every week. I dreaded Wednesdays. After feeling several times during that course like I was drowning, I was elated when the night of the final exam finally came. But I also was dreading the part of the exam that would take place in the water. Following the written test, we all headed to the pool, where the men were told to wait in one bathroom, the women in another, and that one at a time, we would be called out and put through some kind of water "emergency." This test was pass-or-fail. After nearly an hour, I was the last one in the bathroom, waiting alone to be called. Finally, when I walked out, I saw everybody just sitting in the pool bleachers, saying not a word. I looked around and thought, *Is there a body in the pool? Will they jump me? What the heck's gonna happen?* One of the coaches kept signaling to me with his head down, nodding toward the water. For a second, I thought I saw something like a cinder block in the pool. But just then, this six-foot female instructor fell into the deep end and acted like she was drowning. I had to go in after her. We struggled, and struggled some more, until I said, "If you don't relax and let me save you, I'm going to choke your neck and drown you." She finally relaxed and I was able to pull her to the side of the pool. Then she exclaimed in mock alarm, "Where's my friend?" So I jumped out of the pool, ran back to the deep end, jumped in and pulled up her "friend," the cinder block. With that last move, I passed the final! To celebrate the end of six weeks that felt like six years, we all went to Al's bar and drowned ourselves in beer.

———•———

Big Al Caldarelli was the owner of Al's bar which was located in the rough part of town. He was one of our biggest supporters, both of the team and the coaches. Every Friday he insisted on feeding the coaches a pre-game meal. In those days, we didn't feed the kids after school. They'd go home for a home-cooked meal before the game, which doesn't happen in today's football. Big Al would always bring us cigars after the game, and if it was a victory, we'd end up at his place for a nightcap or two.

One night, Joan and I hosted a party at our house for the faculty, and by two in the morning, the beer kegs were empty. What to do except to call Al at home and tell him of our dilemma. He had no problem leaving the bar key under his front door mat and instructing me and a buddy to go inside the bar to grab a keg so we could finish out the night. That kind of trust doesn't happen often today.

Another example of Al's loyalty could've gone horribly wrong. During a big game at Hershey High School, the officials were total "homers." In fact, three of them had been on the Hershey staff the previous year. Because of this, there's no doubt we got cheated out of a deserved win. And the officials, who had called penalties on us where there were none, knew it. The minute the game was over, those guys dashed to their cars and sped away on that rainy night before our fans—in hot pursuit and armed with sharp-tipped umbrellas pointed like spears—could do some real damage. Later as we were all commiserating at the bar, Big Al said, "Just give me the word, Jim, I'll get their names and they'll be floating in the Susquehanna by morning." Obviously, that didn't happen, but we did have some very passionate fans, including Big Al.

Speaking of the Susquehanna, we lived through two springs where it crested and flooded houses on both sides of the river. The first flood occurred when we were living in our original house. Three blocks from our street, folks were being evacuated from their roof tops. The flood occurred after the thaw following a severe winter that had caused the river to freeze many feet deep. The second day of the flood was even worse and culminated with someone running up our street screaming, "Evacuate immediately! A gas line has ruptured!" My thought was to get Joan and the kids out of there fast. I loaded them into the car and sent them to her mom's for a few days. This event of nature was called the "one-hundred-year flood" and it took six months to get everything back to normal. Guess what? The next year, the "hundred-year-flood" happened again with the same results. I decided it was time to move. One of my friends, a contractor, suggested I build a new house. By now, I'd finally paid my parents back the $3,000 we had borrowed for the first house, so I sure wasn't going that route—of borrowing from them again. Fortunately, we had saved enough money to get a construction loan.

During this time, I stayed busy year-around. We still attended clinics every winter, and every spring for a week, we visited a college practice. Our staff traveled to many clinics in order to improve our knowledge and learn new techniques. The Texas trip had been very helpful in establishing our offense, which paid off for many years. In fact, because of that trip, we were written about in several Pennsylvania newspapers. I'll always be grateful to the school board for allowing us to make that journey. I am also thankful to the plasma center in Harrisburg for helping us fund it, as well as many other trips and clinics over the years.

By nature, when the work day is over, I'm a fun-loving guy. But whenever we went to a clinic or spring practice, I required the coaches to be at all sessions and take copious notes, which we all shared at the end of the day. This is how a typical clinic weekend went. I took as many coaches as wanted to go and paid for one hotel room and their registration—provided they had contributed to the plasma center. No free rides. If two coaches went, we each had a bed. If four coaches went, we took the mattresses off and could now sleep four. If eight coaches went, we had to get creative. All of us, myself included, have slept in bathtubs, closets, and on the floor. Food was not a problem because we each brought our own. Mine was simple and nutritious as always: peanut butter and jelly on white bread. "Roughing it" or not, I loved being around coaches and studying football. Our staff worked hard together and played hard when the work was done.

Visiting a college spring football practice every year was the best way for us to learn—and not just because it lasted a week instead of the clinics for just a weekend. There was nothing like having the opportunity to watch film, talk to college coaches, and watch their practices. The Texas trip was our longest, but we also visited North Carolina State, Virginia Tech, and Miami. One big advantage we had at that time was that everyone was recruiting Mickey Shuler, our tight end, who ended up at Penn State and then with the New York Jets for many years. No doubt we got some preferential treatment because of him, especially in Miami. Again remember: the rules in college football recruiting were different in the 70s. Today, high school coaches cannot receive preferential treatment of any kind, such as free meals or lodging.

When we visited North Carolina State, Lou Holtz was the coach, and man, what a fiery coach he was! He was everywhere and involved in everything. One time, when the PAT snapper (the point-after-touchdown ball snapper) was messing up, Coach Holtz impatiently jumped in and became the snapper himself. He snapped it all right, the ball was kicked, and went directly into Coach Holtz's backside, knocking his hat and glasses off. Silence descended over the field, until he collected himself, got up laughing and went on about his business.

The next day after a phone call, Coach Holtz came out and declared, "Well, we just lost a recruit." He explained that the kid had questioned him about his reputation for being too tough on players, and Lou told us, "I gave him an expletive and slammed the phone down in his face." Then he asked us whether NC State had a good shot at getting Shuler. Of course we said yes.

The next year, our spring visit was to Virginia Tech in Blacksburg. The staff there was new and had just come from Alabama where they were running the famous Wishbone offense. Jimmy Sharpe was the head coach there and boy, did they ever work hard. We learned lots of new drills and techniques from this staff, and maybe it was because they were new that they were so friendly and eager to help us. In fact, when we left, they even gave us many copies of film to take back to our school. I thanked them also for letting us eat a couple of meals at the training table. Tasted mighty good after several peanut butter-and-jelly days. As usual, it was full-speed work all day, until about seven o'clock in the evening. Then, "Let's head to the bar." No shortage in Blacksburg—or any college town—of those places to unwind.

Every year, we visited Penn State for its annual spring clinic and practice. Coach Joe Paterno was very kind to our staff as he was to just about everybody. But, like the other schools' coaches, he made it clear he sure wanted to recruit our Mickey Shuler. The Penn State clinic lasted for three days and was beneficial to us, especially on defense. PSU was known as "Linebacker U" because so many pro linebackers were produced there.

One night during a Penn State clinic trip, we ended up at a fraternity party, enjoying free adult beverages, because one of our coaches had been a member of that fraternity when he attended PSU. I've always considered myself young, no matter my age. But when college kids started calling me "Sir," I realized I was definitely getting older.

Coaching Point: When exposed to any learning situation, such as a lecture or a book, it can be overwhelming to try to absorb everything. So look for just one key point and internalize that. When visiting clinics, we aimed to take away the one big idea that would make us better. And it worked. Same as when seeking to model yourself after a person you admire: Choose just one or two of their positive traits that you can emulate.

CHAPTER 14

Football Coaches on a Crazy Spring Break

Joan and I made arrangements to close on the purchase of land for our new house. I bought and paid for the plot of ground where our split-level house would be built. A construction loan was issued to us, which meant the bank loaned out portions of money to the construction company intermittently as construction progressed. Upon completion, the total home loan was signed over to us. To save money, we built just a shell of the house, which meant no painting inside or out, no finished lower-level or landscaping. Plus, all the windows needed to be painted, both inside and out.

The construction company owner allowed me to go to his shop on weekends and paint the windows before they were installed. Joan and I did save a lot of money doing it this way, but I thought we would never get that house finished. Several months later, after the shell was complete, the entire interior of the house still needed to be painted before we could move in.

So I convinced the coaching staff that it would be fun to have a painting party. In each room, I set up all the paint along with brushes and rollers. Each of the seven coaches was assigned a certain area and the goal was to get all the painting done that day. To entice them, I bought and placed everyone's favorite adult beverages on ice in strategic locations. Funny how it seemed the more the coaches painted, the happier they got! Everything was going along great until somebody asked, "Where's Coach Bernie?" He had been assigned a small bathroom and should have been finished already. But when I opened the door, Bernie was lying asleep on the floor and several towel racks had been knocked loose. I guess he'd had one too many of those adult beverages and passed out. Anyway, after all the painting was surprisingly well done, we left to celebrate with a party at Jimmy Beisel's house. Jimmy was a history teacher and a great friend who liked to have fun. By the end of the evening, Jimmy was dancing like a fool as we howled in laughter. What a great—and productive—day.

About a month before we started on the house, I had bought another vehicle, a 15-year-old Volkswagen Beetle that cost me all of $100. The defroster didn't work, I had to rope one door shut and tie down the front hood to keep it locked, but it ran great. I parked it out front because we had only a one-car garage, and the trusty, fixed-up van we used as a camper got the prime real estate. Every morning during the winter, the Beetle's windshield would be frozen solid with ice and I'd scrape off lengthwise about a foot of snow and ice, just enough so that I could see to drive to work. But this beat-up old VW was great to drive in the snow because if I swerved and crashed into a snow bank and dented a fender, so what? It didn't matter.

This car came in real handy in the springtime when I began to landscape the yard. As the ground thawed out, I started raking it by hand. Smoothing out the hard, rocky soil was an extremely time-consuming task. Then I needed to get some sod. Located on a big hill behind the school's practice field, I found an answer to my problem: green grass! Most days after school, I would drive the Bug over there and cut enough sod to fill the back seat. Day after day, I loaded and then laid out the sod until I finally had covered the entire yard. One day, the superintendent spotted me and asked me what I was doing over there. When I told him and also that the principal had said it was okay because "we don't need that hill anyway," he said, "Good for you—you're saving money for your family."

By summer, seeds from the sod had started growing in the backseat of the old green Bug, but after cleaning, the seats were still good, along with the motor, transmission, and tires. But the body of the car was rusting out and none of the doors would close. So at a junkyard, I bought just the body of another green VW Bug for 50 bucks. Then, one Saturday, Bob Shuler and I went to the school's auto body shop, where we replaced the old body by welding on the new, and voila: a new Bug for 50 bucks!

After football season started, if our team was having a bad practice, we would take them to what the kids now unaffectionately called "No Sod Hill," where we'd have them repeatedly and at length bear-crawl up the hill on all fours, then roll down, which they hated not only because it was exhausting, but also because they'd get covered in dirt and mud. I suppose their moms didn't like it either, causing them extra grief because they were the ones having to wash those filthy uniforms. So it didn't take long for the kids to catch on. If their practice was sluggish, all I needed to do was turn my back on them, face 'No Sod Hill," and silently nod my head. Suddenly, their butts were on fire and practice improved 100 per cent.

A few months after we moved into our new home, I had some buddies help me build a deck on the back of the house. My philosophy is, if you don't ask for help, you'll never get it. Then my dad drove up from Virginia several months later and stayed with us for a week so we could finish off the downstairs.

I wasn't just being lazy, getting all that help. I needed it because one of my legendary deficiencies has always been a lack of handyman skills. Every year at the school football banquets, Joan loved it when, following my remarks, the audience called her to the microphone to tell them the latest ways I'd messed up when working on some home project. Like the time Dad and I were insulating the family room walls with Styrofoam, and we had to cut out a thin groove to conceal the exposed electric wires behind the Styrofoam. We were almost finished when Dad saw me grab a knife to trim some of the excess foam, and he screamed, "Stop!" — but not before my knife cut the wire and an electric shock flung me across the room. But, hey, I'm like a cat...nine lives.

Or the time I was installing carpet and I had to cut the bottom of a door to make the carpet fit underneath. I took the door off the hinges, and as the saying goes, I "measured twice and cut once." After I'd sawed off about an inch, I was proud—until I saw I had cut off the top of the door instead of the bottom. After I corrected my error by cutting the bottom, I then had to glue the top piece back on, and repaint the entire door. I admit it: around the house, I can be a bonehead.

Coaching Point: **It's wise to know your deficiencies, and be willing to reach out to others, even professionals, when their talents and skills significantly exceed your own.**

—————

Back at EPHS, many schools were still recruiting our tight end Mickey Shuler, and the University of Miami was among those really hot after him. When somebody from there called me and invited our staff down for spring practice, two things about the invite appealed to me personally. First, I never miss a chance to go and study football. Second, it was about 20 degrees outside and snowing in Pennsylvania, so this seemed like a perfect time for my first trip to Florida.

When I called the University of Miami to accept, they indicated they had an apartment where we could stay. Because of the travel expenses involved, I could take only one of my coaches, Coach Bernie, our defensive coordinator. He was excited to have the opportunity and said, "Let's do this!" So we set a date and began to make our plans. The least expensive way to get there was to drive. Bernie had a Volkswagen bus that got great gas mileage, and he said that if we took out the back seats, we could convert it into a camper. So we did, and then built a plywood platform for a bed across the wheel wells, allowing for food storage and a Coleman stove underneath that we could pull out and cook on. Man, I was excited about spring football and warm Florida weather.

We took off early one morning for our weeklong trip with the initial plan that he would drive and I would sleep. Then we'd switch out and keep going non-stop until we hit Daytona Beach. I remember the moment when we hit the Florida border how everything looked so white and green. The highway was white concrete, the grass was green, and fronds on the palm trees were blowing in the breeze. Back in Pennsylvania this time of year, the sky was usually gray, the grass was brown, and the trees were bare. What a treat to be in Florida!

We pulled the VW onto the beach, took out our sleeping bags and quickly fell asleep. Early the next morning, we were startled awake by loud noises, the sound of cars and buses driving down the beach. This was something I had never seen at any of the East Coast beaches I had visited. We ate several peanut butter and jelly sandwiches for breakfast before heading on our four-hour drive south to Miami and spring practice. When we got to the school, we went to the coaches' office where they welcomed us and showed us around the facilities. Then one of the coaches took us to the apartment where we would be staying. This place was stunning with white shag carpet and a refrigerator stocked with beverages and plenty of food for the week. As the saying goes, "We were living high on the hog."

Our days during spring practice were similar to the routine that we were accustomed to at other schools: into the office early, sit in on some meetings, watch tapes of their team's defense and offense, then attend practice and watch several scrimmages. Despite the beginning of a bad sunburn that first afternoon, I was loving the weather and our accommodations, and the fact that the school was very open to sharing their program's information with us. I felt that, all in all, this was turning into my favorite spring trip ever!

One day when no practice was scheduled, Bernie and I decided to drive an hour up to Ft. Lauderdale and go to the beach there. Little did we know that we were right in the middle of college spring break. When I was in college, I had never gone to a spring break because I was usually working. Well, we got some exposure to what I had missed all those years ago and the fun that college kids had these days. We saw beautiful sand and water and young college students having a blast. We parked the VW on the side of the road next to the beach where an outdoor shower was nearby, and we cooked a meal on our Coleman stove. We had all the amenities: a foam bed on plywood, an outdoor shower, a hot meal, a cool ocean breeze, and the beach just steps away.

We got back to Miami early the next morning, and then attended two more days of meetings and practices. From our beach trip and the afternoon practices outdoors, the sun had fried these lily-white Northerners to a crisp. When it was time to head back to Pennsylvania, we drove the 17 hours straight through, stopping only for gas and bathroom breaks. Despite our painful sunburns, we felt exhilarated.

Once we got home, we could hardly wait to share with the staff all the information we'd learned at the University of Miami—in particular, some great defensive tips and schemes.

For the next few weeks, I kept thinking about Florida and how great it would be to be a high school coach there, with warm weather year-round, and how all year, you can work on drills outside. Also, how in May, all the high schools held 20 days of spring practice.

One day I said to Joan, "Would you be open to looking at moving to Florida?" I remember seeing this quizzical look on her face indicating, "Oh no, here we go again." She reminded me that after a year-and-a-half, we'd finally gotten our new home finished, and that we had already moved four times in less than ten years. Based on my past history, you can guess what happened next.

I began my research on teaching in Florida and how to get certified. I secured a master list of all Florida high schools and updated my resume. For the next six months, I mailed out letters every week in search of a school that might be interested in hiring me. I kept this a secret from everyone but Joan because I didn't want my school or my coaching staff to think I was unhappy. Truth is, I *wasn't* unhappy. I just wanted to coach ball in Florida. All the replies to my letters were, "Thanks, but no thanks," so I was disappointed but undeterred because I had made up my mind I was going to coach in Florida.

Coaching Point: **Even when you think you're settled in a great job, you may discover the grass can be (literally) greener elsewhere, and you can hardly wait to move. And that'll be another time you wish you were a renter instead of a homeowner—and had bought stock in U-Haul.**

CHAPTER 15
I've Got to Get to Florida

In the meantime, as my Florida job search continued, we celebrated Christmas of 1974, in our usual way with the kids having Santa Claus at our house and then loading up some of the kids' presents and heading to both our parents' houses for more celebrations. We felt that since Christmas is about all the family—not just our kids—we made the extra effort to share the holiday with our parents. As a child and even as a teenager, Christmas was always the most special time of the year for my sister Janet and me. Being raised in Annapolis, Maryland, we often enjoyed a white Christmas, and to this day, I always aim to spend Christmas somewhere in cold weather in hopes that it will snow.

My parents provided many special traditions for us at Christmas. Dad and I would always go out into the woods on Christmas Eve, and look for the perfect tree to cut and bring home. Whether or not it was exactly perfect, it sure seemed that way to Janet and me. Mom and Dad always told us that Santa came not only with presents, but he also decorated the tree, so we were put to bed early, usually by 7PM, so that "Santa" had time to get everything done. Today, it's still hard for me to believe all the work that Mom and Dad had to do every year on Christmas Eve, on just one night.

These memories from the 1940s and '50s represent a time when life was very different. I remember one Christmas when I desperately wanted a bike and was really hoping I would find one from Santa under the tree. Of course,

Mom and Dad knew this and had already bought me a bike and stored it at a neighbor's house. Come Christmas Eve after Janet and I were asleep, Dad went to get it and that's when he discovered they'd bought a girl's bike by mistake! At this point, it was probably nine or ten o'clock, so Dad decided he had no choice but to call the owner of the Western Auto store at his home. In true Christmas spirit, the owner agreed to meet Dad at the store to exchange the girl's bike for a boy's bike.

———

Early January of 1975, I started back to teaching while I continued to send out applications and resumes to Florida, still hoping to get a job interview there. Things weren't looking good until on a Friday in late January, I came home to find a letter from Osceola High School in Kissimmee, Florida. The principal, Paul Runge, wrote that they had an opening for a teacher and football coach and requested that I give him a call. By then, it was too late in the day to reach him, so I had to wait until Monday morning. Weekends are often too short, but not this one. When Monday finally came, I called Mr. Runge first thing to make sure that he was truly interested in me as a candidate before I made the long drive from Pennsylvania to Florida for an interview. He assured me that he had already checked out some of my references and yes, he was very much interested in me for the job.

———

I made plans for the drive, knowing that fortunately I would have a place to stay when I got there. Mom and Dad had retired by now and although they enjoyed life in Virginia, they went to Ft. Meyers, Florida, every winter in their big travel trailer. When I called them to let them know that in about two weeks I would be interviewing in Kissimmee, they said they would drive the trailer to Kissimmee and I could stay with them while I interviewed.

Money was so tight, flying was not an option, so I made the 14 hour road trip straight through, arriving in Kissimmee late Saturday night. Then on Sunday, the day before my interview, I drove around to check out the town. Back in 1975, Kissimmee was just a small town with one main road—the two-lane Highway 192, a strip mall, and several hotels. Most of the residents were native Floridians, either white or African-American. Today, Highway 192 is six lanes and the population is multi-cultural, drawn by the many job opportunities at nearby Disney World. Back then, once you left town, the landscape was mainly just palmettos and scrub pines. The key industries were cattle and citrus, and most folks who lived in the area knew each other by name. There were two high schools in the county: St. Cloud and Osceola High. Before my interview, I discovered that Osceola High School's mascot was Kowboy Jake and the nickname of OHS was—and still is—the Kowboys. Not a typo, folks—that's Kowboy with a K!

When I walked into the Osceola High principal's office and introduced myself, I was surprised to see that Mr. Runge had his feet on his desk and that he was wearing pointed-toe cowboy boots, khakis, and a polo shirt. Here I was, dressed in a suit and tie, just like teachers dressed in Pennsylvania. Right away, Mr. Runge said, "You gotta take off that tie and jacket—you're way overdressed for this interview." So from the get-go, I liked this place! He said he knew from my resume and college coaching experience, that I'd been a head coach three times. "But here's the situation," he said. "If I hire you, you'll come in as the head JV coach." I replied, "With all due respect, Mr. Runge, I didn't come here to be a JV coach." He indicated that he wasn't satisfied with the current head coach and that more than likely, he would make a personnel change in November after the football season, and after that, the head coaching job would be open. When I told him that I wasn't comfortable working in that situation, he said, "Do a good job at JV as I know you'll do, and things will work out for you." We closed with him saying, "Go home and think it over. Give me an answer in a week." He also said that if I accepted the job, he wanted me there in April because spring football began on May first. By the time I got home, I was prepared to sell Joan on us moving to Florida. At the end of the week, I called Mr. Runge, told him I was coming, and he replied, "Welcome to the Kowboy family."

———

At the time, my son, Gregg, was 11, my daughter, Jennifer, was six, and they had moved so many times I figured they were probably used to it. I realize in retrospect that this frequent uprooting may not have been so easy on my family, but I was ambitious, and at the time, I put my interests above everyone else's. I justified this, though, by telling my family, "Every move we have made so far has turned out well and we've been better off than before. So I'm betting you will love living in Florida." They did—and they still live there, in Osceola County.

By now, it was February and I had to be in Kissimmee on April 15th. First things first, we had to sell our two-year-old house. It helped that Joan's terrific personality and many friends in our community led to her quickly securing a great realtor. The next week a "For Sale" sign was in our front yard and we were eager for a buyer.

When I told my parents that I had accepted the job in Kissimmee, they were elated. My problem of where to live there was solved immediately. They said, "We'll stay in Florida, bring the travel trailer to Kissimmee when you get here, and you can stay with us." Wow! Free room and board! I'm thinking that as soon as we can sell the house, *everything* will be great.

With much anticipation, I left for my new job in Kissimmee and on my first day as a health teacher, arrived in style, wearing the ever-popular leisure suit. I figured this being Florida I'd need several more, in pastel colors. But when I walked into Mr. Runge's office, wearing my light green leisure suit, he immediately stood up and said, "What the hell is *that* you're wearing?" Then he said, "I hired a football coach not some fancy-pants. Go home and get on some shorts, a tee shirt, and coaching shoes. But make sure you wear some socks with those shoes. Socks are required here."

When I got back to school properly attired, I asked Mr. Runge if he had a copy of my teaching schedule, and he said, "Don't worry about teaching right now. Just take the next several weeks to get familiar with everything and ready for spring ball." I noticed that lots of kids were just wandering around in the halls and outdoors during what I thought would be class time. When I asked the coaches about this, they told me, "We're on a new education plan called something like 'modular education.' Kids can 'opt out' of a class that day and go do independent study at the library, or under a tree." I noticed that several classrooms had signs reading, "This is an opt-out day." Had I died and gone to heaven? Warm weather, shorts, coaching shoes (with socks), no assigned classes, and spring ball in two weeks? NIRVANA!

———

By the end of April, we had an offer on the Pennsylvania house. Because Joan and I had done so much "sweat equity" on it, we actually made a profit on the sale. To save money on moving expenses, I'd drive my trusty green van up to Pennsylvania, load boxes to put in storage back in Kissimmee, then a couple of weeks later, make that same trip again, to get more boxes. Soon I found a house for sale right across the street from the high school. It was a little run down, so I got it for a great price. It needed painting, but with help from Mom and Dad and their friends, Doc and Margaret, I had it all painted and waiting for the arrival of my family.

———

During spring ball in April and May, I installed the Wishbone offense that we had been running in Pennsylvania. Once again, it was helpful having those teaching films from the UT trip (shhh!). The weather was warm, the grass was green, the sun shined every day, and I had some good athletes. I said to myself, *Other than your family, do you need anything else in life?* I didn't even mind being just the JV coach. I had some great assistant coaches who made the job fun. These included Alan Baker, a hard-nosed Kissimmee native, his sidekick Jeff Kessler, a great addition who kept us laughing every day, and Bert Bagley, a retired military man who was finishing his undergraduate teaching degree at University of Central Florida and was passionate about football.

Spring practice went great and we beat our rival St. Cloud in the spring game. Things couldn't have been any better. But two days before my family was to head out to Florida, I got a notice: "All teachers not on tenure will not be rehired." Talk about an explosion! I sprinted into Runge's office yelling, "What the hell is this?" He shut the door and calmly said, "Coach, you're covered. I promise your job is safe. Just keep quiet 'til school is out."

It was a leap of faith when the family and I made our final move from Pennsylvania in June. After those earlier trips in the green van to haul down boxes, I sprang for a company to move our furniture. For its final trip south, the green van was now filled with the last of the boxes, carrying Joan, the children, and me, and towing our old green VW!

Coaching Point: **Trust in fate. If something is meant to be, it will be. I did and it was!**

CHAPTER 16

Kissimmee Kowboys

By mid-June of 1975, we were settled into our newly-painted house on Bruce Street in Kissimmee, Florida. Joan and the kids seemed to enjoy living there because there were lots of new and fun things to do. We lived only about an hour from Melbourne Beach and the Atlantic ocean. Many weekends that first summer, we would take a day trip to Melbourne on the two-lane Highway 192 for a fun family outing at the beach. I'm not sure the rest of the family loved these times quite as much as I did, but we all enjoyed many fun days together. Being a new Florida resident reinforced my lifelong love affair with the ocean. Whenever I was at the beach and either frolicking in the water or just reading a book and relaxing, I was at peace with the world. Many men usually have hobbies, but I never really got into golf, fishing, hunting, or other typical male-type activities. My hobbies—then and now—included going to the beach, reading, and working out. At Kissimmee during the summers, even when I was at the beach, most of my days were filled with studying how to be a better football coach.

The commute to work at Osceola High School required me to simply exit the house, cut across the yard, cross Thacker Avenue, and there I was, standing at the front door of school—all of a two-minute walk. What a great set-up this was and it sure saved on gas. Every day I would go to school and work out with our JV players. We continued to install and polish the Wishbone option offense. Our head coach was Jim Yancey, who had been an all-conference SEC player for the University of Florida Gators. Jim was a great guy. I really liked and respected him.

When school started in the fall, I was assigned to be a health teacher. This was a new field for me and I had to spend some time studying my lesson plans. I suppose I was an okay health teacher, as I enjoyed the subject myself, but of course my passion was coaching football. My first game in Kissimmee was at home and as with all Kowboy home games, was played at the Silver Spurs Rodeo Arena. Naturally, I was anxious about the outcome of that first game, but later that night, we celebrated our first victory!

The Spurs Rodeo Arena was the home of the biggest rodeos in the South, held every year in February and July. The stands of this open-air stadium were covered with a tin roof, and located at each end were chutes where the bulls, horses, and riders entered the arena. These rodeos were big events, and in February, all the local schools designated one Friday as a holiday known as "Rodeo Day." Of course most of the male students didn't need "Rodeo Day" as an excuse to wear cowboy boots and cowboy hats. That was their regular attire every day of the year—in class and out—another cultural adjustment that took me awhile to get used to, especially those hats in class. In July, immediately after the rodeo was over, the groundskeepers began to lay sod and get ready for the Kowboy football season. This was a unique set-up for a high school football stadium, which had the added benefit of intimidating our opponents who weren't accustomed to the earthy smell left by all those bulls and horses. In fact, many opposing players, as adults, have told me over the years that they would never forget the experience of playing in that stadium, and especially that smell.

On Friday nights, before the varsity game would begin, the entrance of the players into the stadium was a thrilling spectacle unlike any I've ever seen or heard of elsewhere in high school football. From one of the chutes at the Spurs Rodeo Arena, out came a horse with a female rider wearing chaps in the school colors of blue and gold and a Kowboy hat, with two six-shooter pistols. Behind her and the horse, waiting to make their grand entrance, was our football team. But first, the horse would buck up and down several times before taking off down the middle of the field with the rider blasting away, left and right, with those six-guns. Our opponents knew to stay well out of the way at their end of the field, until she turned the horse, pistols still blazing, down the sidelines. Without fail, during every home game, thousands of fans went wild, which certainly fired up our football team to win. I'm telling you this was something awesome—all the commotion of the horse and gun-blazing rider, the screaming fans, and the players charging onto the field. In all my years of leading football teams into stadiums, I never again experienced such excitement. Just thinking about this still makes the hair on my neck stand up.

———

After football season was over, Joan and I were getting ready for Christmas, and as much as I loved Florida—the year-round warm weather, the people, and especially the football—when Christmas rolled around, I knew I wanted to be where it was cold and snowing. So Joan and I decided to head north for the holidays, the opposite direction from snowbirds who headed south that time of year. Traveling in the green customized van so the kids could sleep most of the way, we left at 10PM, and drove straight through to Pennsylvania, stopping first in Enola to visit old friends. By the time we got there, it was snowing and with the wind chill factor, about minus 30 degrees. Our friends were glad to see us, but said, "Are you guys crazy? It's 80 and sunny in Florida. Why in the world did you come here *now*?" A really good question, and it's true, we despise cold weather—anytime except Christmas. We enjoyed a two-day stay with our friends, before heading south to Georgetown, Delaware, where we spent a great Christmas with Joan's parents, Norman and Fannie Bell.

At around four in the morning on the day we were to leave, I awoke to a scraping noise. Norman was outside shoveling our van out from under six inches of snow. We waited until around nine that morning before we carefully maneuvered our way home on roads covered with snow and ice. The driving was tense and treacherous for four long hours until we hit Richmond, Virginia, where finally, the roads were clear and we drove ten more hours before arriving home to warm and sunny Florida. By the time we got there, our green van was nearly white because of the salt mix used on the northern roads to keep them drivable. Notwithstanding the stress and length of the drive, we had no regrets about making that journey to have a cold and snowy Christmas vacation.

———

When school started in January of 1976, a buzz was going around that the principal was going to make a coaching change. By the end of January, Coach Yancey was indeed released, and some time later, I was named the head football coach. In between, when Coach Yancey and I talked about his leaving, he was okay with it, saying, "I'm ready to be out of this pressure cooker." I was elated to once again have an opportunity to be head coach and run the show. It was also gratifying to know that my persistence in following my dream to Florida had paid off.

> *Coaching Point:* **According to legendary football coach Lou Holtz, "A river cuts through rock, not because of its power, but because of its persistence." Persistence pays.**

———

I knew from experience, the first thing a head coach has to do is assemble the very best coaching staff available. Football is a game of many moving parts, and it is impossible to do it all by yourself. I highly recommend that you never try. Within a few weeks, I felt that we had hired a staff that would allow us to be successful. Bert Bagley, the military guy who had by now gotten his certification to teach, was the defensive coordinator. Tom Booth was the offensive line coach. George Sullivan was the defensive line coach. Henry Ramsey coached the linebackers. One of the most important coaches because he set the foundation for the entire program was Alan Baker, the head freshman coach, who was instrumental in teaching fundamentals and toughness. In fact, Alan's freshman team went undefeated and amazingly, unscored-upon that season. I have never seen nor heard of this happening anywhere before or since. Some of the credit surely goes to Alan's assistant, Jeff Kessler, also an awesome coach, with one of the best senses of humor I've ever known. Jeff was just naturally witty and always telling jokes. He could take any situation and make it hilarious. He kept us all laughing, even during the most stressful times. Ray Barrette was another valuable assistant coach among several more whose names I can't recall now. (Those I've left out by name, please forgive me; this was 39 years ago.)

Two men had an especially positive impact on me in Kissimmee. Our linebacker coach Henry Ramsey was not only a great coach, but more importantly a great man who also happened to be the best math teacher I've ever known. In addition, he was a rancher who owned and managed a spread of several hundred cattle. How he managed all this, I'll never understand. The other man who inspired me was our lead assistant principal Nelson Winbush. Mr. Winbush was a friend and mentor to me, and also a tough disciplinarian who kept the kids in line with his "adjustment stick." I was blessed to have known both of these men.

————

I was beginning to learn a lot about Kissimmee and Osceola County with regards to the politics in the school system. It seemed that Osceola had the reputation of firing either the football coach and/or the principal about every year or so. Many coaching friends from neighboring Orlando had told me to be careful because "you might be next." In addition, the school superintendent, who was elected every two years, seemed to be replaced every election. I thought, *Holy smokes, I just got hired only to find out that OHS fires its head football coach every year or so?* Fortunately I wasn't among the swift departures. My tenure there lasted for eight years until I decided—on my terms—to accept a coaching job in Texas.

> *Coaching Point:* **It bears repeating that your attitude determines your altitude. My attitude was always positive and that's why I believe positive things happened for me—and not just in football.**

————

I had never been interested in any professional pursuits other than football, until I met several men in Florida who were highly successful in direct sales. They told me that the qualities they saw that made me a terrific head football coach would also make me some money in other ventures. Although I was intrigued to learn more about these opportunities, I simply had no time to pursue them. But my entrepreneurial spirit had been piqued.

CHAPTER 17

So Now You're a Stockbroker, Too?

S everal men visited with me one afternoon in the offseason, and told me about a new company they were forming in Lakeland, Florida. They explained that the company would start out by offering stock in what is known as an IPO—Initial Public Offering. At the end of the offering, the proceeds would be used to start an insurance company. They had seen this done before with a similar company, and said that those who had bought the original stock had done very well financially. Now, they wanted me to go through their new company's training course, pass the stock exam required by the SEC—Security Exchange Commission, and then sell stock issues to some of the many people I knew and others. This opportunity was as far from what my life had been as A is to Z. But because of the excellent part-time opportunity to make substantial additional income, I was very interested and this was the start of my second love, behind coaching football. Soon, being an entrepreneur would become a new passion.

For a couple of months, I traveled to Lakeland, 45 minutes away, to attend classes several nights a week and all day on Saturdays. The training was intense and included information on how the stock market worked, sales techniques, and personal development. This was also my first exposure to many self-help classics, such as Napoleon Hill's *Think and Grow Rich*, which I've read at least 50 times since, and over the years recommended to hundreds of students, including my football players. Looking back, I see that this training was the catalyst for my commitment to personal development and lifelong learning.

Using my new tools, I felt surprisingly comfortable each Saturday when it was my turn to get up in front of about 40 other trainees and demonstrate an actual sales presentation. Throughout this training, I still performed all of my responsibilities as a teacher and head football coach. As a priority, football was still way out in front of everything else. It always had been and would be throughout my career. Even so, I was enjoying this new adventure.

As the training progressed, I believed more and more that this was going to be a great company, and not just because of the extra money I could earn for my family. I felt this was a company I would be proud to represent. After six weeks or so, they told us it was time to prepare for how to pass the SEC test—preparation that would require an entire weekend and likely be the most intense mental training of our lives. The leaders assured us that they had led this training many times previously and they boasted about a high success rate of those passing the test.

We reported to the Holiday Inn in Lakeland, at three o'clock on Friday afternoon. After we signed in at registration and were given packets of information, we were force-fed that information from five o'clock to ten o'clock that night, from 8AM to 10PM on Saturday, then again from 8AM to 1PM on Sunday.

They weren't kidding about this training. Except for brief bathroom breaks, we never left the room the entire time we were there. Even the boxed meals they served were eaten at our desks. This weekend was definitely the most intense learning experience I had ever endured, and by Sunday afternoon, my brain was fried.

Before we were dismissed to go home, we were warned not to look at any of the materials, or even to think about what we'd been exposed to over the weekend. We were told to be sure to get a good night's sleep and then report to the Orlando office at 7:45 Monday morning to take the three-hour exam. They advised us that, during the exam, we should just let our minds flow and trust that the answers would simply emerge onto the paper. And above all, not to try to over-analyze the questions or to change any of our initial answers. Just read each question, they said, answer it, and move on.

At the end of the exam, I felt drained and walked out in kind of a fog. I thought I had known some of the answers, but really had no idea whether or not I had passed. For two weeks, the result was in limbo until I opened an envelope I got in the mail and discovered to my amazement that I had passed the exam with a score of 84 per cent. It suddenly hit me that if I hadn't passed, all those agonizing hours of training would have been for nothing. Then I was elated when I thought, *Oh my God, here I am, a certified stock broker, the same guy who couldn't even pass his first college entrance exam!*

Now having passed the SEC test, I was ready to go make sales and earn some money. But first, I had to buy a suit and some new shoes—leisure suits wouldn't cut it. Passing the exam didn't mean the end of our training, though. Every Saturday, we were required to be in Lakeland for more.

———

I set a goal to make a certain number of sales each week in order to meet my financial goal of making $10,000 in the next three months. Every week, I would usually have two to four evening appointments. I would come home after school, shave in the shower—a time-saver I follow to this day—put on a suit, grab my briefcase, and go off to sell some issues of our company's stock. I actually enjoyed the selling because I really believed we had a great financial opportunity for people who were looking for an investment. Some nights I would come home with checks totaling $5,000 or $10,000, from which, as one of the company's top salesmen, I was paid quite a good commission. It was a bonus when many of my clients would help me out by recommending their friends as potential clients. This was 1976, when my teaching and coaching salary was about $12,000 a year. So imagine how great it felt to be selling stock when I earned that same amount in just three months. School was going well, football was successful, I was making lots of extra money, and life was good.

Along with this extra money came the dream to take my family on a three-week, cross-country road trip. I discovered that as a teacher, I could write off the expenses on our income tax if we kept a logbook of our visits. At that time, the IRS allowed teachers these deductions because this travel was considered educational for our students.

To make this trip, we decided we needed a 20-foot motorhome. So Joan and I went to Ft. Myers, where my mom and dad now lived year-round, and with the money I'd made selling stock, I bought a brand new Mobile Traveler motorhome, equipped with air conditioning, a stove, refrigerator, walk-in shower, two bunk beds in the back, and a queen-size bed over the top of the cabin's passenger seats.

We had an ambitious three-week summer trip agenda. From Kissimmee, our first stop was the beach in Panama City, then on to New Orleans where the kids actually walked down Bourbon Street. In Houston, we went ice skating in the Galleria. In San Antonio we strolled the River Walk. On our way to El Paso, a minor mechanical glitch with the motorhome delayed us for a day near a small town in west Texas. But afterward, it was on to El Paso with a quick side trip to Juarez, a Mexican border town. Back at the El Paso campground, we met a family from Ohio with two kids about the same age as ours, whose parents were also teachers. We really hit it off, especially when we discovered we both planned to make some of the same stops westward. So we followed each other through Carlsbad, New Mexico, then on to Phoenix, Arizona, where we actually fried an egg on the concrete, and in Las Vegas, camped behind one of the big casinos, where as usual, we had electric, water, and sewer hookups. On one afternoon, our son, Gregg, by now an adventurous 13-year-old, decided to swim in every pool on the Vegas strip. Even though Las Vegas was a much safer and smaller place in those days, this was quite an accomplishment for him. I don't remember if we celebrated that night under the awnings of our motorhomes, but if we didn't, we should have.

From there, we headed northwest through the desert in Bakersfield, California, to the cool, beautiful mountains in Yosemite National Park. To get there, each of our motor homes slowly hugged the winding and treacherous road. Up ahead, my new buddy, Bob, knowing I never liked heights and was terrified on this drive, radioed me from his CB, jesting, "Hey Diamond Jim, look to your left, you won't believe how far down it is," to which I replied, "Kiss my ass!"

Without a guardrail and merely by the grace of God, we made it to Yosemite, where we parked for the night alongside a gurgling mountain stream, and slept as cool gentle breezes came through our motorhomes' open windows. From Yosemite, it was on to San Francisco, where we camped at Fisherman's Wharf, and then to Salt Lake City, where we said our goodbyes to Bob and his family as they departed in a different direction.

We turned eastward to Denver and while traveling through Kansas, got stopped in our tracks by a violent thunderstorm packing high winds. Seeking cover, I pulled into a gas station. Then I realized this was a terrible idea. If one of those lightning bolts flashing everywhere hit a gas pump, it would explode and we'd all be history. So I quickly pulled across the road and turned off the key. We watched, helpless, as debris flew everywhere and our motorhome rocked in the wind and rain. All of a sudden, we felt a huge explosion. Turns out, a nearby tall highway sign had shattered, sending a six-by-two foot plastic shard through the side of the motorhome near the couch, like a javelin through butter. We were terrified. But when we saw three feet of that shard inside, we knew how lucky we were to be safe and unhurt. When the storm finally passed, we found an insurance agent up the road who helped us get patched up the next day.

Then we drove through Kansas, Indiana, Pennsylvania, and finally landed at Joan's parents' in Delaware. I left the family there so they could visit, while I drove the motorhome back to work in Kissimmee.

It had been the trip of a lifetime, and we certainly enjoyed it, despite the close calls.

After that, I sold the motorhome and actually made a little bit of money on the deal.

By this time, the stock company was ready, as planned, to turn into a full-fledged insurance company. The company wanted me to go full-time now, selling insurance instead of stocks, and said I could probably make $50,000 or more my first year. Even with the promise of four times my annual salary at Osceola High, I explained that regardless of how much I loved the business experience and was grateful for the opportunity, I was a full-time football coach first and foremost. No amount of money would change that. So I left the company and didn't look back.

But my first experience with entrepreneurship was not my last.

Coaching Point: **Making a lot of money is no substitute for doing what you love.**

CHAPTER 18

One of the Oldest High School Football Rivalries in Florida

When I first started coaching at Kissimmee's Osceola High, I didn't realize the significance of the football rivalry between us and St. Cloud High. At the time, Osceola County consisted of just these two high schools, so whenever they competed, the game created a huge amount of interest in both Kissimmee and St. Cloud. I discovered that this was one of the longest running rivalries in the entire state of Florida. It was always the last game of the year, and whichever team won had bragging rights for the entire next year. At the conclusion of spring football practice in May, this rivalry resumed when we played each other in the Spring Jamboree game for just two quarters instead of four. Even if a school won the big game in November, if the other school won the Spring Jamboree, then that school would always say, "Well, we beat you in the spring, so it's all equal." I never did get that rationale, but we both used it.

During St. Cloud week in November, things got really wild and crazy. Pep rallies were held at the end of each school day and were attended by community leaders and former players whose speeches got the students whipped into a frenzy. In addition, at unannounced times through the day, part of the band would march up and down the halls playing our fight song. They were the Bulldogs, we were the Kowboys, and to say that we hated each other would not be overstating it.

On the day before the fall game, the Osceola County Rotary Club would host a luncheon where both the Bulldogs coach, Tom Greer, and I would get up and publicly challenge each other as to the outcome of the game. Even these business luncheons got wild and crazy. One year, I showed up dressed in full football gear and in front of the crowd, screamed to Coach Greer, "We're ready for you Coach!" The next year, we both dressed up in full football gear and the local newspaper took a picture of us, crouched down helmet to helmet in the classic football stance, looking like we were ready to go to war. The next day, game day, this picture was the entire front page of the paper, the climax of the week's front-page headline stories featuring previous games in the historical rivalry, as well as how the teams seemed to match up this year.

Another year, Coach Greer came to Rotary dressed in a suit and tie, and when he got up to speak, he ripped off his shirt to expose the tee shirt underneath that boasted, "Hell no, we don't eat no crow." This definitely was not a friendly rivalry. On Thursday nights before the annual game, a big parade was held from downtown Kissimmee to the high school, followed by a huge pep rally and giant bonfire, where we burned a St. Cloud Bulldog in effigy. Because in the past, derogatory messages had been spray-painted on our field, it became a necessary tradition for a group of our seniors to stay up all Thursday night on guard. And when the game was held at St. Cloud, their seniors did the same thing.

Regardless of where the game was played, it was always standing room only. And afterwards, there was usually a fight among the competing fans that usually involved adults.

The most exciting game of all time in this rivalry occurred in the late 1970s at the Silver Spur stadium. That year, it was standing room only as usual, with a crowd in excess of 10,000. But this year, the stadium was packed two hours before kickoff. Both teams had had a good year and were hyped up for a win. When I walked onto the field following that traditional dramatic entrance with the horse, rider, and six-guns blazing, I could feel so much electricity my hair stood on end.

The lead in the game went back and forth. And it hadn't helped that my senior field goal kicker, after a knee injury that kept him on crutches and out of practice all week, had shanked a field goal. Why was he even in the game when I had brought up a freshman to be our kicker? Because the senior kicker had come up to me before the game started and said, "Coach, I'm dressing. It's my last game, and I want to be available if you need me." With his missed kick in such an intense, back-and forth game, I was regretting my decision to allow him to play.

By late in the fourth quarter, the game was tied, with only about a minute left. We got the ball on our 40-yard line and I was just running the clock out and playing to get us into overtime. We gained a few yards on first down, but on the next play, our great electric running back Smokey Green, who stood only five-foot-four, broke a long run and as he was tackled out of bounds, the referee threw a flag that advanced the ball 15 yards. So now, we had the ball near the 15-yard line with just seconds remaining. I sent in the freshman kicker for the game winner. But while I was talking to the coaches, they screamed out, "Get him out of there!" The senior kicker, against my orders, had just run onto the field and told the ninth-grader to get out, and that *he* was going to kick the field goal. When I saw that, I lost it!!! I ran onto the field mad as a hornet, and two of my coaches, both about six-foot-three, ran and grabbed me, turned me upside down, and got me off the field just as the ball was kicked. I never saw that kick, but they tell me that time stood still as the ball wobbled off the senior kicker's foot, hit the crossbar, and bounded over inside for the winning score. Our 5,000 thousand fans erupted into delirious joy, while *their* 5,000 fans were stunned into silence.

Two hours after the game, long after St. Cloud had gone home with their tails between their legs, our fans were still on the field celebrating, more than a few with adult beverages in red solo cups. Nobody cared about who was drinking what. We had WON!

————

During my eight years there, we won a lot and they won some. That's how it felt to me anyway, but the truth would be in the record books if anybody wants to check it out.

———

Another year, our opening game was versus the previous year's Florida State High School champions, Haines City High. They were undefeated and loaded with talent. Their star running back was the Florida 100-yard sprint champion. Two brothers named Weaver—one of them nicknamed "Meat Cleaver Weaver"—were so huge that one of my assistant coaches, Alan Baker, said, "Their butts are so big they wouldn't fit into a number-ten washtub!" Both had signed scholarships to the University of Georgia. Most of our Kissimmee fans had the same thought: "Forget *winning* this game. We just hope we have enough players left to finish the season." We had worked our kids, including my son, Gregg, who was our starting center, real hard that summer and we actually believed we could win. No one else shared this sentiment, but by the time the game was over, Smokey Green had run all over them, and we won by two touchdowns!

Coaching Point: **Never underestimate what a team can achieve when they all believe.**

———

But there are times when no matter how many people want desperately to believe they can bring about a positive outcome, their beliefs cannot change fate. One Sunday morning, several parents came to my house to tell me that one of our players, Pat McDonald, had been in a bad car accident the night before. When I got to the hospital, the doctor said that it didn't look good. The entire school was praying that Pat would pull through. The team was so distraught, they didn't really want to practice, much less practice as hard as was necessary for the upcoming game against one of our toughest opponents. And to be honest, I didn't feel much like coaching. I had never experienced such a terrible dilemma. How in the world would we all come together and rise up to prepare for this game? It occurred to me that in life, we all must learn that life goes on even after something traumatic happens. So we continued to practice, somehow getting through day by day the best we could, even as we knew that our teammate was fighting for his life. On Wednesday, that fight took a turn, and they put Pat on a machine to keep him alive. The next morning, the principal came on the PA system and announced that Pat McDonald had died just a few minutes earlier. Suddenly I went numb. And then, over the next few days until after his funeral, I shed more tears than I ever had in my life.

Coaching Point: **There's no way to prepare for the loss of young people before they reach their prime. The only way to cope is to be grateful for each and every day because none of us is ever promised tomorrow.**

CHAPTER 19

How to Rebuild Your Locker Room on the Cheap

I first met Bert Bagley in 1975. At the time, he was just coming out of a 20-year stint in the Air Force and finishing up a teaching degree at the University of Central Florida. He wanted to coach football and I hired him as a part-time coach. The next year, when I got the head coaching job, Bert was completing his last semester at UCF which required him to do student teaching. Because he chose Osceola High, he became my student teacher that spring.

The first day he reported to me, I handed him the roll book and lesson plans and said, "It's all yours." I supervised him some, but I spent most days in my office reviewing films and working on football. He was 40-years-old and I figured he could handle high school kids. But he handled so much more. Hiring Bert was just about the best thing I ever did in Kissimmee. Our success was due to our entire staff of great coaches, but Bert and Alan Baker, the freshman coach, were the bell cows on the staff.

Whenever I hired a coach, I wanted a good teacher of football, and just as important, a good worker. Bert excelled in both areas. Coach Bagley was the defensive coordinator and we made quite a pair, Bert at six-foot-three and me at five-foot-seven were a true Mutt and Jeff. We fought and argued a lot, especially during some of the tight games. I would go up to him and ask, "What's the next play you're gonna call?" He'd look down at me and say "I'm blitzing their ass," and I would say, "Don't call that!" And he would say, "Fire me," before calling the blitz. We loved and trusted one another, and most of the times after whatever play I had argued with him about, I would have to say, "Great call." He would roll his eyes back and assume a posture that said, "Hell, yeah."

One Friday, we were traveling to play an away game against Auburndale. Coach Bagley leaned over to me and said, "What's the first play you'll call if we go into overtime?" I looked at him like he had two heads. But guess what? The game went into overtime and I did call the play he had asked me about. I began to wonder if he was psychic. By the way, we lost that game on a very questionable call. I think the official knew that he had blown it because as the game ended, he was seen sprinting to his car with some of our most passionate fans in hot pursuit.

One day we were talking about our football locker room, known as the Varsity Building, and the practice field, both of which were in terrible shape. Bert said, "Why don't we rebuild the locker room and re-do the practice field?" This wasn't as outrageous as it sounded because I knew he was building his own house on a five-acre plot outside of town. "I'll be the project manager," he said, "and you be the money man, the guy in charge of raising the cash." After he designed the new building, we went to the masonry teacher, John Harmison, who agreed to do all the concrete work, using students in his classes as the workers. John said, "We'll do the work, but you'll have to buy all the materials." For the next four months as this project was in full swing, I was in full swing as a fundraiser. By the end of the school year, the project was complete, except for the practice field and the lockers needed to replace the antiquated ones that had been removed during the renovation. We contacted an old military base over on the east coast to see if they had any surplus lockers. They told us that we could have 50 lockers, but that we would have to haul them to our place. During the entire month of June, we traveled the 140-mile round trip back and forth hauling lockers to our new locker room, where we sandblasted them and spray-painted them royal blue.

While all this was going on, Bert was lining up a company that would provide fill dirt and sod for our practice field. Caravans of big dump trucks made their way down the road before dumping mounds of dirt onto the field. Then, players, students, coaches, and parents all volunteered to shovel and smooth the dirt before laying the sod. Everything was coming together so that our new facilities would be ready for the fall season.

During all this activity, I spent my days looking over the bills that were piling up and wondering how we were going to pay for all this. Whenever I would express these concerns to Bert, he would always say, "My job is to build it. Your job is to pay for it."

Somehow, through donations, begging, and fundraisers such as car washes and bake sales, we managed to pay all the bills. It helped that most of these projects were built with "sweat equity," saving us a considerable amount of money. It was thanks to donors, players, John Harmison's classes, and parents that the Kowboys were given a better football facility.

Just as a new suit can make a guy feel better about himself, our new football facility boosted the team and coaches with new confidence and pride, leading to successful football seasons for years to come.

Coaching Point: **Always look for people's unique qualities, putting them to good use, and never underestimate the value of everyone pulling together to accomplish great goals.**

CHAPTER 20

You Think You Need Water During Football Practice?

I t was when my son, Gregg, entered the tenth grade that he began playing for me on the varsity. Like any dad, I loved my son very much, but on the football team, he was just another player to me. He played the position of center on the offensive line, and in the huddle he was aligned directly in front of me as I called the play to the offense. I am short in stature and fiery by disposition, so when a play got messed up during practice and my temper flared, I would crash the clipboard that I always carried with me over Gregg's helmet, sometimes breaking the clipboard in half. You might think this would have hurt him, but with that hard helmet on his head, he was protected.

Off the field I was a kind and loving guy, but when the whistle blew for practice, another side of my personality came out, and it wasn't always good. Gregg wasn't the only one who suffered my clipboard. I was an equal opportunity coach. But one day, Coach Bagley brought me a big box containing about a hundred clipboards. "I think you're losing some of your fire," he told me, "and I noticed you're low on these, so have at it." Hey, you are what you are.

Smokey Green, our dynamic running back, at just five-foot-four, was very short, but very fast, and very tough. He had an electric smile enhanced by one gold tooth. Every day in practice, he took pleasure in running over the big guys as he screamed, "Hit me harder next time," and he would laugh on his way back to the huddle. Not only because he broke some Osceola rushing records, he was a media darling and a Central Florida star. One Friday, we decided to keep him out of the game because he'd been injured earlier that week during practice. We were about to play Bishop Moore High School, a ritzy private school in Orlando, and as our bus unloaded, many of their white collar adult fans came up to me and asked, "Where's 'The Smoke'? We read that he's hurt, but we really wanted to see him play, so can we at least get his autograph?" Smokey smiled that gold-tooth grin, and obliged each and every one of them.

———

Back in the 1970s, and even before that when I was a high school player myself, the belief was that for safety's sake, the players' hydration should be kept to a minimum. So we carried out to practice every day only one old Gatorade bucket filled with water, along with just one small Dixie cup, for 40 players. Every now and then, as a reward after a particularly good play, we would let a couple of the players use the Dixie cup to get a sip of water. By the time the second or third guy dipped in to get his water, they were also getting some grass and sand left by the first guy. But the bucket usually didn't make it all the way through practice because in a fit of temper after a bad play, I would kick it over, saying, "There's your water for the day." Again, this was years before we knew the benefits of proper hydration and sanitation. In today's world, doing that would have gotten me fired a hundred times over. But I don't think any of my players back then ever fell out due to fainting or cramps because having worked on farms and ranches all summer, they were used to the heat and hard work.

Our medical kit to handle the kids' bumps and bruises consisted of a couple of rolls of tape, some Mercurochrome, and a pair of scissors. Both of my line coaches, George Sullivan and Tom Booth, were huge men who were in charge of treating any injuries. One day a player came to them and said he had a boil. Tom and George looked at each other and told the player to come with them back to the locker room. Wasn't long before I heard a blood curdling scream, and a few minutes later they all came back. Turns out big burly country boys have a way with medicine: a sterilized pocket knife, a bottle of Mercurochrome, and a band-aid. Just like that, no more boil. When the player told the rest of the team what had happened, they all laughed and said, "Well, don't go to *them* for an injury unless a bone's sticking out."

Coaching Point: Remember the wise words of author Robert Schuler, "Tough times don't last, but tough people do."

Our head basketball coach and the principal were in a running feud over just about everything. This had been going on for months and was getting uglier by the day, making things tough for me because I got along with both men very well.

Then one time in the middle of the night, I got a call from the basketball coach who was screaming, "He's gone, he's gone!" It seems the principal went out drinking that night, had an accident downtown, and the woman in the car with him was not his wife. The next morning, the principal didn't show up for work, and two days later, we had a new boss. For various reasons, it seemed that every other year, we would get a new principal. Most of the time that happened because every two years, a new superintendent was elected and he would select his own choice to be the new principal. I saw one person go from history teacher to superintendent and back to history teacher all in a span of six years.

Coaching Point: Bosses may not always be perfect, but in the midst of professional conflicts involving them and your co-workers, it's usually wiser to side with the boss.

CHAPTER 21

Don't Mess with My Wife

When we moved to Kissimmee, my wife, Joan, did not have a job. At the time, there just wasn't anything available in her field of home economics, so I talked to the principal and asked him what jobs might be coming open in the near future. I was told that a science position would be coming open in the fall and he asked me if she might be interested. But after looking over Joan's transcript, he determined she was not certified for this position. He mentioned that if she took four courses in this field over the summer, her certification would be adequate and then he could hire her.

The closest college that offered these courses was Florida State University in Tallahassee, so Joan applied to FSU and registered for the four required courses. Because Tallahassee is about a four-hour drive from Kissimmee, it would be necessary for her to live there for the summer. As you can imagine, this was quite an expense for our family, and one that would put a hardship on both of us. But we agreed that this was what we had to do for the long-term benefit of having two incomes.

I had to learn to be Mr. Mom for the summer, an unfamiliar role to say the least. I don't think I had ever cooked a meal during our entire marriage. But I had always helped around the house and was not a stranger to housework or washing dishes. As a matter of fact, I am an expert dishwasher, both then and now. Breakfast was easy, and the kids could usually fix a sandwich for lunch, but dinner was a challenge. I do remember becoming an expert at instant mashed potatoes. At least we were getting by and nobody was starving. Sometimes Joan would come home for the weekend, and we visited her in Tallahassee a few times.

I was fortunate to get a summer job at the largest motel in town, the Larson's Lodge, probably because I had been the owner's sons' football coach. Iris Larson hired me to be the pool cleaner, so I had to learn how to properly care for and maintain their commercial pool. I suppose I did a good job because I worked there several summers. Two great things about this job: one, I earned some extra money which we needed, and two, the family was allowed to use the pool at any time. Many afternoons each week after my work was done, I would usually bring the kids and let them swim.

With the summer coming to a close and Joan about to complete her courses, we were looking forward to her having a full-time teaching job. On the day before football practice was to begin, Joan received a letter in the mail. When she opened the letter and read it to me, I let out a bevy of expletives! The letter was from my principal who wrote that he was sorry he could not hire Joan as he had filled the position with someone else, blah, blah, blah… "and thanks for your interest."

I'm usually a reasonable person and not one to stir up trouble, but an explosion was inevitable. My feelings are very strong that a man's word is his bond and the principal had told us that if Joan got those courses, she would be hired. Now he'd broken his word and reneged on the offer. I felt that a bond had been broken and that I couldn't trust him on whatever other issues might come up down the road.

I called Coach Bagley and asked him to meet me at the locker room because something big had just happened. Before we even sat down, he could tell that I was furious. I explained the situation and that I was getting ready to resign my football position in the morning. I went home, wrote a letter to the principal, and shoved it under his door. The letter stated why Joan and I felt betrayed, and I closed with, "Go get somebody else to coach your football team." Signed, "Thanks for *your* interest!"

Coach Bagley met the team the next morning and started practice without Head Coach Jim Scible.

I was done and I didn't care. I figured that everything would be okay and that I'd get another job doing something, somewhere, I didn't know what. Around mid-morning, some people showed up at my house unexpectedly, wanting to know what was going on. I remember meeting in my living room with the mayor, several parents, and a few business people. I explained what had happened, that trust had been broken, and that's why I couldn't continue. The mayor said to give him a couple of hours to see what he could do. Around one o'clock, the superintendent's secretary called and asked me to please report to his office. When I did, Superintendent Fletcher asked me right away to explain my side of the story. He then asked me to leave for a while, go get a cup of coffee, and come back in an hour. When I returned and sat down, he said, "First, let me say that you are not the tail that wags the dog in this school district, but I agree, you and Joan were wronged, and it will be corrected. Now go get ready for this afternoon's practice."

Joan started the school year as a full-time science teacher, and continued in that position, as well as other teaching positions in Osceola County where she was a great faculty member for over 20 years.

Coaching Point: **When your basic principles are violated, be willing to take a stand, even if it means losing or giving up your job. After all, integrity is your most valuable asset. In my case, I always figured there were tens of thousands of high schools in the United States, and I had worked in only four....Next?**

CHAPTER 22

So You Want to be a Coach AND a Business Owner?

Around 1978, there was word around town that a brand new strip mall was scheduled to open in about eight months. At the time, there was just one small sporting goods store in all of Osceola County, so I had an idea for a new business and began talking with Coach Bagley about partnering in a franchise called the Athletic Attic. This franchise had been started in Gainesville several years earlier and was very popular. As our talks grew serious, we visited several Athletic Attic locations to talk with their owners.

Athletic Attic was started by the track coach, Jimmy Carnes, at the University of Florida. The Gainesville location had done really well and soon, they were selling franchises all over Florida. The merchandise included athletic shoes of all types, running apparel, and athletic training devices. We discovered that the opening inventory cost was around $100,000. In addition to these costs, there were franchise fees, lease improvement costs, cash register expenses, and other fees which totaled another $50,000. Despite the immediate financial requirements, we were convinced that this venture would be successful because of the location and lack of competition.

The next step was to set up a meeting with the corporate people in Gainesville to ascertain whether they would grant us a franchise. Before we could even qualify to get a loan, they had to do a study to make certain our business would have a high probability of success.

One Saturday, we traveled to Gainesville and spent the better part of the day going over the requirements to be met before we could ask the bank for a loan. A big factor in our favor was that we were coaches. A big negative was that we were coaches who had never started or run a business before. Nevertheless, we must have done a good sales job because in two weeks, Athletic Attic started a feasibility study on our Kissimmee location. It was soon determined that they would give us tentative approval, contingent on our obtaining financing. Bert and I both had home mortgages with salaries totaling no more than $30,000 combined. Both of us intended to continue coaching football and teaching school, while as absentee owners we would monitor the store daily and work at the store on weekends. We planned to hire a full-time manager and several part-time employees.

Now it was time to go to the bank and see if we could get a loan. The vice president of the biggest bank in town was Bob Gee, one of the first people I met when we moved to Kissimmee. Bert and I had coached two of Bob's sons. We developed a detailed business plan including all our projections for the business.

I set up an appointment with Bob, and Bert and I headed to the bank with our business plan for the financial loan meeting. Bob looked over our plan, and in about ten minutes said, "I can't loan you boys any money." I must have looked dejected because he said, "Relax, let me make this phone call to Tampa." I thought he was putting us off when he asked us to leave the room, but actually, he was calling a friend of his who worked with the SBA, the Small Business Association loan office in Tampa. About 15 minutes later, he called us back in and said, "It looks good that you'll probably get the loan, which will be issued by the government's SBA." He said that he would fax the paperwork to them and get back to us in about a week. As we got up to leave, he stated, kind of off the cuff, "You know you'll both have to put your houses up for collateral in case you default on the loan." By this time we were elated, and said, "No problem."

With our homes as collateral, the loan was approved. By now it was summer and we began preparing for a November grand opening. We spent an intensive two days in training at the Athletic Attic headquarters in Gainesville, learning every detail about how to run our franchise—or so we thought.

To save money, we built the inside of the store ourselves. It was wood-paneled and Bert, who had built his own house, hand-made the front counter. As they had with our house in Pennsylvania and here in Kissimmee, my mom and dad again came up from south Florida to help us. Thank goodness, because both my dad and Bert were really good with tools, and me, not so much!

The strip mall was now up and open and we were looking forward to our store's opening about two weeks before Thanksgiving. We hired one of our former players, Roger Cheek, to be our manager and also several students to work part-time.

Based on our annual earnings to break even, we figured we needed to do an average of about $300 a day. On the first day we opened, I called the store about two o'clock and asked Roger, "How we doing?" He said, "Pretty OK." I asked him to run the cash register tab for a dollar amount. He said that wasn't necessary because the total sales so far had been 50 cents for some gum. My worries had just begun.

The first week we were open, we got robbed. While Bert was in the back, a car pulled up, a guy got out and scooped up more than a dozen hangers holding about $1,000-worth of expensive warm-up suits, then got back in his car and sped away. We learned not to put high-ticket merchandise at the front entrance.

But that lesson didn't help us much a year or so later when I got a call one night around 3AM, from the Kissimmee police. They told me to get to the store immediately, and when I arrived, the back door was completely off the hinges. Apparently somebody had climbed onto the roof and entered the store through an air conditioning duct. Once inside, he opened the back door where a truck and driver had parked, and they proceeded to steal about

$5,000-worth of Nike shoes. They could have wiped us out completely—taking our entire shoe inventory of $70,000, but something must have scared them away.

It sure wasn't the sound of an alarm, because we had put off installing an expensive security system to save money. So the next day, we had the expensive security system installed, and Bert built a wooden structure with an elaborate bolt system around the steel back door that he said even John Dillinger couldn't have broken into.

During the five years we owned this business, we made some money, got sued by an accountant who didn't like it when we started doing our own books, had shoes thrown at us by disgruntled customers who tried to return used merchandise, got audited by the IRS, had some laughs, and learned many lessons about owning a retail business.

Throughout this time, both Bert and I continued teaching and coaching football. Football was still my passion, but the business was occupying a significant part of my daily thoughts.

> *Coaching Points:* **Life is full of risks and rewards and highs and lows. Take some chances. You'll never grow unless you do. Yet I learned the hard way the truth of one of my favorite sayings: "Trust in the Lord, but tie up your camels." Or in our case, don't be penny-wise and pound-foolish. Install a security system from the outset—*before* burglars raid your inventory.**

CHAPTER 23

How Not to Run a Dry Cleaning Business

My life was busy, and at times stressful, while juggling school, football, a sporting goods business, and trying to spend some time with the family. I never contemplated whether I was being a good dad to my children or a good husband. I knew that I loved my kids and that I loved my wife, but it's pretty obvious that I didn't put them first in my life. Even under all these circumstances, I found myself on the cusp of adding more to my plate.

About a year after we started the Athletic Attic, a fellow teacher approached me in the off-season with the idea of going with him into another business. He lived in Winter Park, Florida, just outside Orlando, and was interested in buying a laundromat and dry cleaning business in downtown Orlando called Big B. He stated that he was really good at fixing machines and because I was already running a business, he thought we would make a good partnership.

I knew another fellow teacher who owned several laundromats in Kissimmee that were doing real well, so I asked him to let me look over several of his locations. He agreed to give me a quick tour and answer my questions as to how his business worked. One thing that intrigued me was that the laundromat, with the coin-operated washers and dryers, was a cash business that required no inventory, and I liked the simplicity of that. In his opinion, the price to purchase the Orlando business was right, and he said that with my partner good at fixing things, it looked like a good deal to him.

Joan and I went to Orlando and checked out the business, including the books which indicated that the Big B was turning a pretty good profit. In addition to long rows of self-serve commercial washers and dryers, there was a lot of money being made by providing wash, dry, and fold service to an established clientele of individuals and businesses. There was also a robust dry cleaning business that was farmed out, and on the premises, a full-time lady handled the washing, starching, and pressing of navy uniforms brought in by sailors from the nearby naval base. Another key attraction of the business was its convenient location in a strip mall just behind a big mall, which generated a lot of drive-up business.

Several weeks later, my new partner and I closed the deal. Many of the other teachers kidded me by saying, "What are you trying to do? Be a millionaire, Coach?" Boy, did *that* turn out to be off-base. In any event, my plate was now officially full and running over. Both our spouses agreed to help out at the Big B when they could after our day clerk went off-duty, and we figured that would ease our nights and weekend workload.

The first Saturday that we were in business, I was scheduled to work the two-to-nine o'clock shift. When I walked in the door, my partner said first thing that he had left some work for me to do. He indicated that two of our biggest commercial accounts had dropped off some laundry that needed to be finished by that evening. The first account was a big funeral home and there were bags and bags of what looked like sheets. When I asked why they had so many soiled sheets, he said, "Well, looks like they did a lot of embalming this week." Yuck! Piled up next to those bags were many others from the second client, a Chinese restaurant. These bags contained hundreds and hundreds of yellow cloth napkins that had to be washed and folded. So all afternoon and evening, it felt like with one hand, I was holding my nose while loading funeral home sheets into the industrial-sized washer, and with the other hand, folding yellow napkins fresh out the industrial-sized dryer.

I had spent that morning selling Athletic Attic shoes and paying bills, and the rest of the day doing laundry and collecting money from machines at the Big B. All in all, a pretty productive day.

Within the first month, every time I walked into the Big B, I walked into some kind of problem or complaint. One of the worst problems I brought on myself when I shrank an expensive set of living room curtains in half. Turns out they should have been dry cleaned, instead of washed and dried. Who knew? When I tried to fix a broken commercial gas dryer while my partner was out of town, I almost blew up the business. And then there were the irate customers who, on a daily basis, were always unhappy about something, whether they themselves had overcooked a shirt in a dryer that was too hot, or their shirts from the dry cleaners had come back too starched or not starched enough. Boy, this was just about as much fun as I'd ever had.

My weeks were jammed with running to the Athletic Attic to sell shoes, order inventory, pay bills and prepare payroll for four employees who of course expected to be paid every Friday regardless of the cash flow, and then driving the 45 minutes to Orlando four to six times a week to work at the Big B. No surprise that I quickly became worn out and generally aggravated with the world.

Having a business partner, like being married, often takes more than just getting along. And with the physical and emotional drain that the Big B had become for both my partner and me, civility often went out the window. After about three months, we were so fed up with the business and each other, we began talking about selling. That's when we discovered to our shock and dismay why we had gotten such a good deal when we bought the business. Developers at the big mall in front of us had previously negotiated plans to knock down our little strip mall in order to expand parking for their mall. Therefore, in about four months, the Big B would no longer exist. It would be a parking lot. Because my business partner and I had failed to read the fine print in the seller's contract, we didn't realize that we couldn't sell our business; there would be no business to sell. We were screwed.

After constant discussions and arguments, with no solutions in sight, the next week, I made a conscious decision not to wait another four months for the business to be demolished, but to shut this headache down immediately. I've always faced my problems head-on and usually I come up with some viable solution, but in this case, I saw no way out other than to run away from the problem.

The following Saturday night at nine o'clock, at the end of the work week, I closed and locked the doors, went in the back, and instead of being sad, was elated as I wrote on a big piece of brown paper, OUT OF BUSINESS. After taping it to the window, I called my partner and told him the keys were on the front counter. I walked out the rear door and never looked back.

Was this quitting? Absolutely. But I felt more relieved and stress-free than I had felt in ages. I'd deal with the $50,000 debt and bankruptcy later.

> *Coaching Point:* **There's a famous athletic quote that says,** *"Winners never quit and quitters never win."* **But in business, that doesn't always hold true—nor should it. As Kenny Rogers sang,** *"You got to know when to hold 'em, know when to fold 'em, know when to walk away, know when to run."*

CHAPTER 24

How Policemen and Firefighters Cured my Coaching Burnout

The 1980 season found me excited about our football season and the prospect of having a great year. It looked like our big rival St. Cloud was also in store for a big year. As the season unfolded, we suffered some injuries, but we were doing okay. The end of the season was near, and we were getting ready to play "The Game," which was to be on St. Cloud's home turf this time.

The night of the game as we got off the bus, the atmosphere was electric. The stands were packed and fans were lined up around the fence ten deep. Andy Leper was their star running back and he expected to have a big night. For a while, the game was close, but in the end they gave us a pretty good beating. As we were leaving, several of their adult fans came up to the bus and started yelling insults at our kids. To keep kids from getting off the bus and starting a brawl, several of our big coaches stood at the bus door. The scene was tense and finally resulted in one of our coaches and one of their fans getting into a little scuffle behind our bus. Their fan threw the first punch, but my coach finished him off with a punch in the nose just as the cops arrived. We got a police escort out of the stadium and even though our tails were between our legs because of the loss, at least we were on our way home safely.

The next several weeks I did a lot of thinking and decided I was just burned out and needed a break. Along with my teaching duties, I still had the

Big B financial debacle hanging over my head, as well as the daily responsibilities of the Athletic Attic business.

After a long talk with Joan, and then with the school principal, I decided to step down as head football coach. I knew that I wasn't finished with coaching forever, but I needed a break. I had just finished 17 years of coaching, working in five states and six different jobs. That's a lifetime for most coaches. Most coaches with that many years usually quit and go into administration. That wasn't my intention nor my interest. But taking a time-out from coaching was what I needed.

For a while, I was enjoying having fewer responsibilities. Now I could focus on relaxation, teaching P.E., and running only one business. I was honored at the annual football banquet when the booster club gave me a gold watch engraved with words thanking me for my six years of service.

I remember that around this time, Joan and I began having some marital discord. Nothing big at first, but it was a portent of things to come. We had married at an early age and our son, Gregg, was born almost nine months to the day afterwards. Now, 17 years later, I knew that Gregg and our 12-year-old daughter, Jennifer, could sense the growing discord between us. I think that all the moves, the demanding jobs, and the business deals had taken a toll on Joan. It's never easy to say who's at fault, but I'm sure that I caused most of our problems.

———————

One day, in late spring, I got a call from the Orlando police department. They said, "Don't worry, you're not in any trouble." After the Big B, that was a relief. They explained that there was a semi-pro league around Florida that had ten teams comprised of local police and firefighters. They asked me if I might be interested in being their head coach. Several days later, I traveled to Orlando and accepted the job.

So much for my coaching hiatus. I assembled a part-time coaching staff and we began practicing. Most of the players had been former high school football athletes. When I say former, I mean long-ago former, as many of them were my age or older. The quarterback was a captain in the Orlando Police Department and 38-years-old. I had never coached grown men before and I really wasn't sure how to handle them at first. So after about a week, I called a meeting and explained my dilemma. I told them I wasn't being myself and that I didn't really know how to coach them and maybe they should get someone else. They responded that they knew of my reputation and please coach us however you want. The next day we installed the Wishbone offense and I became Simon Legree again. I coached them like high school kids and they loved it.

We won our first two games and we were all jacked up about the season. Things were dramatically different for me as a coach in a lot of ways. For one thing, I wasn't used to seeing my players smoking cigarettes in the locker room before and after practice, or drinking alcohol on the bus coming home from away games. But hey, I figured these were grown men, policemen and firefighters who risked their lives daily. Many times before a game, I saw the team doctor giving shots of localized painkiller to some of the injured players. This would never happen in high school. But I loved coaching this team because there were obviously no discipline issues, or pressure from parents, fans, or a school principal. Plus, I experienced how grateful these men were to have a chance to play the game they loved one more time. And we were winning.

We were now 9-0 going into the biggest and final game of the year. Orlando had never beaten the Jacksonville team, and these guys were pumped for the season's last game to be played in north Florida. We ended up beating Jacksonville, and all the way home, the team celebrated their first undefeated season ever.

A week later, they called to tell me they were hosting a big party at the police lodge in Orlando, and that I was expected to attend. I was advised to have my wife drive me there and they would get me home after the party. There were many adult beverages consumed that night and it was a wild and crazy celebration. At the end of the night, as they promised, I was given a ride home in an OPD police car. A first for me.

In the months following, whenever I was in Orlando, I would sometimes look in the rear view mirror and see a police car on my tail with red lights flashing. As I began to slow down, the car would pull along beside me and I'd see the officers inside laughing and waving at me to move on. I recognized some of my football players messing with me and I loved it. We had a ball.

Coaching Point: **When given another chance to play football, big grown men can be just like kids. In fact, some passions—whether in athletics or the arts—you never outgrow.**

CHAPTER 25

Off to Texas

By now, my marriage was falling apart. And looking back, again I would have to accept most of the blame. It's pretty hard on a family when you constantly uproot them so you can move to another job in a far-away city. No doubt I really loved Joan, Gregg, and Jennifer, but at that time in my life, it was all about me and what I wanted. What made me constantly want change was a mystery. Still is. But I operated on the principle that the grass was always greener somewhere else. I also put huge stress on the family with my constant business ventures. My priorities were only two: football and business. But I did have some good qualities as a family man, mainly the philosophy that I would always provide for them financially. Joan deserves credit for also being a breadwinner, as well as a great person and super mother to our kids.

In 1982, we were legally separated, and even though I hadn't moved out of the house, I spent part of the time living with my good friend and coach, Alan Baker. Alan and Bert Bagley, my other coach, friend, and business partner, were instrumental in helping to keep my emotional sanity intact.

When I had resigned as head coach, Kissimmee hired a new head coach by the name of Ken Baker. Ken had been a longtime college coach, but was looking to get into high school coaching and landed at Osceola High School. Like me 12 years earlier, Ken had wanted to get away from the college coaching grind.

Ken and Bert approached me in late summer and wanted to know if I was interested in working with them on the coaching staff. I once again realized that what I most wanted to do in life was coach football. We decided that I would be best suited as the head freshman coach and during all the Friday night games, would work from the press box communicating via headset with the varsity coaches on the sidelines below.

By this time in my eight years at Osceola, I had completed a full circle of coaching, beginning with my job as the head JV coach, moving up to head varsity coach, and now as the head coach of the freshman team. All this, plus my stint as a semi-pro coach of the Orlando police and firefighters that spring made for a pretty unique track record in the coaching profession. I was fortunate to have enjoyed success at all levels.

———

After I'd moved out of the house completely, and with divorce proceedings in progress, I started dating a young lady I first met while I was coaching the semi-pro team. Suzi was an employee of the Orlando recreation department and loved football. She also worked with special needs kids, taught clogging, and loved country dancing. She was originally from Pennsylvania, where I had lived years earlier, and she had a brother who lived in Houston. Several months into our relationship, she invited me to move in with her, and I took her up on the offer.

So by now, I was living in Orlando and making the half-hour commute to Osceola High School every day. Both Joan and I were still teaching at Osceola, and in the teacher's lounge where the faculty mailboxes were located in alphabetical order, ours were right next to each other. Everyone at school knew about our impending divorce, so this made for an uncomfortable situation.

———

Because I knew I no longer wanted to remain at Osceola High, I began to look at many other coaching jobs in the Orlando area, but was met with the realization that I would have to take a huge pay cut to take any of those jobs. At that time in Florida, none of my 20-year experience in other locations would count toward any seniority, and I would have to start in Orlando at a beginning teacher's salary. When Suzi began talking about moving to Texas to be closer to her brother in Houston, I began to consider taking a job in Texas where that seniority policy did not apply. Out went my resumes and letters of application. But I soon realized why, despite my more-than-ample qualifications, my applications were making no impression. Turns out that Texas coaches were very proud and had very little respect for anyone who had not coached in Texas.

In fact, one of the coaches I talked to on the phone even told me, "If you're serious about coaching here, you'd better come out and meet some people face to face." On one of my first trips and during my first interview in Houston, the head coach spotted my mustache the moment I walked in, and bluntly stated, "Thanks for coming, but we don't hire coaches with mustaches," as he ushered me out the door. I went immediately back to the hotel, put a razor to my lip, knowing I had no future at that school but maybe I would at some others.

I did have other interviews that didn't work out for one reason or another, but the trip wasn't a total loss. I bought my first pair of cowboy boots, and Suzi and I went dancing at my first Texas honky-tonk. As an accomplished dancer and teacher, she had a lot of patience with me on the dance floor, but finally, just threw up her hands and said, "I'm sorry, Jim, but you really don't have much rhythm."

She and I made three more job-hunting trips to Texas to attend many football clinics where I networked and shook a lot of hands. One time, at a clinic in San Antonio, I met—and was fortunate to get an audience with—the president of the prestigious Texas High School Coaches Association. He informed me of what I already knew: that it was rare for Texans to hire a non-Texan. But he told me he liked me and that I could use him as a reference any time. Coach Lynn Etheridge from Tomball, Texas, turned out to be very helpful to me two years later.

But to land my first coaching job in Texas, I still had to break the barrier of being an outsider.

———

Back in Florida, my divorce was final. To save money, Joan and I used the same attorney—against his advice, but she and I were cordial as we managed to work things out more or less to our mutual benefit.

So now I was a single man for the first time in 20 years. I felt relieved, but also sad. After all, my parents at that point had been married for more than 40 years, and by comparison, I felt somewhat like a failure. Not only that, I felt like I was abandoning my children, Gregg, age 19 by then, and especially Jennifer, just 13. But I was hoping that time would heal all wounds.

I still owned half of the Athletic Attic with Bert, but he told me, even as I was still job hunting, "When you cross that Texas border, Jim, you'll begin a whole new life. So go on and go in peace. I'll sell the business and everything will be okay."

One day soon after, I got a letter from Beaumont, Texas, offering me a job. YAHOO, OFF TO TEXAS!

Coaching Point: Sometimes in life, you have to take a lot of steps backward in order to move forward.

CHAPTER 26

Age 42 and Homeless

It was back in 1975, that I had moved my family from snowy Pennsylvania to sunny Florida. Since then, I had been a football coach at the freshman, JV, varsity, and semi-pro levels. I had sold stock and started two businesses.

Now, eight years later, I was leaving Florida with a successful coaching career, two failed businesses, a broken marriage that ended after 20 years, and leaving behind two children. But I was also leaving behind a heavy burden of stress that had weighed me down for years.

———

I had purchased a new Isuzu pickup truck in late May that had what's known as a topper attached to the bed of the truck. This cover allowed the truck to be used as a sort of camper. I built a simple plywood bed into the back which gave me a place to sleep, as well as provided storage space underneath.

It was 1983, and all I had to my name was this truck, a few pieces of furniture, some clothes, and $2,000. But I had a job offer to coach football in Beaumont, Texas, and I was excited.

Suzi and I left for Texas, and of course a U-Haul was involved.

I drove the U-Haul which towed her small car. She followed behind in my Isuzu pickup. Just as we were leaving Orlando and getting onto the ramp of the

Florida Turnpike, her car suddenly had a flat tire. I managed to make it over to the shoulder, and with traffic whizzing by, changed the tire. I couldn't help but wonder if this was some sort of omen of things to come. I surely hoped not. But as things turned out, that omen was correct—at least for a while.

On the other side of Tallahassee, we arrived at a rest stop and pulled in for the night. After eating some sandwiches for supper, we climbed into the bed in the back of the truck under the topper and went to sleep. That truck would become real important to me real soon.

Somewhere in western Louisiana on I-10, I pulled over to call the coach in Beaumont. I wanted to let him know that I was on schedule and would arrive at my new job first thing in the morning. After some awkward hemming and hawing, he said that he was very sorry, but due to budget problems, they would not be able to hire me. Talk about a blow to the gut. I thanked him and told him I still would be heading on to Houston. When we got there, it was raining, and the traffic was beyond anything I had ever seen. Suzi's brother was expecting us, and had arranged a storage area for our belongings that we'd unload from the U-Haul. Then we drove to his house where I met their family, had dinner, and spent the night on the living room couch.

The next morning over coffee, they invited me to stay with them temporarily until I could find a job. I thanked them, but said I had no intentions of imposing on them by staying there, and decided that I would find a campground where I could live in my truck as I went job hunting every day. I had to admit to myself that at age 42, I was officially "homeless," and my truck was my new home. Every night, I would crawl into my bed in the back of the pickup and go to sleep dreaming of finding a coaching job. In the morning, I would walk down to the campground bathroom to shower and shave. Then I would pull out my Coleman stove, make some coffee and cook my breakfast. Unlike camping as recreation, this camping was about survival. But I didn't feel sorry for myself. I'd lie there in my truck, thinking, *At least I'm free, free from the marital stress, the struggle to meet payroll every week, and from doing a funeral home's dirty laundry.*

———————

For the next three weeks, I'd put on my jacket and tie, and head out every morning, driving throughout Houston in search of a job. When I'd call my kids or my mom and dad, I would tell them that I was staying in a motel and doing just fine. In truth, I was getting more and more frustrated each day. But I still believed that things would work out, as they usually did. One day when I called Suzi, she said that her brother wanted to talk with me. So I went to his house, and after dinner, he asked me again if I wanted to move in with them. And again I said, "Thank you, but I'm not going to impose on anybody." He said he figured I'd say that, and then said, "Look, I need my house painted, inside and out, and if you do this for us, that'll take care of your room and board." I thought it over, and because I felt it was a good deal for us both, I gratefully accepted his offer.

I put a few clothes in the downstairs closet, and after they went to bed, I pulled out my mat, pillow, and blanket that I'd brought in from the truck, and slept on their living room floor, in air conditioning versus the humid heat of my Isuzu home at the campground. In the mornings, as I heard movement upstairs, I'd roll up my mat, stash it behind the sofa, and get ready for the day's work. After breakfast—which I did not have to cook—I'd paint for three or four hours, then shower and head out on my job search.

Suzi's family lived in the Spring school district, and they suggested I go to Spring High School to meet the coaches there. So one afternoon, I went to meet the head coach, Alex Decuir. We hit it off right away, and he invited me to come to their workouts that were held in the school stadium. When I saw their facilities, I was in awe. The field was Astroturf and the stadium seated about 10,000. There was a huge brick fieldhouse with beautiful furniture and several weight rooms, a far cry from our sandy practice field and cinder block building in Florida.

I painted every morning, job-hunted every afternoon, and spent my nights at the Spring High School football workouts. I got along real well with Coach Decuir and his coaches. He said that he had looked into hiring me, but there just weren't any openings. He was sure, though, that someone would hire me because of my 20 years' experience and winning track record of over 100 games as a head coach.

But by late July, I was still jobless and getting real nervous. I thought about what might happen if I couldn't get a job. Maybe I'd work on an oil rig, or surely I could get a job as a painter because I was good at it and had lots of recent experience. By now, both the outside and inside of Suzi's brother's house had been painted, and the family was very happy because of the money they had saved getting a great paint job. Of course I was grateful, too, because I had a roof over my head, air conditioning, and free meals. But for whatever reason, I occasionally missed sleeping on my bed in the truck.

———

Football is BIG in Texas. Most of the stadiums I saw there were 10,000 seating capacity or bigger—with red brick facades and artificial turf. About a week before fall football practice began in August, all coaches were required to attend coaching school, held alternately in Houston, San Antonio, Dallas, or Fort Worth. This particular year, coaching school was in Fort Worth and all the Spring coaches told me that I needed to be there.

Money was very tight, but I knew I had to get to Fort Worth as a last-ditch effort at employment in my chosen career. So I told the Spring coaches that I was going to coaching school and I would see them there. They stayed in a fancy hotel close to the convention center. I stayed in a flea bag motel about ten miles outside of Fort Worth. The Spring coaches had a meal allowance. I had sandwiches in my room. Whoever invented peanut butter and jelly sandwiches needs a statue built for them. Seems like I've eaten a million of 'em.

Coaching school is a huge annual four-day event in Texas, with over 10,000 coaches in attendance. There are lecture halls, exhibit areas, and most importantly, two huge rooms for job searches: for coaches wanting a job and for schools hiring coaches. I spent three days and about eight hours each day in these rooms. It was a giant meat market for jobs, and I networked, shook hands, handed out resumes, and interviewed all day. With no cell phones back then, you'd better be there in person, or you might miss an opportunity. And the pace was frenetic.

On the evening of the next to last day, I got an offer from Grapevine High School in the Dallas area. I called Suzi and we celebrated on the phone, but I guess she wasn't really happy for me because by then she was working at a job in downtown Houston, and it looked like I was headed to Dallas.

The next morning, I was on my way to sign the Grapevine contract when I ran into Coach Decuir from Spring. He said, "I've been looking for you because I have a job for you." I told him about the Grapevine deal and he said, "Forget it. Meet me tomorrow in Spring to sign the deal." I went to see the Grapevine coach, turned down his job, and then returned to Houston. Suzi and her brother's family were elated at this latest turn of events.

The next morning, after I met Coach Decuir at his office and signed the contract, I asked him what I would be coaching. He told me that I would be the head JV coach for a semester and that by spring, he would bring me up to the varsity staff. Sounded okay to me and also sounded like something I had done before.

Then I asked him what I would be teaching. He said, "You'll be a permanent sub." I exploded and said, "I turned down Grapevine and a full salary to be a substitute teacher with you? You misled me." He leaned over and said, "You'll have the best job on the staff and at full salary." He went on to say, "Most days you might only work one or two periods a day." That sounded good, but what was the salary? When he told me it would be $32,000, I nearly fell off the chair. I had left Osceola High School where my salary after eight years was $20,000. And now I was starting with a $12,000 raise! Plus, I would no longer be homeless.

Coaching Points: **The old saying is true: "It's always darkest just before dawn." I've always believed God has a way of taking care of you, especially if you do your part by getting up, getting going, making the effort, and being open to God's plan.**

Scible Pegs Lord Eleven As Threat

By RON STEVENS

OCEAN VIEW — Jim Scible, veteran football coach from Anne Arundel County, Md., is the new grid pilot at Lord Baltimore High.

Scible comes to the Ocean View school from Annapolis, Md., where his primary duty was to prepare the weekly scouting report. He succeeds Fred Gainer, who resigned his Lord Baltimore post to accept the basketball coaching job at Laurel.

Scible becomes the third football coach at Lord Baltimore in three years. Dale Farmer was at the Lords' controls in 1962, departing for a similar post at Smyrna. Enter Gainer, who leaves after a brief year's tour of duty, during which he fashioned a 3-4-1 Henlopen Conference record.

COURTESY OF **SCIBLE FAMILY**

First coaching job, age 22: Lord Baltimore High School
Ocean View, Delaware

My first football team
Lord Baltimore High School

Coach Scible with Coach DeSimone and tri-captains
Lord Baltimore High School

Rigors of Coaching

Fans at Delaware scholastic basketball games are rapidly becoming aware that all the action isn't on the court.

Lord Baltimore rookie coach Jim Scible gives you an example of what to expect from the hardwood mentors as he goes through some antagonizing moments in his team's 47-41 victory over Dover Air Base.

In left photo, Scible throws up his hands in disgust as one of his charges has a pass intercepted. In center panel, he anguishly calls for a time out with the score tied and 15 seconds to go. At right, he fills in disbelief as one of his cagers lets go with a 35-footer. It was worth it—it went in.

Coach Scible's one and only head basketball coaching job
Lord Baltimore High School

Coach Scible, age 23, with basketball captains
Lord Baltimore High School

Glazier, Scible Quit Jobs

By RON STEVENS

Two Hexlogenn Conference schools today began the tedious search for new football coaches. Resignations by Frank Glazier at Harrington and Jim Scible at Lord Baltimore leave both schools with major coaching vacancies.

Both Glazier and Scible have accepted positions in the Bergenfield, N.J. system, Glazier as the head grid coach. Scible as his No. 1 assistant. Both plan mid-summer moves to the suburban New York City community and will officially assume their new duties on Sept. 1.

The decision to accept the Bergenfield offer was a difficult one for Glazier, 30-year-old former Baldwin - Wallace athlete, who has been casting an envious eye toward the college ranks.

FRANK GLAZIER   JIM SCIBLE

Coaches Glazier and Scible head to New Jersey

Lacrosse Team with Head Coach Scible (upper right)
Lehigh University, Bethlehem, Pennsylvania

C10—Sunday Patriot-News, Harrisburg, Pa., April 18, 1971

Scible Given Royal Treatment
As Royal Explains Wishbone

By RONNIE CHRIST

JIM SCIBLE did more than just make a wish over the Wishbone.

The East Pennsboro football coach didn't want to be thrown for a loss by the triple option so he went to Austin to learn from the originator of football's newest offensive craze — University of Texas Coach Darrell Royal.

Scible and assistant coach Bill Downs spent a week watching the Longhorns in spring drills, talking to Royal and his aides and looking at films of Texas' games.

They even got a bonus they hadn't expected. They were able to watch one of Austin's high school teams in spring drills — yes, Virginia, scholastic teams have spring practice in Texas — so they could see how the Wishbone looked at the schoolboy level.

"It was the most valuable thing I've even done from the standpoint of learning experiences," says Scible. "I've been going to clinics for eight or nine years and I never was able to learn what I did in Texas.

"I don't think I'll ever go to a major clinic again. I think in the future we'll go to other practices."

Jim Scible . . . East Pennsboro coach charts Wishbone

Coach Scible explaining the Texas Wishbone at East Pennsboro High School
Enola, Pennsylvania

Scible Kowboys' next grid coach

Jim Scible will replace Jim Yancey as the next head football coach at Osceola High School if the school board accepts the recommendation of Acting Principal Chris Colombo Tuesday.

"I have decided to recommend Mr. Scible for the post after reviewing his qualifications and talking with other applicants," Colombo said. The acting school chief said school board approval on matters of this type is usually only a formality. "There's never been one turned down that I'm aware of," he said, adding Scible is certified to teach in Florida.

Yancey resigned last month to take a similar position at Hawthorne near Gainesville. He had back-to-back 3-7 seasons.

Scible, who took over the Kowboy junior varsity reigns last year and finished 6-2 while winning the Orange Belt Conference jayvee crown, is 36

years old and a veteran of high school and college coaching ranks.

He moved to Kissimmee from Euola, Pa., where he compiled a 42-18 record over six seasons at East Pennsboro High Schoo. In 1974 East Pennsboro was 8-2 and confefence champs under Scible.

Scible has been a head prep coach 14 years. He also was offensive backfield coach at Lehigh University for two years and was the college's head recruiter.

Prior to that post he was athletic director, head football and basketball coach in Maryland, West Virginia, Delaware and New Jersey high schools.

Scible is a fan of the triple option and veer offense, using his knowledge to turn around a sagging OHS jayvee program in only a year.

Scible will be the eighth head

COACH JIM SCIBLE
. . . OHS grid boss

football coach at OHS dating back to 1965 when Jack Yearwood departed under fan pressure. The same pressure has also helped claim, in succession, DeWayne Douglas, Don Daniels, Bill Duty, Richard Hagy, Larry Bottom and Yancey.

Colombo said he interviewed three applicants from within the system and received two calls from Kentucky and another from Miami about the post. "Because of our teaching position situations I notified the other callers that the choice would be made from within," Colombo said.

Coach Scible lands his first Florida job
Osceola High School in Kissimmee

(Left to right) Coaches Scible, Bert Bagley, George Sullivan Osceola High School Kowboys

Coach Bert Bagley, my right-hand man and defensive coordinator Osceola Kowboys

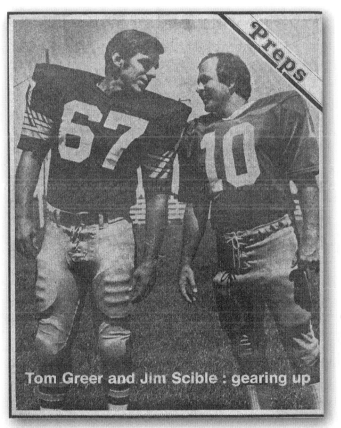

Coach Greer of main rival St. Cloud squares off with Osceola's Coach Scible

2 the little sentinel, Wednesday, December 26, 1979 O

Bagley and Scible look overlook stock of athletic literature · Richard Shepherd/the little sentinel

2 Kissimmee coaches leave sidelines for aisles of a store

By FRANK RUIZ
Osceola little sentinel

KISSIMMEE — In August 1978 two local football coaches sat at a coaching clinic in Gainesville work-

beige walls and a large display of shoes fills the entire back wall.

"We also specialize in shoes for active people," says Bagley as he reaches for a Nike Trailwind sam-

Coach Bagley and Coach Scible open Athletic Attic store in Kissimmee

Head Football Coach Jim Scible explains the offense at Channelview High School
Channelview, Texas

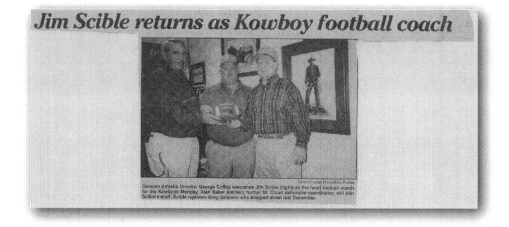

Jim Scible returns as Kowboy football coach

Osceola Athletic Director George Coffey welcomes Jim Scible (right) as the head football coach for the Kowboys Monday. Alan Baker (center), former St. Cloud defensive coordinator, will join Scible's staff. Scible replaces Greg Johnson who stepped down last December.

Coach Scible addresses the Kowboys after 1997 semi-final loss to
Rutherford High School in Panama City, Florida

Assistant Coach Gregg Scible and Defensive Coordinator Coach Alan Baker discuss a 4th down call, Osceola Kowboys

Osceola Kowboys entering University of Florida Field ("The Swamp")
for 1998 Florida High School State Championship game

(Left to right) Coaches Alan Baker, Gregg Scible, and Victor Buxton
Osceola High School

Florida State High School Championship 1998, Kowboys ahead with one minute left in the game, Coach Scible proudly holds State Championship cap

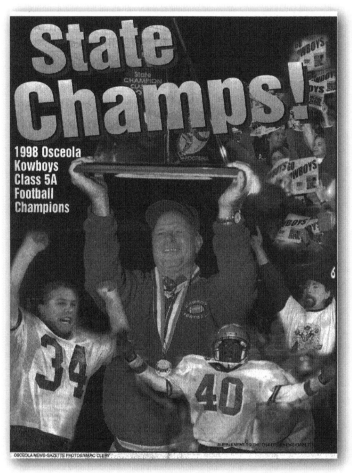

1998 Osceola
Kowboys
Class 5A
Football
Champions

OSCEOLA NEWS-GAZETTE PHOTOS/MARC CLERY

"NUFF SAID"

Coach Scible is interviewed post-game of 1998 State Championship

Coach Scible wearing 1998 State Championship medallion celebrates
with his wife Pat (left) and his sister Janet Kerins (right)

Pre-game contemplation before winning my 200th football game

Pat with daughter, Jennifer Scible Cousins, and grandson, Caleb Cousins

My beloved parents, Walter and Ruby Scible

Celebrating retirement with my cherished wife, Pat

CHAPTER 27
My First Texas Job

As I've said, I've always had the belief that things will work out, no matter how gloomy they look. And that 90 percent of what we worry about never happens. I've tried to live by this philosophy, although not always successfully. But during this time in my life, that philosophy was certainly reinforced. After all, I had gone from being homeless to getting a $12,000 annual raise. So things were looking up.

After I got hired, I finally was able to get my own place to live. I rented a second-floor apartment and furnished it with what little furniture I had brought from Florida. The apartment even had a small fireplace and a balcony. After two months of sleeping in my truck and on a living-room floor, it felt like a million-dollar mansion.

———

Before the school year started, when the Spring High School and middle school football staff met for the first time, I was stunned to see 31 other football coaches there. Under the control of the Spring High School head coach/athletic director were a seventh grade A and B team, an eighth grade A and B team, a freshman A and B team, a sophomore team, a JV team, and the varsity team—making a total of nine teams, 32 full-time coaches, and over 500 players. Each of those teams played a full 10-game schedule. We were in the Texas 5A division, the biggest at the time, but we were far from a powerhouse program in the district, much less the state.

As the head JV coach, I had a staff of three other coaches. We practiced on a separate field from the varsity, so it was great that I had my own team, even though everybody on all nine teams ran the same plays.

On my first day of the school year, I reported to Ms. Donna Grier, who was the principal's secretary and in charge of substitute teachers. Since I was hired also as a permanent substitute, I was the first name on Ms. Grier's daily list of classes requiring a sub. However, the man who was my actual boss was the head football coach, and he had instructed me to agree to substitute only if I had no football duties that day. In those years, Texas schools were unique—and may still be—in having what they called "off-season" classes for football, from seventh through twelfth grade, year round. In fact, the master schedule for all the school's courses was built around these off-season football classes. One of my football duties was to be at each off-season class workout. That meant I was to attend each of the freshman, sophomore, JV, and varsity team workouts. Each of these teams met during different periods throughout the day with their respective coaches, working on drills, weightlifting, and agility exercises. With six periods in the school day, and four of those periods involving these off-season team workouts, plus the required planning period without an assigned class that each teacher was guaranteed, that left just one period when I would be available for Ms. Grier to schedule me as a sub. I remember all the times she'd roll her eyes at me when I told her that I was already booked for most of the day. Eventually, I was off her sub list completely. We still got along well, but she understood, as did I, the realities of where my bread was buttered.

It seemed when I got to Spring High, people were either divorced, getting a divorce, or single. This wasn't totally true, but it was close, and some of the coaches on the football staff certainly fit this description. As a result, going out with them after hours, I got exposed real quick to lots of Texas honky-tonks and dance halls. Coaches and teachers would go out regularly to Friday night Happy Hours, especially before and after football season. But the coaches, under orders from the district athletic director, were to stay away from those dance halls on Kuykendall Road because locals would be there, and it didn't look good for coaches to be seen hanging out in bars. But it's no fun to always follow the rules.

So one night, after a long, hot practice, a few coaches took me to one of those forbidden dance halls and ordered me a Long Island Ice Tea. Because I didn't know what that was, and because it tasted like sweet tea, I ordered two more. Soon after, I was dancing like a fool on top of a table. Next thing I remember, my buddies were tucking me into my bed. The next morning, a district-wide in-service meeting was scheduled and all the district's teachers were there. I sneaked in late and stayed in the back of the room, trying to keep my eyes open until we left for practice. When I saw the coaches, they all laughed like crazy and asked how I was feeling. I replied, "No more of that damn New York tea for me."

———

About this time, Suzi was getting agitated with me because I was either working on football or out with "the boys." She and I were real close friends, and I enjoyed her company, but I wasn't in love and not interested in a more serious relationship with her.

As I was walking down the hall at school one day, I met a female teacher by the name of Pat. She told me that Coach Decuir had told her all about me and that he had said, "Guess what? I've just hired this great coach from Florida who has 20 years' experience and he's going to be our head JV coach." Of course, my ego swelled up, and I thanked her for relaying this to me. Pat then said that she was a former home economics teacher and now was running a program call HECE, which was a home economics co-op class. I had no idea what she was talking about, but she was very attractive, friendly, and loved football: three very good qualities in my mind. Plus, she had a knockout Southern accent. Along with other coaches and teachers, we hung out during some of the Friday night Happy Hours. Much later we began to date casually.

Little did either one of us know that one day, we would be married.

———

Spring High had a really good JV season that first year, and the varsity did okay. At the end of the season, Coach Decuir called me in and offered me the offensive coordinator position on the varsity staff, a huge jump in responsibility and also a little more money in my pocket. Just before Christmas, I was told I would have a new teaching position the second semester. I would be the assistant to Coach Alvarado who ran the In-school Suspension program for kids who'd gotten in trouble. Coach Alvarado welcomed the help, and I was about to get a lesson in how discipline was handled in Texas.

Rather than suspend these kids from school right away, the first step was to isolate them from the rest of the students by assigning them to a separate room for a length of time determined by their offense. This place was no joke. And no fun. The kids had to sit up straight all day, feet flat on the floor, and complete their special assignments. If they talked, fell asleep, or even nodded off for a second, Alvarado would yell, "You got another day!"

At 10:30AM on the dot, he would tell them, "Stand up—girls first—and go outside, line up, single file, next to the wall." The boys were next, lined up on the opposite wall. We stood in the middle between them and would march them to the girls' and boys' restrooms where each student went in one at a time. A female teacher's aide would come and monitor the girls' bathroom. Then at lunchtime before the rest of the students came in for lunch, they were marched, single-file, to the cafeteria, where they sat down and ate their bag lunches in total silence. A cafeteria worker would bring each student a carton of milk. After eating, they were marched back upstairs to resume their studies. Most of these kids were not bad kids, but every now and then we would get a wild one, who would be placed in a separate locked room, like in a prison's solitary confinement. My duties during this second semester were not only to assist Coach Alvarado, but also to rewrite the offensive playbook, which is what I spent most of my days doing. In fact, this was the main reason I was assigned to the quiet seclusion of In-School Suspension.

———

During that first year, I visited my own kids two or three times, and they came to Texas once or twice. We talked on the phone at least once a week and

I was glad that they seemed to be getting along fine. Gregg, now 19, was going to college and working part-time in various jobs. Jennifer was 14, and in the ninth grade. I felt that she was still hurt because I had left her during her most formative years, although we never talked about it directly. I suppose I could have stayed in Florida, but I chose to leave after the divorce because I just needed a change in every way. As I've said, I've always been somewhat of a selfish person and the truth hurts. But I hoped that as the years passed, my kids would forgive me and I had to keep reminding myself of that. I loved my new life in Texas, but especially during those quiet times when driving to and from work or before falling asleep at night, I would sometimes feel sad, missing my family, including my parents.

That second season, 1984, went well for Coach Jim Scible and also for Spring High School football. But by December, I was ready to start pursuing a head football coaching job in Texas. I met with Leonard George, the athletic director for the entire Spring district, and told him about my desire to become a head coach again, as I had been in every other state where I had worked. He said, "Now that you've proved you can coach in Texas, we'll help you out in this pursuit."

By this time, Pat and I were serious and very much in love.

Coaching Point: **Remember blessings come sometimes when you least expect them.**

CHAPTER 28

If You Want a Texas Head Coaching Job, You Still Gotta Network

O nce the season was over, and Spring was not going to the playoffs, Pat and I began to go to other schools' playoff games every Friday night and all day Saturday. The first playoff game we attended was in the Houston Astrodome, and the attendance was in excess of 40,000. In all my 20 years of coaching, I had never seen so many people at a high school game. Sometimes there would be three games at the Astrodome on Saturday, and sometimes we'd spend the entire day there. On Friday nights, we could attend two different games at two different sites, and sometimes we did. It takes a special woman to go along with watching that much football, and Pat was that special. She loved football almost as much as I did.

Beginning in December, 1984, I was in a full-scale hunt for a head coaching job. But I was always aware that you continue to work hard at your present job because if you stop paying attention to your present job, you may end up having no job.

I updated my resume and tried to network with other area coaches every day. As I've said, Texans are very proud people, and the coaches were even more so. Most still considered me to be an outsider, so I had a big hurdle to climb in getting my foot in the door for any interviews. In fact, most of the really big jobs in Texas high school football coaching didn't even accept applications. The school board selects the top five candidates by prior reputation, and those candidates get invited for an interview. To get an interview at any Texas school required several things, including experience as a coordinator or head coach, a proven track of success, and lastly, being a well-known Texan. At the time, I had the first two qualifications and was working on the third.

When I first moved to Texas, I fell in love with cowboy boots, and just a year-and-a-half later, was the proud owner of five pairs of exotic boots. At that time, most Texas coaches wore starched Wrangler jeans with their boots, so of course, I did too.

Everybody born in Texas seems born with the ability to do the two-step and the Texas waltz. Pat and I loved to dance, and we spent many weekend nights at honky-tonks with her trying to teach me the two-step, all to no avail. We even took dance lessons to try to improve my dancing skills. I did my best, but I just wasn't very good. Pat was the second woman to tell me, "Jim, you just don't have any rhythm." But I loved wearing my boots and starched jeans, drinking long necks, and dreaming of seeing myself glide across the dance floor.

During the spring while I continued to network for a head coaching job, we had some really fun times. Mom and Dad visited us for several days and we took some trips visiting places such as San Antonio, Austin, and the Galleria shopping mall in Houston. Dad was really getting into Texas when he bought his first pair of cowboy boots. He strutted around like a little banty rooster. In San Antonio, we visited the Alamo, walked along the River Walk, and ate the obligatory Mexican food. The next day, we visited the LBJ ranch outside of Austin, where Mom and Dad saw their first Longhorn steer. One Saturday, while at Houston's Galleria, Dad saw Marvin Zindler walking toward us. Marvin was a famous local TV reporter best known for his restaurant reports, and very few establishments escaped being criticized for having "slime in the ice machine." Having watched Houston's local news during his visit, Dad recognized Marvin Zindler right away, and said, "There's the slime man," as he walked up and introduced himself. Dad, like me, was never shy around strangers. Mom and Dad talked about this trip for years, and even though they came to visit us four or five times in Texas over the ten years we lived there, I think this trip was their favorite because they were so awed by their first exposure to the Texas landscape and lifestyle.

My children, Gregg and Jennifer, also visited us several times and we always enjoyed showing them around Houston and Austin. One time, we took a side trip to College Station to visit Texas A&M University. For a while, Greg considered enrolling there, but instead went into the military, and later attended University of West Florida, before earning his doctorate at Auburn University. I think on these trips to Texas, Jennifer most enjoyed shopping at the Galleria.

Pat and I got along so well because we had so much in common. We were both teachers, we loved football, going dancing—or trying to, eating out, reading, and going to Galveston Beach. Unlike the beaches in Florida, the sand at Galveston was darker and the water wasn't always clear, but we loved going there and having great seafood at Gaido's. One night, early in our relationship as we were getting to know each other, we got so involved in conversation at Gaido's, that our server came up and kindly said, "Hey you lovebirds, you're gonna have to leave now—we're closing." We couldn't believe it was nearly 2AM when we closed the place down.

Pat and I traveled to many weekend football clinics around Texas that spring. I went to the lectures and networked while she spent her days reading, shopping, and waiting for me to take her to dinner. She especially loved the Franka clinic because it was in San Antonio and we usually stayed at a hotel on the Riverwalk. There is a lot to do in San Antonio and 30 years later, it's still one of our favorite places. During one of these clinics, I met the Deer Park High School head coach, Ron Lynch. He was very successful, and had heard of my struggles to get a head coaching job. I also remained in contact with Lynn Etheridge, the president of the Texas Coaches Association and the head coach at Tomball High School. Both these men were very influential coaches in Texas, and very soon, would have a major impact on my career.

The school year was coming to a close and I had managed to get several interviews on my own, but nothing was working out. By the middle of June though, a job opened up at Channelview High School, which was located on the east side of Houston near Pasadena and close to the oil refineries at the ship channel. This was a 4A Division school and had experienced modest football success. I called Coach Etheridge, who told me that it wasn't a great job, but it might be a good start for me. He said, "I think you might have a chance to get this one."

He made some phone calls on my behalf, and I called Coach Lynch at Deer Park High School seeking advice on how to get that job at nearby Channelview. He told me to come see him at nine the next morning. Soon after I arrived, Ron took me to the Deer Park superintendent's office. After a few minutes, the superintendent said, "Ron has told me that you're a good guy and a good football coach." The superintendent then asked if I really wanted this job, and I answered, "Absolutely." As we shook hands, he told me to go home and expect a call from Channelview in the next day or so. On my drive home, I was thinking, *Wow, what just happened here? After six months of this job search, am I finally going to get my foot in the door?*

Sure enough, the next morning, the superintendent of the Channelview district, Billy Hamlin, called and asked me to come in for an interview. Two days later, I met with Mr. Hamlin and the athletic director Bill Neal. After the interview, I was driving home, smiling and singing, and when I got there, burst in the door telling Pat, "I've got a really good chance at this one." Then I called Coach Lynch and the Deer Park superintendent to thank them for their help. He asked me again, "Do you really want this job?" And again I said, "Absolutely." As before, he told me to sit tight and expect a call tomorrow from Channelview.

Mr. Hamlin called me the next day and asked me to come back the next evening to interview with the school board which turned out to be a very intense two hours, but I left feeling elated and nervous. The next day, I got the final call from Channelview and they offered me the job. I accepted, and the day after that, I was back at Channelview discussing salary and many other pertinent things related to the job. At last, I was a head football coach in Texas!

It's true that I was a good coach with 22 years' experience in coaching at all levels, but I found out later what really triggered my getting this job. The Deer Park superintendent and the Channelview superintendent were best friends and also twice-a-week golfing buddies. I will always be grateful for Coach Ron Lynch's help in getting me into his boss's office. Landing a head football coach's job in Texas sure involved way more than being a good coach. As the saying goes, unless you're a big name coach and already established in Texas, "It's not just what you know, it's who you know."

Coaching Point: **Never be afraid to pick up the phone and ask for help. Because if you don't ask for it, you can't expect to get it.**

CHAPTER 29

Living the Texas Head Coaching Life

L ate June and early July of 1985, was a very busy time for me. After over two decades of coaching, I was now the new head football coach at Channelview High in Channelview, Texas.

Two years before, I had arrived in Texas as an unemployed and homeless person. Then, after two months of daily searching, I finally got a job and worked my way from a head JV coaching position, to becoming an offensive coordinator, and now was finally a head coach.

Because I had been hired so late in the year, I had lots to do and a very short time to get it done. The first order of business was to assemble a staff. I could hire only two new coaches since all but two teaching positions at Channelview High were already filled. So I hired Bob Wiegand and Steve Hurth from Spring High School. Bob became the defensive coordinator and Steve was his assistant. Bob also held the title of first assistant to the head coach, which resulted in a good pay raise for him. Plus, he was in charge of all strength and conditioning for our entire program. Coach Hurth was in charge of all areas dealing with equipment, the most demanding off-the-field job of the entire staff. I was very fortunate to have inherited a great staff already in place, which included Coaches William Jennings, Charles Chargois, Gene and Art, whose last names I can't recall.

One of our most important staff members was not a coach but a jack-of-all-trades who was called "Chief." He was a retired Chief Petty Officer in the

Navy and his full-time job now was to care for our building and do laundry for the football team. He had a body that was completely covered with tattoos and a personality to match. I could write a book just about "Chief" because he had been around the world and had some great stories from all of his travels. His favorite story was when his ship had sunk after being blown up in the attack on Pearl Harbor. He drifted in the ocean for days and eventually hooked up onshore with some Marines for six months, before being reunited with his Navy unit. Now, he was in his mid-60s, and highly respected by both staff and players for his work ethic and pride in maintaining the Channelview High fieldhouse. Our building was so clean you could eat off the floor. And he took it upon himself to wash and fold my coaching gear every day. He told me during my first week on the job, "Just leave your dirty practice clothes by your locker and I'll take care of them." I said, "I don't want you doing that, Chief. I don't need you to wait on me," but he insisted. And sure enough, each morning, I would arrive to find my shirts, socks, shorts, and underwear all neatly folded, military style, on the corner of my desk. Pat especially liked Chief!

Another important member of our staff was "Doc," who was our sports medicine person in charge of treating all injuries and rehabilitating our athletes. "Doc" also served as the team's spiritual leader, talking every day about his faith in God and how God would help the players in their school life, their personal life, and on the football field. His daily prayers with the team kept us all spiritually inspired, focused, and unified. Completing our staff were several full-time teachers who also coached our seventh and eighth grade football teams.

Our field house was a big building located behind the school. The back doors opened onto our track, game field, and stadium. Our stadium had a capacity of 6,500 seats and was painted blue and gold, our team colors, which happened to be the same colors as when I coached the Kowboys.

Behind our stadium were three manicured practice fields: one for offense, one for defense, and one for the freshmen team. Unprecedented in my career, I had a maintenance crew at Channelview that lined the fields, painted all the field equipment, painted the stadium, and took care of any other outdoor physical needs. I would tell them what I needed done, and each week they would do it, gladly. I often thought back to Florida, when we coaches would spend three or four hours lining the game field Thursday afternoons, and sometimes paying for the paint out of our own pockets. I remembered all that Bert and I had done both financially and physically in refurbishing our rundown practice fields and locker room. And now here I was, living in the lap of football luxury with a guy laundering and folding my coaching clothes every day, and a crew that took care of all of our facilities.

During my first week on the job, Coach Hurth, who I'd brought from Spring and was in charge of equipment, asked me to take just ten minutes out of my schedule to come take a look at what was called the auxiliary equipment room. As we walked in, I couldn't believe my eyes and exclaimed, "Holy shit!" What I saw were rows and rows of brand new uniforms, practice clothing, shoulder pads, and boxes and boxes of new footballs— more gear than I had ever seen anywhere. Hurth said, "We probably won't have to buy any uniforms or equipment for years." To which I replied, "Oh yes we will. I've got a big budget and I've got to spend it. Use it or lose it." This budgetary practice from prior years probably explained the surplus we were staring at now.

Soon after, I got a call from our superintendent, Mr. Billy Hamlin, asking me to stop by for a meeting. He talked about several things pertinent to my job and his expectations. He said, "There are three things here that are very important for you to know, Jim. Your football budget is so generous, we do not allow any fundraising. So if you have any further needs over and above your budget, come to me and I'll get them for you." I knew again that I had made the right move coming to Channelview, Texas. He continued, saying, "There are two other things that I want you to impart to your staff. The first is, if you want a drink, then get it somewhere outside of Channelview. And secondly, I don't want any scandals, so tell your coaches 'Don't get your honey where you get your money.' And you know what I'm talking about." When I relayed this to the staff they laughed like crazy, but they knew he was serious. And so was I.

———

When Pat and I had worked at Spring High School, it was a district rule that a married couple could not work at the same school, but now that I had left Spring and was in Channelview, we were determined to be married. By now it was nearly the end of July—I had been at my new job for three weeks, and the annual coaching school and start of football practice were literally just days away. So I bought Pat a wedding ring and we made an appointment to be married by a Justice of the Peace. It certainly wasn't a fancy wedding and the only attendees were the judge, a witness, Pat, and me. But we were in love, happy to have tied the knot a year-and-a-half after we met, and celebrated our wedding at the elegant Brennan's Restaurant in downtown Houston. Pat told me that a fancy wedding was not important to her and that as a matter of fact, she hadn't had a fancy wedding when she married her first husband, Bob. What was important to Pat were her two sons, Jason and David, who'll come into the story in the next chapter.

The morning after our wedding and dinner, I gave Pat a big kiss, and drove off to meet my staff in Channelview before heading to coaching school in Dallas. Our honeymoon started a few days later when Pat drove to Dallas where we stayed at a nice hotel located on a street named, appropriately enough, "Lovers Lane." During the several days we spent in Dallas, I'd come back to the hotel after coaching school and we'd enjoy dinner and each other's company as husband and wife, at last. When coaching school was over, we headed back home and I started football practice.

A big issue was where we were going to live. Pat was still teaching at Spring, enjoying her job, and intended to stay there. We agreed that we needed a place about halfway between her job and mine. We looked for weeks and finally stumbled on a house for rent in Atascocita, which was just about 20 miles from her job and 20 miles from mine. It was a two-story house, with open windows in the back, and located on a golf course. We called the owner to set up an appointment. We agreed on the rent, signed the contract, and prepared to move into our new home on the 18th fairway. Some of my coaches helped us pack and then unpack the ever handy U Haul truck. Pat loved that the entire back of the house was windows, and even to this day, can't stand houses without lots of natural light. As we were unpacking, one of my coaches commented, "I bet you're going to have lots of broken windows from golf balls—the tee box isn't that far from your house." As a matter of fact, the first day we were in the house and while Pat was in the living room unpacking, a golf ball exploded through the window and whizzed by her head. Understandably, she was shook up when she called me at work to explain what had happened. But we got used to it, and kept the glass company on speed dial for the ten years we lived there. In all, we figure we had more than 50 windows broken, including two on one day.

In 1985, Houston was going through tough economic times due to oil industry problems and the savings and loan debacle. In our neighborhood, about half of the houses were vacant or had foreclosure signs out front. Fortunately, we weren't among those affected. We had found our dream home on the golf course and it fit our needs beautifully. In fact, several years later, we bought that house for a great price while the housing market was still somewhat depressed.

Fall practice began and we were working on installing my tried-and-true Wishbone offense and the 5-2 defense. During a water break one day, I stepped back and looked over our three manicured practice fields and felt a tremendous sense of accomplishment about where and how I had ended up.

The athletic director at Channelview was a man by the name of Bill Neal. Bill was about six-foot-five and not just tall, but large. Being that I'm ten inches shorter, I really looked like the classic cartoon character, Jeff, to his Mutt, as we walked down the hall together. Bill was very supportive of me, and our relationship was always very good. He was a jokester too. I will never forget the time he deliberately passed gas right in front of my desk, ran out fast and slammed the door, leaving me with tears in my eyes. He was that kind of guy.

On the first day that teachers reported to school before classes actually started the next day, a lady walked up to me and introduced herself. She said, "I'm Dottie Morgan and I'm the principal." In most states, the principal is instrumental in hiring everyone. In Texas, the school board and the superintendent make those decisions regarding hiring head football coaches, so we had not met until that moment. She welcomed me aboard and said, "You handle the football program, I'll handle the school, and we'll be just fine."

At Channelview, the school day started at 8:45 with all students reporting to homeroom for 15 minutes before classes started at nine. My homeroom consisted of all the junior and senior football players, and I started each day with lessons from a well-known and highly-regarded program called "The Making of a Champion." I wanted to instill in our kids the qualities described in the program that help make a person successful, and hoped that those qualities would carry over to the classroom and football field.

My first season had lots of ups and downs. We were playing an away game at Brenham High School (home of Blue Bell ice cream and the "contented cows"), and things weren't going well. I had called a bone-headed play that hadn't lost the game but sure didn't help our cause. After losing the game, as I was walking by the stands and into our locker room, I felt water gushing over my head. I looked up and saw Bill Neal and Bill Hamlin with empty water cups in their hands, laughing at me. My heart sank as I thought to myself, *Is this over before it really gets started?* I called the AD the next day and he said, "Forget it. We were just having fun with you." He said they were pleased with the direction of the program. And I thought, *Well, a water bath is a funny way of showing it.*

On the tenth and final game, our world exploded in a good way. Huntsville High School and its legendary coach who also played golf every week and was the best buddy of our superintendent, came to our stadium with a 50-game winning streak. They were big, fast, and had the best punter and field goal kicker in Texas. Because they were favored in this game by over 40 points, everybody thought we would get slaughtered—everybody except our kids and our coaching staff. On a cold and rainy night, we scored a few times, blocked two punts, and kept them from crossing the 50-yard line until late in the game, when we blocked their attempted field goal. So it was a shutout. We won one of the biggest games in Channelview history!

Our superintendent was so thrilled at the outcome—and that we had shattered his best buddy's 50-game winning streak—he said, "We're keeping that score on the outside marquee for a month." And so we did, even during the beginning of basketball season. I had won my first big Texas football game.

Coaching Point: Confucius said—or he should have, "Maybe if you get water dumped on your head, it's a sign good things come to you later."

CHAPTER 30

The "Southern Cruise" and How It Paid Off

Pat's son, David, was in middle school, and her other son, Jason, was beginning his senior year at Westfield High. That was the sister school of Spring High where Pat and I had met and worked together and where she still taught. No doubt these young men were terribly hurt when their parents' divorced, but David and Jason seemed to be managing their feelings well. I attribute this to the fact that both had qualities which helped them cope. Both were, and still are, intelligent, hard-working, and kind. Pat loved her sons with all her heart, as did their dad. The boys lived with their dad during the first two years of our marriage, but when David began his sophomore year in high school, he came to live with us, transferring to Humble High School where he joined the football team. By then, Jason was attending Texas A&M University and visited us most weekends. Both boys were a pleasure to have around. They were good students and avoided the shenanigans that some teenage boys typically get into.

When you have stepchildren, those relationships can often be delicate. But I think that because I was a football coach and they were avid sports fans, our situation was eased somewhat. We got along real well as fortunately, I was not involved in disciplining these boys. Thank goodness neither Pat nor I had to be concerned much with that part of parenting as they were *that* well-behaved, and most of my conversations with them were about sports or school. Before David began playing football at Humble, he attended many of our games at Channelview. I felt really good having him there because it added extra excitement to the game for me.

David became friends with one of my coach's sons, and they often ran around together during the games. Coach Watson Wright's son and David were about the same age. One night, while we were playing an away game on Halloween, Pat looked around and couldn't find David. She became worried, but was soon relieved when the two boys walked into the stadium with bags of candy. They had decided to sneak off and go trick or treating, and it appeared they had been successful, as those bags were chockful. David and his friend got a pretty good scolding from Pat as this was not the safest of neighborhoods. But I told her that it looked like the boys had just figured out how to attend an exciting game and get some free Halloween candy to boot.

Following our great win against Huntsville High, it was time to get back into the research and development mode, so in January, I was interested in the offense that Georgia Southern was running. Their Spread-Wishbone was an updated version of our Wishbone that had been so successful. I made a detailed proposal to the school board on why we needed to take our staff to Georgia. The board quickly approved the needed funds for the weeklong trip, and gave us the school station wagon to use for transportation. Unlike the R and D trip we made 15 years earlier from Pennsylvania to the University of Texas, we didn't have to sell our blood to fund this trip.

Coaching football was never just a job to me. It created an excitement in my life that I always craved. I loved the practices, the planning, the strategizing, the interaction with young men, the thrilling highs, the devastating lows, feeling my heart pounding before a game, working all night on the game plan, the arguments with coaches in the staff room, and the constant studying and research and development that typically happened during the winter clinics and spring college visits.

—————•—————

When I called Georgia Southern's Irk Russell to ask him permission to come visit, this burly, bald-headed, tobacco-chewing, head-butting football coach—who later became a legendary character for his unique winning exploits—said, "Hell, boy, you don't need our offense. You just need our quarterback." As I hung up after getting his permission to visit, I thought how astute and profound that was. It's not the type of offense, it's the type of players running it.

Nevertheless, off we went, four of my coaches and I, to Georgia Southern. Our route took us through Alabama, where we decided to stop at Troy University for a day and look at *their* offense. Troy had just won their division's national football championship, and they, too, were using the Wishbone offense. When we arrived unannounced, the staff greeted us with true Southern hospitality, placing several coaches at our disposal and offering us anything and everything we needed or wanted—copies of their films and playbooks—for the study of their offensive system.

When word spread that we were on campus, many of their players showed up in the coaches' office, saying, "If we can help you in any way with individual techniques for different positions, just let us know." The next day, the quarterback even cut class and spent the whole morning with us to help us better understand their system. We never made it to Georgia Southern. We spent the entire week at Troy, as within two hours of our arrival, I knew we would. We stayed at Troy's Holiday Inn, and worked long hours, staying late every night before heading out to dinner and some R and R at the Holiday Inn's bar and a local honky-tonk. But we did have to behave ourselves. We weren't exactly inconspicuous, riding around town in the marked "Channelview Independent School District" station wagon.

—————•—————

That impromptu stop in Troy turned out to be one of the best professional visits I ever made. Looking back, I see that experiences in just three places defined my football system: the Troy visit in 1986 during my 23rd year of coaching; my prior experience coaching at Lehigh University from 1966 to 1970; and of course that key trip to the University of Texas in 1971. These ended up defining my football system for the rest of my 46-year career.

That program at Troy had an impact not only on me and the coaches I brought from Channelview; many of the players on that Troy team we met that week went on to become football coaches themselves. Throughout the years ahead, several of them would visit wherever I was coaching to recruit our players. One year, four coaches showed up at the same time. We laughed and howled as we shared old stories from that Troy visit when they were players. We'd also gossip about other coaches and their "war stories"—past and present—as we coaches always love to do.

———

After returning to Channelview, we were excited about teaching our players those new techniques that we had learned during our week at Troy. We later found out that while we were away, many of our fellow faculty members had commented, "It must be nice to take a week off from school, and go on a SOUTHERN CRUISE." Trust me, "Southern Cruise" or not, the school district definitely got its money's worth from that trip, as would become clear during my second season there.

Several games that season were of monumental importance. Liberty High School had a quarterback who had committed to the University of Florida Gators. He was about six-four and sleek. It was a cold night and I remember meeting him in pre-game. I thought, *This guy is going to cause us some trouble tonight.* Unfortunately, my assessment was correct.

Every time Liberty got the ball, they scored against us in just two or three plays. But we had a big fullback by the name of Billy Borten, who, even though he was only about five-ten, weighed about 230 pounds. It seemed that about 200 of those pounds were in his butt and thighs. He was a beast to tackle and was a great runner. I figured that the only way we could win was to give Billy the ball every play. Liberty would score in two plays, and then we would drive and score in 15 plays. By the end of the game, we won because Billy had carried the ball 55 times for over 300 yards. This set a Texas high school record, and Billy is still in the all-time Texas record book. After the game, a reporter asked me if I had overused Billy with those 55 carries. I replied, "Hey, the ball weighs only about thirteen ounces and he weighs two-thirty." The reporter didn't much like my answer, but Billy and his mom were happy, and we had won! What else mattered?

Going into the last game that season, we were playing the powerhouse Dickinson High School for the 4A playoff spot. But the previous year, before a big enrollment shift, Dickinson had been a 5A program, coached by Texas legend Dub Farris, and had progressed deep in that division's playoffs. This season, they had many returning players and a very special quarterback, Andre Ware, who would go on to star at the University of Houston and win the Heisman Trophy. He later played pro football and went on to become the famous TV football commentator that he still is today.

According to the way the playoffs were set up that year, we not only had to beat Dickinson, but we had to win by 21 points, or else Friendswood High would win that playoff spot. The game was to be played at our home stadium, but we still had a formidable task to win by 21 points. At our Saturday and Sunday staff meetings before the Friday night game, I told my staff, "I believe we can win, but 21 points is going to be tough." By contrast, I revealed no doubt whatsoever when addressing the kids that week. "We are absolutely going to win," I told them, "and we will win by 21 points or more." They seemed to believe.

Our inspirational leader on defense was a player named Jason, all heart and guts. But he had been in a wheelchair all week because of a knee injury. Somebody rolled him around school to help him get to his classes, and then they even rolled him out to the practice field. During each practice all week, he would be sitting in that wheelchair, constantly screaming and yelling, "I'm playing Friday night and we're gonna beat their ass!" He even fired me up, but I thought to myself, *No way, Jose.*

Friday night came, the stands were packed. Electricity filled the air. In the field house, "Chief" had hung Jason's uniform in his locker. A player pushed Jason's wheelchair to his locker, and as I walked in and asked, "What the hell is going on here?", Jason was putting on his uniform while repeatedly yelling what had become his mantra, "We're gonna kick their ass!" Our trainer, "Doc," who, unbeknownst to me, had been working and praying with Jason daily, assured me that Jason was good to go. Who was I to argue?

On that cold November night, from the moment of our kickoff, I had the feeling that I was witnessing this game like an out-of-body experience. I was calling plays, Jason was tackling, the defense was on fire, the offense was scoring, the fans were wild, and with one minute to play, we were leading 28 to zero. Until then, Dickinson had crossed our 50-yard line only once. But with ten seconds to play, they scored, and lined up to kick the extra point. At 28 to 7, we still would have won by our 21 points. But to knock us out of the playoffs, they changed their plan suddenly and decided to go for two—a two-point conversion. If successful, the spread would then be only 20 points, and we'd be done.

As the play unfolded, Andre Ware was sprinting to the corner pylon of the end zone, and Jason was in hot pursuit. It was obvious that Jason wasn't going to be able to run him down, when, out of nowhere, "Peanut" Brown, our star safety, looked like he was moving faster than the speed of light. He exploded into Andre at the six-inch line, knocking him out of bounds. I fell to my knees, time stood still, the fans erupted, and Jason piled onto me at the sideline, yelling, "I told you so! I told you so!"

Coaching Point: **Never underestimate belief. It can move mountains—and an injured player out of a wheelchair.**

Thirty minutes later, I was sitting in my office chair, physically and emotionally spent. The phone rang, and it was the Friendswood coach asking me, as if he figured Dickinson beat us, "What was the score?" I screamed, "WE WON BY 21 POINTS. WE'RE GOING TO THE PLAYOFFS. YOU'RE GOING HOME," and hung up the phone. Another great moment of the night.

I never heard any more putdowns about the "Southern Cruise."

We had some terrific kids on that 1986 team. Just to mention a few besides Billy Borten, "Peanut" Brown, and Jason: Henry Coleman, Elmer Laird, "Big Neil" Friesland, and Marcus Norman. Billy and Henry went on to become Texas high school coaches, Neil became a college professor in Kansas, and Marcus is now a successful lawyer in Dallas. I loved that entire team, and regret that after all these years, I can't remember more of their names, or Jason's last name. I do know that Averion Hurts, another good player that year, is now the head coach at Channelview High, as he has been for many years. And his son, Jalen Hurts, as of the fall of 2016, is the first true freshman in decades to be the starting quarterback for the University of Alabama Crimson Tide. What are the odds of that?

Coaching Point: **Throughout my career, I've been blessed to have many great players on several great teams. Even so, I appreciate the wisdom of University of Alabama softball coach, Patrick Murphy, who has said, "Uncoachable kids become unemployable adults. Let your kids get used to someone being tough on them. It's life, get over it."**

CHAPTER 31

Six Years of Super Surprises

In Texas, to avoid giving any one team the home field advantage, all playoff games are scheduled at a neutral site. Once the teams are determined, it's a mad rush to secure the best and biggest stadium that you can get. The day after our playoff opponent, Wharton High School, was announced, I met with their head coach to make plans for the upcoming game's location. The biggest schools usually end up playing in the Houston Astrodome, at Texas Stadium in Dallas, or at a similar-sized facility. We were able to book the stadium at Katy ISD (Independent School District) which was the biggest and best stadium our players had ever played in.

This was the first time Channelview had been in the "big dance," so it was a big deal. The kids, the town, and the school administration were all excited. I couldn't help thinking back to where I had come from in Florida. Football is big in both states, but nothing could top what I was seeing in Texas. I suppose I had become fully "Texanized." Yes, I loved cowboy boots, starched jeans, chicken fried steak, Mexican food, country music, the Texas 2-Step, but more than anything, I was really loving this bigtime football experience.

On Saturday morning, all the kids reported to the field house at eight o'clock. This was just like a normal in-season Saturday, except this was to be our eleventh game—uncharted waters, for sure. Like every Saturday, the coaches had already arrived at seven that morning and graded last night's film of the game. The junior high coaches began to compile and make copies of the opponent's scouting reports, and the JV coaches took the players to the track to warm them up with stretches and light runs as the sports medicine guys checked for injuries. While the players were outdoors, the varsity staff stayed inside to look at the Wharton films. Wharton's players were big, fast, and talented. On my desk was a computer printout about three inches thick, compiled by a coach whose sole duty was to have this compilation of all the plays and statistics of Wharton's last three games on my desk by 7AM. To do this, he had started at 10PM and worked all night until I arrived and checked to make sure we had everything we needed. Then he was free to go home. By about 10AM, the other coaches and I met with the players to give them their grades for last night's game. After that huge win, of course the team got an "A," but not all the players did. The staff and players received the ten-page scouting report on Wharton, and then we all studied one game film. After the kids left at lunchtime, the staff would continue to work until around two o'clock that afternoon, when they finally left to go home.

After that, I usually stayed for another hour or so, and then drove the 45 minutes home to be with Pat. After we ate, I would sit in my recliner with a stack of yellow legal pads and work on the game plan, sometimes until two or three in the morning. I didn't get much sleep during playoff week.

On Sunday morning, the varsity staff met at ten, and worked on the game plan until usually around six or later. Not only during playoff week, but throughout the season, our wives had to be very understanding. They didn't see their husbands much on weekends.

We booked two charter buses for the trip to Katy stadium. This was a big deal as we usually traveled on what's called "the yellow dogs," regular school buses.

The playoff game was exciting, but we had several injuries, including our star fullback, Billy Borten, who sprained his ankle. We lost a close one, but it had been a great second season.

———

In December, I heard about a head coach job opening at Westfield High where Pat's son, Jason, had attended a few years earlier. Since this was the sister school to where I had coached at Spring High, I knew the district's athletic director really well, and called him to express my interest in the job. The school was 5A, so it was bigger than Channelview and the salary was better. The job would be a step up. Over the next month, I went to several interviews and felt confident that I was going to get this job. But one day, I got a call from the AD who said that it didn't look good for me. They had picked somebody else and were waiting for him to accept their offer. I felt crushed and thought, *Who could be better than me?*

The answer was in the next day's *Houston Chronicle*. Westfield had picked Emory Bellard for their head coaching position. WHAT?! This was the inventor of the Wishbone at the University of Texas, the man I had gone to visit in 1971 to study his new, revolutionary offensive system, and one of the coaches I had most admired in my career. He had just been fired as the head coach at Mississippi State, but he wanted to continue coaching. I called the AD and told him, "Wow, what a great choice!"

By that time I had developed a pretty good coaching reputation around Houston. Soon after the Westfield disappointment, another big 5A job opened, this one at Katy Taylor High School. This was in the district where we had played our playoff game in that huge stadium with fantastic facilities. I was excited when I got a call for the first interview and a week later, the second interview. Katy was a great place to live and Pat was getting really excited thinking that perhaps she could transfer to one of the Katy high schools. She had earned her counseling certificate and was working as a counselor at Spring High, so she now had three different types of certificates. She felt she was marketable enough to obtain either a counseling or teaching position in such a large district. The next week, I got my third and final interview. As I was driving home, I thought to myself, *I nailed this one*, and was expecting a call offering me the job. Self-confidence has never been a problem for me, but sometimes my opinion of myself far exceeds what others may see in me. I just *knew* I had this job! Several days later, I got a rejection letter instead, indicating that I had come in second and thanks for your time. When the *Houston Chronicle* came out with the announcement that Katy had hired a coach with the first name of "Bubba" —and that Bubba had been a long-standing Texas high school coach, I sat down and cried out, "Why wasn't I born a Texan?"

———

Pat's son, David, had been living with us now for two years and all was going well. I knew several of his coaches at Humble High and I hoped that this had helped to make his transition to his new school easier. He played on the sophomore football team in tenth grade and the JV team his junior year. Pat and I had lots of fun watching him play. Like me, David wasn't always the best athlete on his team, but he had a great attitude and his teammates loved being around him. Unlike me, David was very smart—particularly in math.

David and I continued to get along well, but I knew he had a great dad so I never attempted to take on a fatherly role. David had lots of buddies and they were always either at our house or at another buddy's house. Pat was usually the one to pick up David and three of his teammates after practice. They all enjoyed regularly attending the Channelview games. Going into his senior year at Humble, David quit football because he felt he wouldn't get much playing time on the varsity. After Pat and I finally talked him into trying to rejoin the team, the next day, David and I took a trip to see the head coach. He agreed to let David back on the team, and it was a good decision, both for David and the team. He got to experience homecoming and at the end of the season, David was awarded the Fighting Heart Award, emblematic of the player with the most heart. This was quite a tribute and we were very proud of him. I was able to watch David grow into a fine young man and experienced lots of milestones with him, such as helping him get his first car and watching him enroll as a freshman at Texas A&M. Unfortunately, that first year at A&M he majored in building the Aggie bonfire and forgot to go to class. Things worked out fine for him though. He transferred to Sam Houston State University where he earned his degree and met the love of his life, Tammy Pore, whom he later married. For the past 20 years, David has enjoyed a successful career in Dallas in information technology.

David's brother, Jason, is four years older, and when Pat and I got married, he was attending Texas A&M as a freshman. Because he was in college,

Jason and I weren't able to spend nearly as much time together as David and I did. Jason did spend several summers with us while he worked part-time and continued taking courses in summer school at a nearby community college. One summer, he got a job washing boats and he'd be filthy when he got home. Working outside in the Houston summer heat was a tough gig, but he made a "boatload" of money. Jason earned his Bachelor's degree from A&M in accounting, went to work as an accountant for a few years, then went back to A&M to earn his Master's in commercial real estate appraisal. Like his brother, he, too, has enjoyed a successful career for the past 20 years in the Dallas area.

My son, Gregg, despite his high I.Q., was in and out of college multiple times and took on several jobs before finally finding himself after he joined the U.S. Army. During his four-year military career, he was selected to be in the famous 82nd Airborne—an elite parachute outfit—and jumped out of airplanes hundreds of times. I hate flying and couldn't understand why someone would get *on* a plane, much less jump *out* of one. After Gregg got out of the Army, he completed his college degree at the University of West Florida, where he majored in math. His goal was to be a college math professor, and after earning his Ph.D. in math from Auburn University, his dream came true. He now teaches at Valencia Community College near Orlando. I assumed he got this interest in math from his mother because I always hated math and only barely passed every math course I ever took.

My daughter, Jennifer, five years younger than Gregg, attended Valencia Community College decades before Gregg began teaching there. She was in the paralegal program for a while, before leaving the program and working successfully in property management, where she excelled because of her strong organizational skills and ability to work well with others.

——————

Back to Channelview. Our football seasons the next couple of years in the late 1980s, were just average. In my many previous jobs, if we weren't winning enough and having a super exciting, successful season, I would conclude that it was all my fault. Sometimes this was true, but sometimes it was simply that the talent of our "Jimmies and Joes" didn't match up with the opponents' talent.

One day, after reaching my limit of discouragement and frustration at our lack of success on the football field, I went into Bill Neal's office and told him that I thought it was time to make a change and that they should get a new coach. I also told him that, if I could, I wanted to stay on as a teacher, which in Texas, I knew was almost unheard of. When coaches quit or get fired in Texas, they're immediately shown the door. But I asked to be the marketing teacher because I had heard that position was about to be open. Several days later, Neal agreed to accept my resignation, and because I had had prior experience in owning two businesses, offered me the teaching job I asked for. But to become certified as a teacher of marketing, I was required to attend the University of Houston and take 18 hours of marketing courses, six courses in all. Pat was not happy that I had not discussed any of this with her until the day I came home after telling Bill Neal I wanted to resign. She was, of course, concerned about my leaving coaching and worried that things wouldn't work out for me. Although I knew she always had my best interests at heart, I had made up my mind and there was no turning back. After those few days in limbo waiting for Bill Neal's decision, we were both hugely relieved when I was offered the teaching position.

Little did I know that getting certified as a marketing teacher would have major benefits for me, not only in Channelview but also in a future location.

Until my courses at UH were completed in two years of night school, I was working as an uncertified marketing teacher which was allowed because I was actively pursuing certification. A big part of the marketing job was being the sponsor of the DECA club, a business development student organization for marketing students. The students would develop projects and then would compete with students from other schools in organized contests. The first step was a local contest, then a state contest, and then a national contest. During the next few years, two of my students won the local and state contests and advanced to the national competition. The first student got to go to Denver for three days, and of course I had to accompany her and her mother as their sponsor. The next year, I accompanied the second student and her husband when she competed at the national convention held in San Francisco. Besides the school district paying all our expenses for these trips, I loved the travel, except for the flights, and had fun seeing these kids compete. I thought at one time that maybe I was destined to be a well-known DECA teacher. Then thought, *NOT!* Because at heart, I knew I was still a football coach, just on a hiatus that I happened to enjoy.

———

One of the benefits of being a teacher and not a coach was more free time during the school year and summers off, with no stress. This gave Pat and me the opportunity to travel, and we took a two-week cross-country road trip to California, went skiing several times in New Mexico, and visited her brother's condo in Panama City Beach, Florida. On some of these ski trips to Red River, New Mexico, we took Gregg, Jennifer, Jason, and David. We also often traveled with our Houston friends, Joe and Susan Euresti. We were able to visit Pat's mom and dad, Selburn and Annie Ruth Parsons, many times during this hiatus. They lived in Fort Payne, Alabama—home of the world-famous band Alabama— located in the northern part of the state, 50 miles from Chattanooga, Tennessee. Fort Payne is a picturesque small town in a valley between two mountains. We would sometimes visit the beautiful, natural tourist attractions on Lookout Mountain: Little River Canyon, Desota Falls, and the Desota State Park, but mostly, we just spent hours rocking on the Parsons' front porch and talking. During these relaxing and fun times, we really enjoyed life, family, and friends.

> *Coaching Point:* **Sometimes when you don't know where life is taking you, just slow down and enjoy the ride.**

CHAPTER 32

Family Dramas Including the Texas Pom-Pom Mom Scandal

As I've said, the Atascocita subdivision where we lived had many foreclosed and empty homes as a result of the economic downturn in Houston and elsewhere due to the savings and loan debacle. Pat was now working as a counselor at Spring High, a huge change for her, but she had accepted the stress and long hours that go with this position because she wanted a change from teaching. Although I was still not coaching, I continued to keep my foot in the coaching door by attending several football clinics during the winter.

One Friday I was waiting for Pat to get home so we could leave to go out of town to a clinic together. She was late and I was getting more impatient by the minute. She called and told me she was going to be *really* late, and then quickly detected the anger in my response when I told her I was leaving without her, which I did. Even so, we were both troubled that after nearly five years of marriage, this was our first big tiff. In the middle of the night— actually about two in the morning—she was awakened by sounds of sirens and people screaming. The vacant house two doors down was burning to the ground. Some neighbors came over and stayed with her because she was afraid since it was suspected that there was an arsonist in the neighborhood. She called me the next morning and I came straight home. The next night, just after midnight, a second home was on fire. There were police, fire trucks, and investigators everywhere. The next evening, the house next to us had its back deck set on fire. The whole neighborhood was scared to death!

All the men in the neighborhood met the next day and set up a patrol schedule from six o'clock in the evening to six the following morning. We used golf carts—two men on each cart with one man being armed with a pistol—to patrol the neighborhood. For about two weeks, we traded shifts every two hours until we were informed by the police that probably the owners were the ones burning the houses down in order to get insurance money. We were told that for those owners who were unemployed during the downtown and could no longer afford their mortgages, or who wanted to move but couldn't sell their houses during this economy, arson was apparently their only way out. After hearing this explanation for all the fires in our neighborhood, we now felt safer, but it had been a really scary time.

High school cheerleading is big in Texas and very competitive. The candidates would try out and those who were selected by an outside committee of cheerleading sponsors from neighboring schools made the final cut. Then they would spend two weeks politicking among the student body prior to the school assembly where the students would then vote for the final team. In 1991, I had two girls in one of my ninth grade classes who were friends but were considered the top competing candidates. These girls were kind and sweet to each other, but one of the mothers, Wanda Holloway, had decided that she would ensure her daughter's winning spot by putting out a contract with a hit man to kill the other mother! Later, it came out that Mrs. Holloway thought that her daughter's competitor would be so shattered after her mother's death that she would drop out of the competition. Fortunately, the hit man panicked and went to the police. When the story broke locally, suddenly the national news media descended on Channelview to cover what became known as the Pom-Pom Mom scandal. One day as I was driving to work on Sheldon Road, I saw police cars and TV news vans from NBC, CBS, and ABC, all parked across the street from the high school. Reporters were there trying to get interviews with the students as they arrived for class.

After about two weeks of this mayhem, the principal announced one day that the cheerleading election would be held in the gym the following morning. Sure enough, the next morning what seemed like hundreds of Harris County police officers were on campus, especially concentrated around the gym. Only students and teachers with special ID badges were allowed inside. My best buddy, Hugh Long, who taught across the hall from me, said only half joking, "Jim, let's sneak in a video camera, tape the election, and sell it to NBC or the highest bidder." We laughed, knowing we could probably have retired with the proceeds, but we realized, of course, that this wouldn't be such a good idea.

After both girls won their cheerleading spots and the media went away, school settled down. Wanda Holloway, the Pom-Pom Mom, went on trial and was convicted to 15 years in prison. After serving only six months, her conviction was overturned due to a technicality of the court selecting one of the jurors who had a prior cocaine conviction. In 1993, an HBO movie was made about the scandal and became a hit—no pun intended. Holly Hunter went on to win an Emmy award for her portrayal of Holloway. For years afterward, no matter where I happened to be visiting in the country, whenever people would ask where I had worked and I said "Channelview," their reply would inevitably be, "Oh, the home of the Pom-Pom Mom." Channelview became world-famous and not just because of its multitude of oil refineries. And the scandal didn't diminish the importance of cheerleading in Channelview, Texas, by one bit.

The 1990s would continue to be a dramatic decade in my life. Everyone's life is full of beginnings and endings, joy and pain, suffering and conflict, and in the early 90s, two things happened that demonstrated these cycles of life for us. While I was in San Francisco at a DECA conference, I got a call from Pat that her dad was in critical condition in a Birmingham, Alabama, hospital. I immediately left for the airport, got on a plane bound for Birmingham, as Pat left Houston at the same time. Her dad was indeed in bad shape. Things did not look good for him. After being informed that Mr. Parsons might linger for several weeks or longer, we left two days later and returned to Houston on a Sunday night. On Wednesday morning, Mr. Parsons died, and we headed back to Alabama for his funeral. Pat has always regretted that she didn't stay with her dad during his final days, but she was fairly new in her counseling position and with a demanding boss, felt she needed to get back to her job. I had learned early in our relationship that Pat had just as strong a work ethic as I did.

As it turned out, on the same Saturday that Mr. Parson's funeral was scheduled in Alabama, my son, Gregg, was to be married to Lynette in Florida at a ceremony that had been planned for months. I was honored to have been chosen to be my son's best man, and no way would I have missed their wedding. No way, of course, that Pat would have missed her father's funeral, so she stayed with her family and I left to be with mine. One beautiful life had ended while another beautiful relationship was officially beginning. It was a bittersweet day for both Pat and me when we could not be together to support each other during such momentous family events.

———————

Mrs. Parsons left her home in Fort Payne, Alabama, several years later and moved south to Dothan. I'm sure this was a gut-wrenching decision for her at the time, but one that she later agreed worked out very well for her. She was living closer now to her son, David, his wife, Gayle, and three of her grandchildren. Mrs. Parsons spent the rest of her life in service to others, one year even winning the city's Volunteer of the Year Award at a big ceremony at Dothan's Civic Center where she made a wonderful acceptance speech. She also was known for making quilts for hundreds of people, not only family members, but practically everyone she ever met in Dothan! She surely was one of God's favorite children.

———————

In 1993, my daughter, Jennifer, married Dennis Cousins at The First United Methodist Church of Kissimmee, Florida. The whole family was there and it was a beautiful wedding. I cried as I walked my daughter down the aisle.

Remembering when she was born in 1969, I was so proud of the grown woman she had become. Maybe I'd live closer to her sometime in the future? We'd have to see…

———

In 1995, Pat's 20-year-old son, David, was now in his senior year at Sam Houston University in Huntsville, Texas. David and the love of his life, Tammy, were to be married that year and I remember Pat asking him, "Aren't you too young to be doing this now?" I believe David then told his mom, "Tammy is the one for me and now is the time." Pat said no more about it because she trusted David's judgment. They were a perfect match and after graduation moved to Dallas and began their careers. To this day, they are still happily married.

———

In 1991, on December 23rd, I would turn 50 years old. It seemed that my life had been a blur, but I did not want this milestone to go by in a blur, so during the prior year, I made big plans for everyone in my entire family to join me in celebrating my 50th and then to stay for Christmas. I picked Red River, New Mexico, a ski town where we would all gather. I pushed and prodded until I got full commitments from everyone to be there, with the exceptions of Pat's son, Jason, and my son, Gregg, and his wife, Lynette. Jason couldn't get off from work, and Gregg, being a newlywed, agreed to spend their first Christmas at his in-laws. My cajoling that I'd have to strike them all out my will had no effect!

I was pumped up and excited about fulfilling this dream of spending my 50th with family and all of us enjoying an old-fashioned Christmas complete with lots of snow, a crackling fireplace, downhill skiing, and a hand-cut Christmas tree. Family members who would be able to come included my daughter, Jennifer, Pat's son, David, my mom and dad, my sister, Janet, along with her husband, Jack, and their three children, Ryan, Craig, and Andrew. And of course, the birthday boy and wife, Pat. We needed to rent a really big place and I found the perfect five-bedroom house which was near downtown and the ski area. My sister and her family had the longest trip to make because they were coming from eastern Pennsylvania.

Mom and Dad flew in from Florida to stay with us at our home near Houston for a few days before we'd drive to New Mexico. I'll never forget one of those days when Pat and I came home from work to find every square inch of every kitchen counter covered in hundreds of home-made cookies of every variety, including a batch of gingerbread men that my mother always made for me every Christmas since the day I was born. Pat and I had no idea that they had spent the entire day baking until the moment we opened the door to the kitchen from the garage and were hit by the wonderful aroma of more cookies than I had ever seen in my life. These cookies were placed with loving care in dozens of tins that would be part of the cargo bound for New Mexico. Also in that cargo: food for many meals, Christmas presents, and brand new matching ski outfits that my elderly parents had bought for their first—and only—ski expedition. They were ready!

It took two cars packed to the gills to get us there: a big Cadillac I rented for Mom, Dad, and me, and our silver Thunderbird that Pat and David drove. We stopped in Amarillo to pick up Jennifer who'd flown in from Florida, and my sister, Janet, and her family would meet us in Red River.

In my mind, this dream trip would be centered around just three things: family, Christmas, and snow. Had to have snow. But as we drove into New Mexico, and were just a hundred miles from Red River, there was no sign of the white stuff. With each mile, I was getting further down in the dumps— where was the snow? We gotta have snow! We were driving up a big mountain 20 miles out, and *still* no snow. But descending that mountain, I spotted the resort in the distance, and it actually looked white. Was this a mirage? Wishful thinking? No! The closer we got, the whiter it got, and we arrived to more snow than I had seen since my Pennsylvania days. Hooray!!!

The house was perfect too. Janet and her family soon arrived, and then all the men and boys climbed up the mountain behind the house in snow that was knee-deep searching for the perfect Christmas tree, following a tradition Dad and I had enjoyed every year since I was a young boy. Suddenly, there it was: the most beautiful Christmas tree I had ever seen. After we all helped cut it down, we dragged the tree down the mountain, still in knee-deep snow, and set it up in the living room. Everybody had brought ornaments from home, and we spent Christmas Eve decorating the tree as a fire blazed in the big fireplace.

For the next five days, we celebrated my 50th birthday and Christmas with much love, laughter, storytelling, eating, and skiing. Mom and Dad, in their seventies, decked out in their full matching ski apparel, were precious to watch as they played around on the bunny slope. The rest of the crowd was more adventurous and headed for the Black Diamond slopes. Pat and I skied on the intermediate slopes together, but I fell a lot, and she, being more experienced and skilled, didn't miss the opportunity to tease me about that before she left to join the others on the Black Diamond slopes.

In my 50 years to date, this was the most glorious time I had ever experienced. Snow, family, Christmas together—PRICELESS!

Coaching Point: **Just because you take a break from your career doesn't mean you take a break from life. In fact, by taking a break, you may realize how much you've been missing.**

CHAPTER 33

After the Call from Football Clinic Founder and Legend Frank Glazier

It was in the fall of 1990, that I got a call out of the blue from my old friend and mentor, Frank Glazer. "You're still in Texas, right?" he asked. "Because I'm bringing my clinics to Texas and I want your help." I knew that since Frank and I had worked together in New Jersey, where he'd suffered the first of many heart attacks—and recovered each time—he had been enjoying great success as the founder of the nationally renowned Frank Glazier Football Clinics. For the past five years, these were held every February and March throughout much of the country, but not in Texas.

As our conversation continued, he wanted to know what was the biggest football clinic in Texas, and I said, "It's the Henry Franka clinic in San Antonio." He said, "Go and see how many coaches are there and then scout out the biggest and nicest hotel that's closest to that clinic. Because same time next year, I'm bringing my clinic to go head-to-head with the Franka clinic."

Knowing his personality and ambition, I wasn't surprised by his plan, but I had my doubts. Because he was a native of Boston and had the heavy accent to prove it, I wasn't so sure from my own hard-fought experience breaking into Texas football coaching, that Texas coaches would cotton to such an obvious outsider as Frank Glazier.

But Frank had no doubts. He knew that with his track record in major markets much bigger than San Antonio and with his top-notch speakers already on the roster, it wouldn't take him long to be a hit in Texas. So the next year, as he'd planned, he went head-to-head with the Franka clinic. Franka hosted its typical 1,000 coaches, and Glazier, the newcomer, hosted only about 200. But the following year, those numbers reversed: the Glazier clinic had about 1,300 attendees and the Franka clinic, maybe a little over 100. Texas coaches knew quality and after that first year, they spread the word. In subsequent years, Glazier clinics in Texas exploded and were held in Dallas, Houston, and Corpus Christi.

Certainly Frank wasn't surprised by this. Early on, after he was put out by the mediocre, lackadaisical quality of so many clinics he had attended, he was driven to reinvent the way football clinics were conducted. So he started hiring the best college and pro coaches to speak, and demanded that they teach the full three-hour sessions, with no filler—no jokes, no folksy stories, no over-reliance on old game films—just all strategy. His clinics lasted three days, usually for nine, ten, or more hours each day. And they were all football, every minute. That was the Glazier rule. The speakers loved it because Frank paid them well, and the attending coaches loved it because they knew they were getting more than their money's worth.

I helped Frank open Texas, and for the next 15 years, I was on his staff as one of three national clinic directors. He also hired Pat to handle the front end of the registration process, among other duties. He paid us both very well and we usually worked about four clinics a year.

Over the years, Pat and I worked at Glazier Clinics held in Detroit, Minneapolis, Orlando, Boston, Los Angeles, Seattle, Portland, Houston, Dallas, and Denver, to name a few. The venues were always at the best and biggest hotels in each city, and we would stay in big penthouse suites where the speakers could hang out between sessions, having lunch or snacks. Pat served as hostess during these breaks, and was greatly appreciated by the coaches for her friendliness and engaging personality, not to mention she actually understood a lot of the football lingo and could keep up with their conversations. That she'd respond in her Southern accent also charmed them.

Pat and I would fly out from home on a Thursday afternoon after school, arrive at the hotel, and then make sure that the hotel staff had set up the conference rooms as requested. This meant with the proper audio-visual equipment, including overhead projectors and microphones, correct lighting, seating, and coffee and water service available in the back. Each room was selected in advance based on the anticipated size of each speaker's audience. Just a myriad of details, not to mention organizing my team of graduate assistant coaches responsible for the speakers' round-the-clock airport runs—to and from—which were often delayed in certain cities by inclement weather that time of year.

Even though we were accommodated in lap-of-luxury penthouse suites—in one, we counted 13 phones, three bathrooms, and six television sets—we really couldn't enjoy them much, working so many long and demanding hours. On Sunday afternoons, we would either fly straight home, or decide to stay another day or so to relax by visiting special locations nearby, including Santa Barbara, San Diego, La Jolla, and Palm Springs in California; Pike's Peak outside of Denver; Seattle and then nearby British Columbia in Canada; Windsor, Canada, outside of Detroit; the Mall of America in Minneapolis, the nation's largest, and other places that are just a blur.

But the coolest thing I loved about working the Glazier clinics was being around my beloved football non-stop. I got to meet and become friends with some pro coaches and most of the big names in college coaching—assistants mainly—who would become even bigger names in the years to come. At the time, they were struggling assistant coaches who just wanted to make a little extra money. Now, many are head coaches and millionaires.

———

During one of the clinics, Frank sent a young man named Andy Lutz to help us run things. At the time, Andy was just a graduate assistant somewhere on the West Coast. But Frank loved the guy so much and was so eager—even insistent—that Andy come work with us, we found ourselves wondering what Frank's agenda might be. But within ten minutes of meeting Andy, we, too, loved the guy. He had a great personality and was such a great help to us that we three worked every clinic together from then on, for more than a decade. Andy ended up as a coach at Ole Miss and then at Auburn, followed by a stint at Texas Tech, and most recently, at Georgia Tech. For several years after working the clinics together, our friendship continued away from the clinics when Andy would manage to get complementary tickets to the Daytona 500 NASCAR race, and he'd invite me to go with him for the weekend. This was an annual event that we each looked forward to, even more during those years when our tickets were in the Gatorade Skybox and we also had pit passes. We loved those races: the roar of the crowd, the smell of burning rubber, and of course, the obligatory adult beverages.

———◆———

I'll never forget before one clinic, Pat and I arrived in good spirits at the Kansas City airport. We were picked up by one of the other clinic directors, and after we got in the car, Pat asked him if he knew when Frank was coming during the weekend. The director looked surprised as he turned to me and said, "You folks don't know?" I said, "Know what?" He replied, "Frank had a heart attack and died last night." Later on, I would cry like a baby, but in this moment, I was too shocked, and we had a clinic to run.

For the next several years, Frank's children ran the clinics, and even though they treated us well, it was never the same,

The way it had worked: Frank would usually fly into every clinic and stay awhile, collect the money, and leave. But after his death, if one of the children couldn't fly in, they'd ask that we just bring the money home with us and send them a cashier's check the next day. Pat was put in charge of this, and we got on many planes with up to $20,000 cash in our possession. She'd go to the bank Monday morning to purchase a cashier's check and send it for overnight delivery, but until that money was out of her hands, she was one nervous gal.

September 11th, 2001, changed everything for the clinics. Due to the massive changes in airport security, we could no longer pick up and drop off coaches at the curb, so getting all these speakers for the clinics in and out of town quickly became a logistical nightmare, greatly complicating schedules and personnel.

A couple of years later, we got a call from Frank's children indicating that they had sold the clinic operation to a big conglomerate, with the stipulation that Frank's name remain in the company's title. Indeed, the company is still known nationwide as Glazier Clinics, and has expanded beyond football to include several other sports, offering instruction both online and at weekend seminars.

God rest Frank Glazier's soul.

Coaching Point: **Leaving a legacy like Frank Glazier's involves not only having passion but also high standards. If you're lucky enough to work with such a mentor, be grateful, and soak up all you can.**

CHAPTER 34

You're Going Back to Kissimmee?

During my last several years in Channelview, beginning around 1994, I was talking to Pat about moving back to Florida. My rationale this time was that I needed just two more years to vest my Florida retirement. That, and the fact that I was itching to get back into football. Those clinics had reignited the bug.

Another thing that triggered this desire was when the principal at Osceola High School in Kissimmee, where I had coached for eight years in the 1970s, would occasionally ask my daughter to have me stop by to see him the next time I was in town. Hearing this, I surmised that maybe he was interested in getting a Texas coach for his football team.

Pat and I would sit on our deck in Texas, overlooking the golf course, and she would sometimes ask me why I was so unhappy. I would say, "I'm not unhappy. I just think it might be a good idea to get back to Florida. I should pick up the last two years I need to be able to collect retirement when the time comes. Otherwise, my eight years there that have accrued funds toward my retirement will just be left on the table. We can start collecting my Texas retirement in two more years when I turn 55, and then I can go earn the two years I need to qualify for Florida retirement. You can start building another retirement in Florida, and hey, have you seen those Florida beaches?" Of course she had, many times. And she would reply, "Hey, I've got a good job here and my kids live here." I would reply, "Well, there are good jobs in Florida, too. Your kids are grown, and of course we can fly back and see them at any time." On and on and on I went, sounding like a broken record.

———•———

What put Florida on the back burner for me was in the spring of 1995, when the head coaching job in Channelview opened up again. I applied, and for some reason, didn't get the job. But the new coach, Mitch Gray, asked me to be his defensive coordinator. I accepted and became a football coach again. Immediately I was happier and so was Pat. This meant I'd finally stop yapping about Florida. Plus, I was back doing what I was supposed to do. Pat's son and daughter-in-law, David and Tammy, would come from Huntsville—about 90 minutes away—to many of our games. With and without the kids, Pat and I developed a tradition of stopping after each game on our way home to chow down on Sonic burgers. Our life felt like it was back to normal, but in the back of my mind, I was still thinking about Florida, especially after football season ended in November.

———•———

Through reliable sources in the high school coaching grapevine, I had heard that the Osceola head coaching job was opening up again and I was being seriously considered. This motivated Pat and me in January of 1996, to drive to the Texas teachers' retirement office in Austin. We wanted to verify that we both could retire and I could start drawing my money at the beginning of the next year. During this meeting, we discovered that I could buy ten years of out-of-state teaching experience to apply toward Texas years, and that if I did this, my Texas retirement would increase by as much as a third. Wow. However, for this to happen, I would have to pay the State of Texas a lump sum of $10,000. But I didn't have $10,000. So we went to Pat's mom, who'd been a saver all of her life, and I explained the situation. She said, "Let me lend you the money, interest-free, and you can pay it back every month over the next three years from your Texas retirement check." This offer helped us immensely—then and ever since.

———•———

The rumor I'd heard became true when Osceola High called me in February to ask me to come for an interview. When I went back to Kissimmee, and the interview went well, I told them that I wanted to hire Alan Baker who'd worked with me successfully 15 years ago, as my defensive coordinator. If the powers-that-be agreed, and if Alan accepted, I told them you've got a deal.

Alan and I had already talked, and when the offer came, he accepted. He had made a name for himself as a stellar defensive coordinator not only in Osceola, but also at its chief rival at St. Cloud. Our return to Osceola was big news, announced at a press conference when I went back in March to sign my contract. My old buddy, former assistant coach, right-hand man and business partner, Bert Bagley, was also at the press conference and hugged my neck. It was just like old times. When the press conference was over, Bert and I walked down to the varsity building to look things over at the facility that we had refurbished some 20 years earlier. My interview visit had been so rushed, I hadn't seen the place. Hadn't occurred to me to look. In my mind, it was like I had left it 15 years ago. But when Bert and I walked inside, I was stunned. It looked like a bomb had gone off. Not a pretty sight. The building was in shambles. I turned to Bert and said, "The hell with this. I'm not taking this job. I'm going back to Texas where they take care of their facilities and do things right."

He said, "Don't panic. I'm gonna get this fixed. I'm gonna make this my personal project. I'm gonna re-do it just like we did 20 years ago, except better. I'm gonna gut the building, throw out everything, have it painted and ready to go just the way you want it, by spring practice." When he told me this, everything changed, all in just 30 minutes. I trusted that man with my life and knew his word was his bond. He had never let me down and even though it would be a mammoth task to accomplish all this in just two months before the start of spring practice, I knew he wouldn't let me down now.

While I was back in Texas, Bert got a crew together and they gutted the building. He got a couple of doctors and other community leaders to donate $18,000 for new lockers and supplies, and sure enough, by spring football, the building was ready, and so was I.

Pat and I were working to sell our house in Texas, but were having no luck. I was talking about my concerns to a friend, and he said, "Just get a St. Joseph statue at a Christian supply store and follow the instructions." When I opened the box, I was scared because the instructions telling me what to do seemed like voodoo. I was supposed to bury the statue upside down with the face toward the house and the feet pointing to heaven. Then, every morning, I was to go outside and over the statue, recite the enclosed prayer. When I told Pat about this, she looked at me cross-eyed. But the next day I did it, and continued saying the prayer for a couple of weeks until one day, Pat came home and told me that two ladies from school were coming to look at the house. When they saw it, they liked it, as well as the price, and soon after the routine legalities were completed, up went the "Sold" sign. At the time, I didn't really believe that St. Joseph had sold our house, but I've since come to believe that by believing, the universe finds a way to make it happen.

> *Coaching Point:* **Whether or not it's using a St. Joseph statue to sell your house, or longing for a new job, or any goal that seems out of reach, the power of intention can work wonders.**

Before it was a done deal, in our conversations on the deck and elsewhere, Pat had said, "Well, if we do go to Florida, I'd sure like a house with a pool on the golf course." Now that we were heading to Florida and I was going back to the same job in the same office I had left 15 years ago, I told her, "Let's see what we can do about that house." But first, we moved into an apartment while we could figure things out. My immediate priority had to be the job. Osceola Kowboys here I come! I was excited and also a bit anxious about how I would be accepted after all this time. Did I have enemies when I left in 1983? Time would tell. There's an old coaching adage that goes: "You lose ten percent of your support and fan base every year you're there." I had been there for eight years, so maybe when I'd left, I had only 20 per cent left. Again, time would tell. But this time, with all the hoopla, I hoped I was starting with a clean slate.

My daughter, Jennifer, was very happy that her dad was returning to Kissimmee. But she told me on many occasions, "Dad, it's not the same Kissimmee that you left." I could see that was true. Kissimmee had grown from a cow town with two high schools to a relatively big city now with five high schools, as well as more diverse ethnicities. Jennifer worked in property management and helped us secure our apartment. She knew we wanted to build a house and had picked out the neighborhood for us. But we hadn't even moved from Texas yet, so I said, "Hold on, girl!"

During April and May, I drove back and forth from Houston to Kissimmee several times to make sure I was ending up the Channelview school year in good shape, as well as getting things off to a good start at Osceola. I was sure happy to see Bert, man of his word, making such good progress on the varsity building, while I was meeting the kids, parents, and booster club, and hiring assistant coaches.

Meanwhile, Pat was very worried about finding as good a job in Florida as she was leaving in Texas. So she started aggressively networking to land a job in Kissimmee or Orlando. Her resume was outstanding. She had two Master's degrees and 20-plus years of experience in several academic areas, in addition to certifications in counseling and vocational administration, as well as teaching certifications in marketing and occupational education, career technical education, and English. Not surprisingly, despite her worries, it wasn't long before she got a job offer in counseling at Orlando's Cypress Creek High School, which turned out to be about 15 miles from the apartment where we later moved. Her school was located in the Orange County school system, while my school was located in the adjacent Osceola County system. I was happy that she would be away from my district, so she wouldn't have to listen to the criticism about me when it started, as I knew it would. People like to talk and complain about their football coaches, and Kissimmee certainly wasn't any different, nor did I expect it to be. Thick skin was always a job requirement.

Coaching Point: **Worrying is like a rocking chair, to quote a proverb. It will give you something to do, but it won't get you anywhere!**

Spring practice began May 1ˢᵗ and lasted 20 days. The first day, I saw two young men standing on the sidelines watching us practice. It was very hot, so both of them had their shirts off. Because they looked almost like grown men, I asked them why they hadn't come out for football. They said that they were just eighth graders now, but would be with us in the summer before they started high school. I asked their names and one said, "I'm Smokey Green." I had coached an outstanding player named Smokey Green here at Osceola 15 years earlier, and I casually remarked, "You must be his brother." He said, "No sir, I'm his son." I had forgotten that I had been gone that long! Unlike his dad, who was a five-foot-four, 140-pound dynamo, Smokey, Jr. was about five-foot-nine, 180 pounds, and ripped with muscle. The second young man introduced himself as Chad Mascoe. He was about six-foot-two and just as muscular. They weren't the only impressive physical specimens I saw that first day of practice. I was looking at athletes unlike any I had seen in my career anywhere, including Texas. I thought to myself, *Jim, you made a great decision coming back to Osceola.*

During those 20 days while Pat was still working in Texas, I stayed with my daughter and her husband, Dennis. It was nice coming home after school spending time with my daughter, whom I hadn't been able to spend a lot of time with since I'd left 15 years ago.

That twentieth day was the spring game, called the Jamboree, which didn't count for the record, but because we were playing longtime rival, St. Cloud, it was a big deal for the players, coaches, fans, and the community. That rivalry was just as intense now as when I left. As the game unfolded, we battled back and forth and were tied with just under a minute to play. I thought to myself, *Please don't lose to these guys on my first game back.* The next play, our junior running back, Cory Glee, broke for an 80-yard run and the winning TD. It was like we had won the Super Bowl! Our fans and players were jumping up and hollering and celebrating just like the old days. Back at our locker room, the players gave me the game ball with all their sig-natures on it. I left for Houston about midnight and drove 16 hours straight through. I had the windows down, the radio blaring, and the game ball in my lap. I just wanted to get home. When I finally got there, Pat told me that Jennifer had called her, screaming, "You shoulda been here! We won! We won!" Pat was just beginning to experience the importance of the Osceola versus St. Cloud football rivalry.

By the end of June, with yet another U-Haul packed and us about ready to leave, I walked around our backyard that faced the golf course and stood between two of my favorite oak trees. Suddenly it hit me that for 11 years, I had nurtured those trees, cut a lot of grass, and spent many meaningful hours with Pat on that back deck. Saying goodbye had me suddenly crying like a baby. I'd moved from many homes before, but leaving never felt like this. Was it the nostalgia that comes with age? I was now 55. Was everything going to work out, especially with Pat leaving a job she'd had for 16 years? I was sad, apprehensive, and yet excited, all at once.

On our way to Florida, we stopped about ten hours into the trip to spend the night with Pat's mom in Dothan, Alabama. The next morning, we were off in the biggest U-Haul I'd ever driven, headed for Kissimmee. I had driven a U-Haul on every one of my moves, but driving this one, a 26-footer, had me nervous the whole way. At one point, wedging the truck through some heavy construction on I-75, I somehow got the right rear wheel off the edge of the shoulder and almost flipped the truck. I sure was happy when we finally pulled into K-town!

The next morning, some coaches and players met Pat and me at our apartment and helped us unload the truck. I spent July at school and in our weight room. Our staff was intact by now, and we were awaiting the arrival in August of the first day of fall practice. I had a great staff, with Alan Baker handling the defense with his hand-picked assistants, and me working with the offense. Doug Nichols was my right-hand man helping with the running backs and working with the wide receivers. Doug had been at Osceola for several years and had a great relationship with the kids. Jamie Baker, Alan's son, was a new hire and he coached the offensive line. To think that before I left for Texas, he had been our ball boy at Osceola. Another reminder how time flies.

One day I was talking with the staff regarding how we would handle the Friday players' pre-game meal. Alan remarked, "Kathy wants to talk with you about that." His wife came in the next day and told me that she would like to handle the pre-game meal. I wasn't looking for a cash donation, but she replied, "No, I'm going to form a Mom's club and we're going to cook a home-cooked meal for these boys every Friday." Well, she did just that, and more. Our food at the pre-game meals became legendary for the remainder of my time at Osceola. The meal always included lots of meat—usually fried chicken, some kind of pasta dish, a salad, and the kids' favorite dessert, Rice Krispy treats. Nothing was store-bought. Kathy was our Team Mom and without a doubt, the most beloved person in our program. She handled not only all the pre-game meals, but also post-game food—subs or pizza, as well as our travel arrangements and our famous football banquets held every year either in January or February. She was worth more than a bunch of coaches put together. On every bus trip to an away game, she was seated in a place of honor: the front seat of the defense players' bus. Kathy came by her great work ethic not by accident. She was the daughter of one of the founders of the Osceola County cattle industry. And if Coach Alan Baker ever reads this book, "Hey, Alan, make sure you get those water coolers cleaned on Thursday night." Echoes of his wife, Kathy.

Thanks to my marketing certification—and that I had finally earned my Master's degree while in Texas, I was assigned as a teacher in the students' job academy program. For our football teams, I instituted a program called the Academic Game Plan developed by Coach John Baxter whom I met at football clinics when he was coaching at Tulane University. The program taught players how to study and how to be successful in all academic areas. We were one of the first teams in Central Florida to have our football players in this program which featured a dedicated two-hour class for weight lifting and academic achievement, the same as high schools throughout Texas had offered. The program I instituted was run by Osceola coaches Jamie Baker and Doug Nichols. We had a program for physical development, and just as important, a comprehensive program for monitoring the students' academic progress through the Academic Game Plan. The players had to keep a daily notebook with their assignments due, and their teachers had to sign off on it every Thursday that those assignments had been completed, and what grades they had earned that week. If a player didn't have that notebook, or if it was incomplete, or if he had a failing grade, he sat out on game night. Couldn't play. This program, patterned after what I had done in Texas, was very well-received by the teachers, administrators, and parents here. I believe it was a critical factor in building our successful program at Osceola.

We had some great players that first season, including Cory Glee, and freshmen Smokey Green and Chad Mascoe—the two I'd spotted when they were watching our spring practice--and many other players too numerous to mention. Willie Green (a.k.a. "Smokey") was as advertised, a very special athlete, but as a ninth grader, he didn't start every game. One day, after he hadn't played much in a couple of games, his mom met with me and asked if he could be moved to the JV, so he would have more playing time than he did with the seniors. I agreed, but told her I thought it was a mistake. Sure enough, in the next Thursday night's JV game, Smokey rushed for nearly 400 yards. The next day, his mom called me, acknowledged that she'd made a mistake, and asked for him to be moved back up to the varsity team. A great decision for all concerned.

Our second game that season was tough and our fans, even tougher. We were losing, when Pat heard one of our fans scream out, "Go back to Texas, Scible." She had never before responded to a fan's criticism, but this time she turned to the screaming man and said, "Sir, Coach Scible is my husband and you are hurting my feelings." The man had no response, and for the rest of the game, spoke not a word.

Things got better real quick that season and we finished with a record of seven and three. This earned us a post-season bowl game, which we won. All in all, a good start for my first year back in Kissimmee at Osceola High.

Coaching Point: **Sometimes when you take a chance on making a big change, you can wind up not just happier,**

but feeling like you won the lottery. Never underestimate the power of luck and how well things can fall into place when you're at the right place at the right time.

———

While everything was going so great, including that Pat loved her new job, there was one frightening event we certainly could not have predicted. While in Texas, Pat had developed a dark brown spot on her left earlobe that didn't look good. She had been so busy during her last few months there, that she had ignored it. She planned to have it checked after we moved to Florida, but her insurance didn't kick in until November. She was able to get an appointment in early December with a dermatologist who did a biopsy. It was a terrifying shock for both of us when the biopsy revealed that the spot was a melanoma. Her doctor removed the spot, and then recommended that she have a brain scan and lung x-ray to see if the cancer had spread. Fortunately, it had not, but for many years, she suffered a great deal of anxiety that the melanoma would return. Thankfully, it has not.

Coaching Point: **If you change jobs and there's a lag in your health insurance coverage, make sure that you have a bridge policy which covers you until your new health insurance takes effect. Life can throw you a curve when you least expect it.**

CHAPTER 35

"Those Georgia Peach Pickers are Tough, Coach"

One day while I was at school, Pat called me and said, "Get home quick!" When I pulled into the apartment complex, she was sitting in her car, looking frantic, almost in tears. I thought someone had died. When she saw me, she started screaming, "Snakes! They're at the front door!" The entrance to our apartment was in back, next to some woods. As I walked up to our doorstep, I saw two thin black snakes—the harmless kind—just lying there, like they were sunning themselves. Once I got there, they just slithered away. Pat told me, "If I continue to see snakes around here, I'm going back to Texas!" Yeah, right, like there are no snakes in Texas.

When we sold our Texas house, we made a nice profit, so we decided we would build a house in Kissimmee. We had picked out the lot, thanks to Jennifer knowing the area. It was in a new subdivision called "The Oaks," which was a beautiful golf community. We picked out a lovely lot on the golf course, and secured the financing on a three-bedroom home with a screened-in swimming pool. I remembered that back in Texas, Pat had said several times, "If we go to Florida, I'd sure like a house on a golf course, with a swimming pool." *Voila!* Done! After all, we were living in the land of the Magic Kingdom where all dreams come true!

For the next six months, we spent many a fun evening driving by to see the progress of our new house being built, from the foundation up. I think Pat was kinda liking this Florida living! She had a good job, we were winning our football games, we had season passes to Disney World, the beach was only an hour away, and as the superintendent once told me, "When you guys retire, you'll be all right. You'll get six checks a month to live on: two from the State of Texas, two from Florida, and two from Social Security." Not bad for a former "homeless" guy.

What happened next made life in Florida even better. My mom and dad who were living in Ft. Myers, about a two-hour drive from Kissimmee, dropped a bombshell on us during a visit one weekend. A good bombshell. Out of the blue they told us, "We've decided to sell our house and move to Kissimmee." "What?!" I couldn't believe my ears. How great was this? The circle is complete. My kids close by, and now, my parents!

At first, Mom and Dad rented an apartment, and very soon after, bought one of the townhomes being built about five blocks away in our new subdivision. Dad really looked forward to coming to my practice most days, as well as being on the sidelines during the Friday night games. All the coaches got to know him well and liked him a lot. My parents were fun people and we all enjoyed each other very much, spending holidays together, and just lovingly watching over each other. Dad also was happily on standby as our personal handyman, fixing a faucet, hanging curtains, building shelves, and later, even helping me repaint the house, inside and out.

———

My football office was about as big as a postage stamp. Just down a short hallway, about six steps in, was the one bathroom and shower used by all eight coaches. Anytime a coach showered or used the bathroom, I was constantly yelling, "Shut the door." I didn't want to enjoy the aroma. One day I was complaining about something, saying, "Well in Texas, we did this…." and Coach Nichols promptly retorted, "Well, you ain't in Kansas anymore." That was the last time I talked about how we did things in Texas.

Although it was tiny, I loved my little office. It was jammed with a desk, two chairs, and most importantly, a big white board where I could draw plays during my offense staff meetings. With two more coaches in there, it was even more cramped, but that's where I had held those meetings in the 1970s, and the way I wanted to hold meetings now in the 1990s.

My first eight years in Kissimmee during the '70s, we had played all our games at the Silver Spurs rodeo facility. Upon my return in 1996, we christened our own on-campus stadium when we played our first home game that year. Kowboy stadium wasn't the biggest stadium, but it was new, and it was ours.

———————

Hugh Holmes, a senior linebacker for the Kowboys my first year back, was one of the top high school linebackers in the country. So he was being heavily recruited by Florida and Notre Dame. Both offered him full-ride scholarships: tuition, room, board, and books. In his close-knit family, his mom, dad, and sister were die-hard Gator fans. During a home visit by Florida Coach Steve Spurrier on the Friday in February before Wednesday's signing day, Hugh made a verbal commitment to Florida. And at the big signing day press conference, his mom and dad were decked out in orange and blue Gator gear from head to toe. The room was electric when the media said, with their cameras poised to record the moment, "Okay, Hugh, put your college cap on." Hugh looked back and forth between the Notre Dame cap and the Florida cap, then put on the Notre Dame cap! I was the only one in the room who wasn't in shock. His mom lost it. She started yelling, "Oh no, you're not! You're not going to Notre Dame!" And she loudly insisted that I take Hugh back to the locker room and make him change his mind. I knew that wasn't going to happen, even though we made a show of departing the news conference for the locker room. I guess we both needed a break from all the turmoil. But why wasn't I surprised? Because earlier, just before the news conference, Hugh had informed me of his decision to go to Notre Dame. When I asked if he'd told his mom and dad, he said, "Nope." And I said, "Oh boy." He replied, "Football is football, but I like the academics at Notre Dame better." Now, for the second time, we walked into the news conference. When his mom saw us, she yelled out, "Son, where you going to school?" And he calmly replied,

"Notre Dame, Mom." She stormed out of the room, as his dad stood up and said, "Go Irish." A house divided. Hugh did play at Notre Dame for a year or two until he got injured. Even after that, he continued with his education and completed his degree in business marketing.

> *Coaching Point:* **As I've told my players thousands of times, don't count on playing pro ball, because the numbers are astronomically against you. If you do make it in the pros, that's gravy. But if you get your degree, that's your ticket for the rest of your life.**

———

Our first grandchild, Caleb Cousins, was born in May, 1997. This was a joyous occasion for Pat and me, and of course, for his parents, Jennifer and Dennis. They brought little Caleb to most of the home games, and I sure loved hugging my grandson when those games were over. We were grateful to have so many members of our family come to Kowboy games, including Jim and Anne Parsons, Pat's brother and sister-in-law, who lived in nearby Lakeland. Once a season, David and Tammy Blake, Pat's son and daughter-in-law, would come from Dallas. That was really special for Pat, and I loved it too because they were our lucky charm. Every time they came to a game, we won. If I had been rich, I'd have flown them in for all ten games every season. My mom and dad never missed a game, and combined with all the other family, I had good backup on those occasions when a fan or fans got too rowdy against their head coach. Sometimes fans would holler nasty things from the stands, like "We've seen that play, Scible. Run something else!" Fans can get unhappy about most anything, but especially if their son isn't playing enough or at all. Even though I usually didn't hear those shouts during a game, my family sure did, but they knew better than to respond in kind.

After home games, we'd all meet at a wing restaurant called PG's. Celebrating with coaches, players, fans, and family members were memories I will always cherish—especially after the wins. Maybe not so much after games we lost, but even then, hey, "Misery loves company."

Coaching Point: **As Olympian champion gymnast Mary Lou Retton said, "A trophy carries dust. Memories last forever."**

————

Every program needs a signature win to put it on the map. And in 1997, ours came against West Orange High School. The week before we played them, they had beaten nationally-ranked Evans High School, also out of Orlando. In front of a standing-room-only crowd, we put on an awesome show, and won decisively. Now we were on the map.

We ended up the season stomping our historic rival St. Cloud and going to the playoffs. Because of a weird playoff bracket, we would play our first game, versus Mainland High School, on the road. Osceola had not been in the playoffs for several years, so there was a big buildup of community excitement. Mainland was a longtime powerhouse program, we were underdogs, and most of our players and fans were just happy we were getting to play a post-season game. Smokey Green ran wild, and we won decisively. The next game, versus Ocala, was also away, and again, we were underdogs. This game was closer than the last one, but we still ended up with our second post-season win.

With things now going so well, my wife wasn't hearing any more insults from the stands, such as, "Hey Scible, go back to Texas!" The community's excitement ratcheted up even more notches as the Kowboys headed to Jacksonville to battle our third-round opponent, Ed White High School. The Ed White Commanders were coached by Dan Disch, a Florida legend, and for the third week in a row, we were underdogs. The Commanders were big, fast, and no strangers to post-season playoffs.

Jacksonville is about two-and-a-half hours north of Kissimmee. I discovered that many of our kids had not traveled very far north of Orlando, 25 minutes away. And I'd have to add that some of our kids weren't too up to speed on their geography either, or understood the structure of the state playoffs. Because on Tuesday, one of our defensive linemen came up to me and said, "This is going to be a tough game, Coach. Those peach-pickers sure play good football." When I asked him, "What's a peach-picker?" he replied, "You know, those Georgia boys." I laughed and said, "Well, they're tough all right, but they're not from Georgia. We're in the *Florida* playoffs, son."

As our buses arrived in Jacksonville, many of our diehard fans, already drunk on adult beverages or the excitement of the game or both, walked off the buses hollering boastfully, "The Kowboys are IN the house!" In front of a standing-room-only crowd, in a very close game, with just several minutes left to play, we were down by six points. A quick glance at our team looking so discouraged got me to thinking that maybe this game was the end of the line for us. Several plays later, though, the Commanders fumbled the ball, and our fans, echoing a scene from the popular movie of the same name, began chanting, "FREE WILLY! FREE WILLY!" That's when tenth-grader Willie "Smokey" Green—one of the kids I'd spotted on the sidelines two years earlier when he was big enough, but too young then to play—ran up to me and said, "Gimme the ball, Coach. I'm gettin' ready to score and we're gonna win this game!" I did. He did. And the legend of Smokey Green had begun. "Crazy" is too tame a word to describe the jubilation that followed and carried us all the way back to Kissimmee with plenty of momentum for the next game. We had beaten the "peach-pickers."

We were going to the semi-finals, and again, to be on the road, this time versus Rutherford High School in Panama City. Saturday morning, I woke up elated at our victory from the night before, and then suddenly got in a sweat that our fourth postseason game on Friday would be played nearly eight hours away. This would require an overnight stay on Thursday which presented two major obstacles. One, was our lack of $10,000 to pay for two charter buses, seven meals for nearly a hundred coaches, managers, medical staff, and players, plus hotel rooms for everybody. Two, and just as formidable, was somebody to arrange all these logistics.

At the end of some storms, there's a rainbow, and our rainbow was, not surprisingly, Coach Baker's wife, Team Mom Kathy Baker, who'd helped feed our team each week all season long. On Saturday afternoon, she said, "You guys take care of the coaching. I'll get the money and take care of the travel arrangements." By Tuesday, Kathy had organized a community fundraiser that resulted in more than the $10,000 we needed. She had booked a hotel in Panama City Beach and made all the meal arrangements with local restaurants. She had set up our entire two-day itinerary, in writing, and in so doing, relieved me of a huge burden that freed me up to focus on the game.

If traveling the two-and-a-half hours to Jacksonville the week before had been a big deal to our players, this was like a trip cross-country. All week they kept saying, "Coach, Coach, we're playing in another time zone!"

In order to break up the eight-hour trip and also to get in our Thursday practice, we contacted the FSU football office in Tallahassee four hours up the road to see if they'd let us work out on one of their practice fields. We were grateful when they agreed, and our plan was, after practice, to eat some sub sandwiches that Kathy had gotten for us, while on our way to the hotel in Panama City Beach.

Thursday morning at eight o'clock, two charter busses were waiting in the parking lot as our kids walked down the long hallway flanked by the entire student body, with the band playing and TV crews everywhere. The atmosphere was loud and electric, and the players were pumped up as they boarded the buses and we got underway.

When we pulled into FSU to have our practice, our kids' eyes were as big as saucers when they saw the stadium and nearby practice field, and when they got to suit up in the college players' visitors' locker room. We had a great practice, not only because the kids got to stretch their legs after four hours on the road, but also because they were so exhilarated by the environment. After practice, Kathy brought out submarine sandwiches, chips, and drinks for everybody which we had to eat outside in the parking lot when we found out from the bus driver that the bus company wouldn't allow food on the bus. But the bus company must have allowed unscheduled, unannounced stops, because two hours past Tallahassee, the bus driver decided he suddenly needed a smoke break. I was so infuriated, I demanded that he keep going, but he took the keys and had his smoke break anyway.

When we finally pulled into the hotel on the beach at Panama City, the kids couldn't believe their eyes, seeing such a big hotel on white sands on the Gulf of Mexico. Before leaving the bus, I stood up and announced, "Don't forget to set your watches back, boys. We're in another time zone." This made the location seem even more exotic to them. Once off the bus, the weather was another shock because they weren't used to wind blowing in 35 degrees, uncharacteristic for the beach even in December, versus the typical winter temps of 65 to 70 in Orlando.

After Kathy and her contingent of parents who'd followed the buses in a caravan got everybody checked into the hotel—no mean feat in itself—she and the parents went to Wal-Mart. They nearly cleaned out Wal-Mart's inventory of gloves and ski masks which they bought and brought back to the hotel. The players were thrilled to put on their new attire before going outside to board the bus for dinner. What a surprise for the Panama City TV stations' reporters and cameramen waiting at the restaurant when our kids made their entrance wearing ski masks! And what a visual for the viewers of the 10 o'clock news later that Thursday night, asking themselves, *Who* are *these guys?!*

Rutherford was a great team. They were big, fast, and much more experienced than we were in that game, especially on their home turf. Overmatched, we lost that night, but this was the beginning of a long and successful run for the Osceola Kowboys. No longer an unknown team, we had made a name for ourselves.

The Kowboys then—and still to this day—like to chant during warm-ups before the games, "Rain or Shine – Kowboys do it all the time." Well, they didn't quite get it done that night, but buckle up your chinstraps, because the real fun for our team was about to begin!

After the Rutherford game, Pat had two choices for getting back home to Kissimmee. She could travel on the small plane in which she and the team doctor, Chris Chappel, and his wife, had flown to Panama City earlier that afternoon, or she could ride back on the bus for the next seven hours with me and the team. Even though the weather looked threatening, she decided to fly back with the Chappels. For the next hour-and-a-half, that plane felt smaller with each mile, Pat later said, as it bounced around in a ferocious rainstorm amidst non-stop thunder and lightning. She said she was terrified and feared for her life, especially when she saw Dr. Chappel administer oxygen to the pilot so that he would be more alert.

I, of course, knew nothing of this ordeal until I got home around 7AM, and although we both were exhausted, we stayed up and talked for hours—about the game and about her horrible flight. Even though we'd lost the game, we'd gone farther that season than anyone ever expected. But of course, after her flight, football was the least of our blessings we counted that morning.

———

Following the Kowboys' remarkable football season, I received many awards and special recognition, which I always attributed to the hard work and dedication of the kids and our coaching staff.

In March, I received another special award, this one from the Houston Astros, whose headquarters for spring practice was in Kissimmee. I was invited to throw out the first pitch at the Astros' opening spring game there. Not being a good athlete, coupled with the limiting effects of rotator cuff surgery I'd had years earlier, I practiced pitching for several weeks. Now, on the verge on my big moment, I glanced up to the stands and saw Pat—who was a long-time die-hard Astros fan, along with my mom and dad, my son, Gregg, and daughter-in-law, Lynnette, my daughter, Jennifer, with her husband, Dennis, as well as many friends looking on. I took a deep breath, wound up for the pitch, and let her rip. And watched embarrassingly as the ball bounced low on home plate, a few inches in front of the catcher. He gathered it up, met me halfway, shook my hand, and with a smile as he gave me the ball, said, "Good thing you're better at coaching than pitching." I still have that ball, with its red dirt and all. Thanks for the memories.

CHAPTER 36

"I Want to Coach with You, Dad"

By 1998, my son, Gregg, was in Alabama, working on his Ph.D. in mathematics at Auburn University. One day he called and dropped a shocker on me. He said, "When I was young, Dad, I never wanted to be a coach. But now, I know I want to come work with you at Osceola and coach football." This struck me as really strange because at age 34, he was halfway to completing his Ph.D., and here he was, wanting to move from teaching calculus at Auburn to teaching ninth-grade math in Kissimmee? What was up with this? When he came down to talk with me about it, I told him straight out, "Look, as much as it would be wonderful to have you working with me, you're probably gonna be working as defensive line coach with Coach Baker. That's where we have an opening." I knew that Alan Baker would demand 100 per cent total commitment year-round, seven days a week from Gregg, as he did all his coaches, and I told Gregg, "Look, I judge my coaches on their performance, not their blood lines. You sure you want to do this?" Gregg was adamant and said, "I'm ready, Dad." So, with high school math teachers being in high demand, he got the job at Osceola almost immediately after he applied.

I knew Gregg was smart, but his work ethic impressed even his old man. With the same passion that he'd studied for his Ph.D., he now applied toward being a student of the game of football. He soaked up everything like a sponge. He was not only smart, he was tough, kind, loving, had a great sense of humor, and was popular with everybody. Not many dads get to coach their sons in high school, and then 15 years later, wind up at the same school working together in the highly competitive coaching arena.

It was ironic that while Gregg worked with Coach Baker on defense, Alan's son, Jamie, worked with me on offense. And heading up the crew was our Team Mom, Kathy Baker. A family affair.

During my first two years of coaching at Osceola in 1996 and 1997, the finances required to pay for equipment, uniforms, field maintenance including paint and fertilizer, fees for home game officials, and team travel expenses, were in fairly good shape. We'd made some money due to the previous season's post-game playoff receipts and various local fundraisers including discount cards, car washes, and candy sales. Unlike in Texas, Florida schools had to fend for themselves. But our team finances were about to escalate to a whole new level. When a local businessman, Steve Johnson, asked me if he could form a Touchdown Club to raise a lot more money for our team's expenses, I was all ears. He told me that I would never have to be involved with meetings or fan parties, that he would handle everything, and it would work like this. "I'm gonna get 200 people to be members," Steve said, "and every time Osceola scores, each member will owe $5, with a maximum of five touchdowns per game, so they'll never owe more than $25 a game." He got our football secretary to agree to bill each member by mail every two weeks. And if a member missed a payment, that member would be kicked out. Steve said that my only responsibility as head coach was to "score touchdowns and spend the money well." Steve's Touchdown Club went on for years and turned out to be the best high school football fundraiser in history. Whenever I would explain Steve's concept to the out-of-town professional fundraisers who were always pitching me on their deals, I'd ask, "Is your deal better than this?" They'd all laugh, sigh, and have to say, "No." I knew that in order to make this kind of deal work as successfully as it did, we had to have a football-crazy town, a superfan organizer like Steve, and a team that consistently scored a lot of touchdowns. We had all three. The kids got so aware of how the Touchdown Club worked, that if a player fumbled the ball on the two-yard line and we didn't score, the other players jokingly ribbed him afterward by saying, "That was a thousand-dollar fumble!"

Coaching Point: It's no less true for being trite: "Necessity is the mother of invention"—and innovation.

On the first day of school in 1998, hundreds of kids arrived wearing gold tee shirts that read, *"The Stomp in the Swamp."* The "Stomp" was the State Championship game and the "Swamp" was the University of Florida football stadium where the game would be played on December 18th. The school was ready to win a championship and so were our players, even though we had yet to play the season's first game.

Each day at the end of practice, the players would chant, "Going to the Swamp, going to the Swamp." And each day, I would give my same message, "It's a long season boys, so don't count your chickens until they hatch, and then I'll have the buses ready for the trip."

We were virtually unstoppable that year and we scored unrelentingly, often leading by 40 or more points. Against one opponent, we were ahead near the end of the game 79 to nothing. With about four minutes still left to play, it was 3rd down, and much too early to take a knee, but so as not to score yet another touchdown which would have been a sure thing, I called for a highly unlikely 40-yard field goal attempt from a young kicker named TJ Bell. TJ was the son of Tom Bell, one of our assistant coaches, who was in charge of equipment—and kickers. I said, "What do you think, Tom, can he make it?" "Probably not," replied Tom, "But he could use the practice." Whether to impress his dad or just make the most of this opportunity, TJ outdid himself, and to everyone's amazement—BOOM! The ball split the uprights down the middle. Final score: 82–zip. Not for the reason you'd think, that was a field goal heard around the world—or at least throughout Florida. The next morning, newspaper reporters all over the state pounced. Following the lead of the *Orlando Sentinel* sports reporter, they editorialized that I had no class, that in all of our lopsided victories, I just loved to run up the score and humiliate our opponents. The truth was that I did love for our team to score, but I certainly wasn't expecting points on that play. And I called the *Sentinel* reporter saying what a low blow that was, since our starters were on the bench after the first quarter when we were 30 points ahead. The rest of the scoring came from our second and third stringers. It wasn't my fault that our opponent couldn't keep up with us.

The Osceola Kowboys were now ranked #1 in the state. We had the highest scoring offense in the state and our defense was stifling opponents. During the week, there was usually a TV reporter or two at our practices. And during our home games, TV news helicopters hovered above the field, shooting video of the pre-game warmup, and many times landed in the end zone to shoot video up close. What a rush this was for our players and fans. Osceola was ranked in the top five high schools by *USA Today*, as well as by the Fab 50. Talk about fun—this was fun on steroids!

Our pep rallies were wild, the fans were delirious, the TD Club money was rolling in, and then…then we played a game, our eighth game, at home, against Auburndale High School, and we LOST! Talk about a wake-up call! All of a sudden, we faced adversity squarely in the face. How would we respond?

The next game was an away game in Tampa, versus East Bay High School. The shine was off our team because of the previous week's upset. Fans were talking and players were chipping at one another. Although we had many great players in 1998, and several super stars, the bell cow was Willie "Smokey" Green. During this game, Smokey took a bad hit on his knee and was sidelined for the rest of the game. We were far from a one-man show, but that injury was a major psychological blow to the rest of the team. We suffered a 28–26 defeat. The long ride home to Kissimmee was deathly silent. No one made a sound. Here we were, on a two-game losing streak.

The next week, Osceola dropped from #1 in the state to unranked. The community was abuzz about what was wrong. I'm sure at the forefront of all the conversation was criticism of me and the coaching staff and whether we had lost the team. All those gold tee shirts proclaiming *"The Stomp in the Swamp"* were a vision of the past.

To make matters worse, we were now about to play the tenth game against our longtime bitter rival, St. Cloud, and at their place. Smokey was still injured and we were skating on very thin ice. I thought, *Is the dream dead?*

We arrived at St. Cloud to a wild, sold-out crowd on their side of the field. At stake: if we win, we go to the playoffs. If we lose, we go into a three-way sudden-death shootout on Monday night, with two other teams, one of them St. Cloud—at their place.

No longer were helicopters circling above the playing field, and the game was covered now by only one reporter instead of a pack. We had gone from the penthouse to the outhouse in two weeks.

St. Cloud played the first half like sharks with blood in the water, and we sort of just hung around, but at halftime, the game was tied. During the 15-minute halftime break, our players looked glassy-eyed. I even asked Smokey if he was able to play at all with that injury, and he shook his head dejectedly, and said, "No, Coach." About five minutes before we were to take the field for the second half, just before I was about to start my best impassioned halftime speech, our quarterback, Bobby Sippio, stood up and started going berserk. He was screaming and yelling and grabbing players as he shouted, "We've come too far and worked too hard for this bullshit to be happening...." *Would this be the wake-up call the team needed?*

We kicked off to St. Cloud and they got the ball on their 15-yard line. On the first play, our linebacker, Chad Mascoe, hit the runner in the backfield, with a thud heard all over the field, and the ball popped up what looked like about 20 feet in the air. One of our players grabbed it and sprinted to the end zone. The rout was on, and for the rest of the game, *we* were the sharks in the water. What would have happened if Bobby Sippio had not stepped up to the plate? We'll never know. I do know this:

Coaching Point: **In football as in any venture, you need leaders on your team, and when they step up, good things usually happen.**

The 20-minute ride home to Kissimmee was delirious as we drove our buses through St. Cloud, with our kids yelling out the open windows to the St. Cloud faithful.

The first playoff game was at home against Spruce Creek. During the pre-game warmup, I was walking around the field and inside the big "O" painted on the 50-yard line, I looked down and right in the middle of the "O", was a big shiny nickel. I put it in my left pocket and thought, *Nickel...five cents... five games to win the championship. Could this be a sign?*

Smokey Green was still injured. Spruce Creek ran the opening kick-off back for a touchdown. Not a good start. The rest of the first half was back and forth with us holding on to a slim lead at halftime. Walking back to the locker room, Smokey came up to me, grabbed my arm, and said, "Coach, my grandmother just told me that she had had a dream, and that God had told her my knee was fine, and that I'm ready to go." I said, "Fine, Smokey, let's go to work." And go to work he did.

We won that game going away. Smokey ran wild.

The second game of the playoffs was also at home. And in a déjà vu "all over again," moment, Belleview High ran the opening kickoff back for a touchdown. What kind of a weird pattern was this, two games in a row? But no problem. We scored the next 68 points, which at the time, was a playoff record.

Game three, again at our place, was against Gainesville High School for the Regional Championship. They were big and fast and their star was running back Clinton Portis, who later played at the University of Miami and for many years in the pros. This game was billed as the showdown between two super running backs, Smokey and Clinton, although we had many other stars, as they did, in addition to two outstanding defenses.

Both running backs had a sub-par game, but both defenses played lights out. Very late in the fourth quarter, and with the game tied, I called a very special play that we had practiced every week for 13 weeks and never used in a game. It was a pass down the middle to our blocking fullback, Quentin Smith. Every time we had practiced it, Quentin dropped the ball. Now, seeing that Gainesville was consistently playing man-to-man defense, I knew that Quentin would be wide open down the middle of the field. I called the play, and sure enough, as expected, Quentin was wide open 40 yards down the field with no one anywhere close to him. Bobby Sippio threw the ball 50 yards downfield, the ball bounced off Quentin's shoulder pads, and with the crowd suddenly quiet, Quentin bobbled the ball several times, and then finally secured it as he sprinted over the goal line for the winning touchdown. The crowd erupted, and same as the year before, we were off to the semi-finals.

The fourth game was at Mainland High and it was a rout as we led 32 to nothing at halftime and never let up. Everyone in the state of Florida had predicted we would play Lakeland High in the Swamp for the State Championship. With two minutes left in the game, the announcer came on and said that Estero High School had upset Lakeland, and it would be Osceola versus Estero for the 5A championship next week in Gainesville.

The *"Stomp in the Swamp"* tee shirts suddenly reappeared, as the town of Kissimmee was in a frenzy.

It was December 18, 1998, and we were entering the Swamp at the University of Florida. The dream was coming true, and what a moment as the kids looked up and saw themselves on the big Jumbotron screen in the end zone. Seeing is believing!

Alan Baker's son, AJ, was publicly recognized before the game for receiving the student athlete award, having the highest GPA on our team. Alan, who was so focused on coaching the defense while his son was a lineman on the offense, looked at me and said, "I never realized he was #64." Coach Baker was the best defensive coordinator I ever worked with. I felt that essentially we had two head coaches, one for offense and one for defense. I never made a big personnel or discipline decision unless we both signed off on it, a strategy that always worked well for us.

Chad Mascoe, Smokey Green, and Bobby Sippio played great that night. The offensive line blocked like crazy and the defense gang tackled for another typical great night. Robbie Beach and Lab Varnado made two key plays that saved the game.

With a minute to play and with us leading 28-14, the Championship hats were broken out and the kids went wild. The Jumbotron flashed, "1998 5A State Champs: Osceola Kowboys." The party was on!

Standing in the middle of the Swamp, amidst a crowd of reporters, I held the trophy high and proudly exclaimed, "I wouldn't take a million dollars for this moment!"

In the stands, were my wife, Pat, my mom and dad, my sister and her husband, Jan and Jack Kerins, who surprised me by coming all the way from North Carolina, Pat's brother, Jim, and sister-in-law, Ann Parsons, my daughter and her husband, Jennifer and Dennis Cousins, my son's wife, Lynette, and thousands of jubilant and crazy Kissimmee fans.

And, at midfield, my son and fellow coach, Gregg Scible. He and I danced and hugged like we had just won a State Championship. WE HAD!!!

After a press conference and big steak dinner with our players and fans, the buses headed from Gainesville back home. I was happy, drained, proud, and every other positive emotion you could think of. As we approached our exit on the turnpike, I saw flashing lights at the exit for Kissimmee. I thought maybe there had been a bad accident because four or five police cars had blocked the entrance. Turns out, they were waiting to escort our buses through the city, with their sirens blaring. It was two o'clock in the morning. Our season's journey was complete.

Coaching Point: Never, never give up. After those two losses, I had doubted whether we would win the Championship. But the kids never doubted, and that was all that mattered! Sometimes a coach can benefit by being coached by his players.

CHAPTER 37

Florida State Champs

After we won the State Championship on December 18th, Pat and I decided to get out of town for a few days during the Christmas break just to unwind. We headed to north Georgia to a small mountain town by the name of Helen. On the drive up there, Pat and I reminisced about all that had happened in the three short years since we moved from Texas. I felt like I was on top of the world and I doubt anybody could have slapped the smile off my face. After spending two days in Helen, we decided to stop in Atlanta on our way home to take in a Sunday Falcons game. We had a ton of fun, and it was a welcome relief to be watching a football game in which I had no personal or professional investment.

An end-of-year bonus appeared as a full supplement magazine in the *Osceola Sentinel* dedicated to our 1998 season and the Championship game. I had always had a good working relationship with the local media, as far back as my first stint in Kissimmee in the 1970s. A reporter named Frankie Carroll was my favorite then, even though we had our disagreements. Over time, we became close, and I appreciated the way he reported news about me and our beloved Kowboys. Upon my return in 1996, I worked closely with another local reporter whom I admired, Rick Pedone, who took it upon himself to create the special supplement magazine dedicated to our historic championship season. For many people, including me, this magazine became a keepsake.

Not just the State Championship, but everything in our lives seemed to be coming up roses. Pat's good job was about to get even better. Mom and

Dad had moved to Kissimmee. We had a new grandson, Caleb. I was finally reunited with both my children, who were living nearby. I was thoroughly enjoying working with my son on our coaching staff. We had a new house with a pool on the golf course. Our finances were in good shape. Did I mention we had won a State Championship? Pat's son, David, and his wife, Tammy, visited us a lot, not just because they loved us, but also because we happened to live down the road from Disney World. And Pat and I loved living close to the beach. Pat's son, Jason, though still working hard in Dallas, was able to visit a couple of times a year. And to put the cherry on top, Pat's sister, Linda Shaddix, who wanted to start a new life in Florida, moved from North Carolina to Kissimmee after getting a job in the same school district where Pat worked. She built a new house right around the corner from us, just two blocks further down from my mom and dad's townhouse. All in all, just one big happy family. I guess if we had also won the lottery, it would have been nirvana. But this was close enough.

Pat entered a career nirvana when she took a new job as the Tech Prep Coordinator for Cypress Creek High School. This job was custom made for her as it involved some counseling—her professional expertise, as well as almost daily visits to the big hotels, to Disney World and to other resort properties, where she talked to employers about potential jobs for Cypress Creek students. For years, when I would ask her where she was going that day, she might say, "Having lunch at Disney." Or, "Meeting an HR rep at Sea World." Or, "Seeing someone at Universal Studios." I remember kidding her sometimes that she didn't have a job, she was on a perpetual vacation. Is it any wonder that I heard no more doubts about our move from Texas to Florida?

Coaching Point: **Better to lose count while naming your blessings than to lose your blessings by not counting them.**

———

After the Championship, the first project in January was to pick out the school's Championship ring. That was fun. Not so fun was figuring out how to pay for them all: 80 rings at $250 each, totaling $20,000. But true to form, the community stepped up and raised this money in a very short time. The City of Kissimmee recognized the Kowboys in *many* ways for their accomplishment. On every streetlight in town a big, five-foot banner was placed proclaiming Osceola High as the State Champions. As head coach representing the team, I was presented a Key to the City, as well as Proclamations in honor of our team from the City and the State of Florida. In February, a parade was held with the players, coaches, and cheerleaders smiling and waving from a dozen floats. Missing from this celebration was the head coach. Because of my duties as a national director for the Glazier Football Clinics, I had to be out of town that weekend, a real disappointment. But what a thrill for the city, which had been our 12th man.

———

After the parade and a few days before the ring ceremony, tragedy struck. One of our most beloved players was shot and killed in a drive-by shooting. AJ Jones was a team leader and a young man with an infectious smile and personality. For his funeral, the First Baptist Church was packed. His closed coffin lay in front of the congregation, and as I stood up at the pulpit to present his eulogy, the casket was opened and raised for everyone to see. Looking down, I, too, was seeing AJ for the last time. With my voice cracking, I tried to console the mourners—and myself—in our sadness that a young life was taken from us way too soon. The next hour or so was gut-wrenching as I watched everyone in the church file past AJ's body and break down in tears. On the way to his gravesite, the funeral procession wound through Kissimmee—cars with headlights on that seemed to stretch for miles.

A small monument was built on our practice field with AJ's #3 engraved in tribute topped by his helmet. To my knowledge, that monument is still there. And for many years, his #3 was worn by various prominent players in memory of his life and what he stood for.

———

Several days after the funeral, a large crowd including parents, media, and dignitaries attended the ring ceremony held in the school auditorium. The players made a dramatic entrance marching in from the back of the auditorium to behind the stage to music blaring from the speakers, Queen's iconic recording of "We Are the Champions." Onstage, the ring manufacturer had built a big replica of the ring, from which each player emerged when his name was called to great applause to receive his ring. After their moments of glory, and after all the players were onstage wearing their rings, I then called a very special guest to the stage where I presented the last ring, what would have been AJ's ring, to his mother. Pat was in the audience and later told me that she had never seen so many sad boys at such a happy occasion.

The final event celebrating our championship season was our annual football banquet, held as usual in the school cafeteria. Thanks again to Team Mom Kathy Baker who characteristically made sure that all food and decorations were first-rate, this banquet topped them all: WE ARE THE CHAMPIONS!!!

During March, I was very busy after I was contacted by the big three universities in Florida and invited to be a guest speaker at their spring football clinics. On consecutive Saturdays I spoke at Florida State, the University of Florida, and Miami University. It was fun and I enjoyed wearing that Championship ring that signified what a lot of our young men and coaches had so proudly accomplished.

The ring was big, but not in the same category as an NFL football Championship ring. A pro ring is about twice the size and embedded with real jewels, so about a hundred times more expensive. But most people haven't seen either type of ring, so to most folks our ring looked really big.

I wore it every day, not to show off—well, maybe just a little—but mainly because when I looked at it, memories would come rushing back and make me feel really good. Out in public, in restaurants, at athletic events, or wherever, I was always delighted at how much attention it brought from strangers. One time, when Pat and I were in Texas, attending a Dallas Mavericks basketball game, I noticed as we were leaving that several people were looking back and forth at me, and chatting with each other. Finally, a lady came up to me and asked, "Excuse me, is that a Cowboys Championship ring?" I couldn't help myself and decided to have to have a little fun. I replied, "Why, yes, it is." She ran back to her friends yelling, "It IS a Cowboy ring!" When I got outside, Pat's and my kids who'd come with us to the game asked, "What was *that* all about?" I told them, and then explained that in fact, it *is* a "Cowboy" ring— just that in Kissimmee, we spell Cowboy with a K. So it's a Kowboy ring.

> *Coaching Point:* **A Super Bowl winning player once gave me some wisdom when our paths crossed in a New Orleans restaurant and he noticed my ring. To my remark, "Well, it's not like your ring…," he replied, "It doesn't matter what level—whether high school or college or the pros—everybody wants a ring. It's the ultimate prize and that's *your* Super Bowl ring. You should wear it as proudly as we do."**

CHAPTER 38

Traveling to a Football Game in Pick-ups

I was hired at Osceola High School by the principal, Mr. Chuck Paradiso, who had several nicknames. He was "Mr. P," "Chuckie P," and the coaches' favorite nickname, "Jerry Jones." The real Jerry Jones, owner of the Dallas Cowboys, has always been very hands-on. And our "Jerry Jones" was like a General Manager of the Osceola Kowboys. He loved being a part of everything in our program and during many weeks would even come to the locker room and suggest a play we might want to look at. Even if we didn't like his suggested play, we had no doubt: "Chuckie P" was the boss.

He was a great principal and ran a very innovative school. He also was very helpful in helping us get the best staff possible for Kowboy football. If I had an opening, he would do all he could to find an open teaching position to fill with the football coach I wanted.

Chuck had heard a lot of football stories about some of the hijinks during my first stint at Osceola High during the 1970s. Chuck came to me one day and said that he wanted to get all the old timers together and hear first-hand all the "war stories" from back in the day. Most of my first coaching staff had moved on to other jobs, but many of them still lived in Osceola County, and Chuck invited them all to come. He said, "I'll buy the beer, we'll go down to a campground in the woods, barbecue some burgers and hot dogs, and let 'er rip." So we did. It was a crazy and fun night. One guy would tell a story, then another guy would try to top it. Laughs and more laughs. When one guy started telling a story about me, I interrupted and said, "If you go on with that, I'll have to tell *two* stories about you." The rest of the guys started chanting, "Tell it! Tell it!" But he and I exchanged knowing looks. Then he admitted, "Some things are better left unsaid." And I agreed, which was met by groans all around from the rest of the guys. Suffice it to say, names have been omitted from this tale to protect the guilty.

> *Coaching Point:* **Before you take a job, make sure you investigate your boss—or in my case the principal. If you have a good one, take the job. If not, run for the hills! "Chuckie P" was a good one.**

The thing I most liked about coaching was the day-to-day interaction with the players and the coaching staff. I often thought how lucky I was to be doing what I had wanted to do ever since ninth grade. No two days were the same. One night I would go home as mad as a hornet, and the next night I would bound into the house with a big smile on my face. Every day was a competition between the offense and the defense. Most of my years I coached the offense, so if we had a good day, all was right with the world. On the days when the defense kicked our butts, I wasn't a happy camper. Our practices at Osceola were highly competitive and that's what made us such a good team.

I used to think that Alan Baker and the defensive coaches sat around at night dreaming of ways to get my goat. They knew that every day I planned, in detail, all the offensive plays that we would run in that day's practice, and in which sequence. I called it "the script." Many times, when the defense would be kicking our tails and it seemed like they knew exactly what play we were running, I would get so angry, trying to figure out what the heck was happening. Finally, after several plays, and just beside myself, I'd look over at the defense in time to see them start laughing like crazy. Then it hit me: they had stolen my script—again—and that's why they knew every play we were running. My son, Gregg, and Alan Baker were always the instigators behind this tomfoolery. Knowing I was so intense all the time, they enjoyed messing with me, just to break the tension of practice and to have a little fun.

Once a year they'd play another trick on me that was far worse, and it always caught me by surprise. At some predetermined point in a practice, after one of our key players was tackled, that player would roll around on the ground yelling in agony, "My leg's broke! My leg's broke!" Or he'd grab his arm, and yell, "I broke my arm!" My heart would sink as I yelled, "Trainer! Trainer!" while running, scared to death, up to the star player who I envisioned was so seriously hurt he'd have to be out for the season. A minute or so later in all this commotion, with other players, coaches, and the trainer hovering over him, the star player would suddenly bounce up to his feet, grinning from ear to ear, yelling, "I'm fine, Coach! I'm fine!" as everybody—except me—roared with laughter. It was all a big prank at my expense. Their laughter rolled on as I would chase Alan and Gregg around the field, hollering amidst many expletives deleted, "You guys have a warped sense of humor," although I couldn't help but laugh with them. Try playing that prank on your Wall Street boss. But all this tomfoolery really worked to the good for everybody, giving us a break from all the tension and competition between the offense and defense. Not to mention a lot of laughs. I can still see what a charge the kids got out of these times and remember that special camaraderie among our rare group of coaches. Good stuff.

———

I also loved seeing players mature right before my eyes. Many times we would have a player who was big and strong, but just not aggressive enough, even though I knew he had it in him. So I'd say, "Hey, football is not a game for the timid. Today you're either going to become a football player, or you're gonna decide that football isn't for you." After a series of competitive one-on-one challenges in front of the whole team, I saw many make the transformation to becoming real football players in just one two-hour practice. One of my mantras was, "Hey, football isn't for everyone. You have to be a little crazy to be out here in this heat, with all that heavy equipment on, and still love it. And, you also have to be a little off to coach it." When it would be 95 degrees and 95 percent humidity, I'd often say in jest, "Hey, guys, can't you feel that cool ocean breeze?" They'd look at me with a scowl on their faces. Hey, we did what we could to bring some levity.

Coaching Point: **Just as in military boot camp, football and other strenuous athletic experiences can turn boys into men. They learn that quitting is easy. Fighting is hard. And that if they stick with it through all the difficulties, they'll like who they become.**

We started the 1999 season ranked #1 in the state. Like so often in life, it's more fun getting there than it is maintaining what you have accomplished. And once we had obtained that ring, it felt like the bullseye was on us every week. But if you don't like the heat, then get out of the kitchen. We turned the heat up real high.

The TV news helicopters still circled above our Friday night games, and most days, TV or newspaper reporters—even more than they had the previous season—were on hand to cover what was happening on the practice field. The kids were used to this by now and so was I.

Every year—and this year especially was no exception—newspaper and TV people would ask my assessment of how I thought we would do in the upcoming season. My answer was always the same: "It depends ultimately on the chemistry of the team—that's the X factor." When they would ask, "Do we have the X factor this year?" I would tell them, "I can't say yet for sure, but when we have it, we'll know. Now team chemistry alone won't cut it. You can't win the Kentucky Derby with a mule, nor a State Championship with small and slow kids. But when you have racehorses, leadership, *and* team chemistry, you can win it all."

In the third or fourth game of the season, we traveled to play Lake Wales High School in Polk County. They were ready for us, and in the first half, they dominated the game while our kids seemed lethargic. As we headed to the locker room at halftime, something happened that had never happened to me before. When we were about ten yards from the locker room door,

233

Chad Mascoe came running up to me, grabbed my arm, and said, "Coach, I got this halftime. Please keep the coaches outside." He kept repeating the same statement over and over with a determined look on his face. Chad was our team leader, and at six-three, 220 pounds, could also, if need be, physically whip any player on the team. I looked at the coaches, they shrugged their shoulders, and I finally said, "Okay. Get your butt in there." Before going inside, Chad then said, "I'll call you when we're ready." For the next ten minutes or so, we heard loud voices and what sounded like banging on the lockers. The other coaches and I just stood out there, listening in suspense, waiting to be summoned. The door opened, and Chad said, "You can come in now." The team was seated in a circle, surrounding Chad who was standing in the middle. They made not a sound, just sat there with glazed-over expressions on their faces. I didn't know what to think, or what had gone on, so I just said, "You boys ready?" None of them said a word, just nodded their heads yes.

The second half was as if a tornado had landed on the field, and the tornado was called the Kissimmee Kowboys. It was a resounding victory for us. Our bell cows typically were Smokey Green and Chad Mascoe, but that night the bull in the ring was Chad alone.

———

Coaching Point: **Sometimes you have to lose control to gain momentum.**

———

We had many great players on that team. But our quarterback, who had been a great wide receiver the year before, was struggling in his new position. By the middle of the season—might have been the Gainesville Buckholz game—I decided at halftime to move the quarterback back to receiver, and insert Chad Mascoe at quarterback. Chad had played many positions, and in practice had served as backup quarterback, taking only 10 to 15 plays in that position each week. Now, I was asking him to open the second half of this game as quarterback. He immediately demonstrated his leadership by doing something totally different and unexpected. During practice we'd always snap the ball on a "Hut 1" because when practiced on a "Hut 2," our kids on offense would always jump off sides, which in a game, would result in a five-yard penalty against us. So we gave up practicing on a "Hut 2" and never did it in a game. That now made no difference whatsoever to Chad. On the opponents' nine-yard line, it was 4th down when he snapped the ball on a "Hut 2." But at our typical "Hut 1"—and what the opponent's defense was expecting—it was our opponents who jumped off sides and incurred the five-yard penalty. I looked at my coaches and said, *"That's* never happened before." The ball was now at the four-yard line, and after we scored the touchdown, when Chad came off the field, I asked him about the "Hut 2." "Why did you *do* that?" I asked. He replied, "It was to our advantage to do it, plus I told the offense if *they* jumped on the 'Hut 1,' I'd beat their butt in practice on Monday." Never underestimate the power of fear!

———

Coaches try not to have favorites, but I have to admit that Chad was one of mine, and almost like a son to me. He was one of the best players I ever coached and certainly the smartest when it came to football. In four years, he learned every position and played most of them. He was a wide receiver, a linebacker, a running back, a defensive back, a defensive end, and he ended his senior year as our quarterback.

One day during his sophomore year, I got word that Chad had suddenly moved with his mom to Georgia where her family lived. She and I had grown close because she was occasionally in my office discussing her concerns about his grades and his inconsistencies in the classroom. I was shocked and confused about why they had left town without letting me know. For weeks afterward, I was distraught. I missed both Chad's personality and his leadership. Several weeks later, a player burst into my office, screaming, "Chad's back!" I said, "What? Where is he?" "Up by the cafeteria." I took off running down the hall as fast as I could, and when I saw him, I jumped in his arms and we hugged like father and son. Later, at his graduation, his mom, Cynthia, and I hugged jubilantly, saying to each other, "We got him through!"

Chad got straightened out in school and was offered scholarships to many colleges including FSU. Long story short, he eventually transferred to University of Central Florida and played football there. I'm happy to say he is now married and has four children. I suspect his two sons, now in junior high, are going to be very special football players when they grow up. They sure have a fine role model in their dad.

Whenever we played an opponent outside the county, we traveled in two charter buses. But for the in-county game against Gateway High School, located about five miles from Osceola High, our line coach and athletic director, Jamie Baker, had scheduled for us to ride to Gateway in two yellow school buses. For such a short distance, the expense of hiring charter buses didn't make sense. I admired Jamie and not just because he was reliable. He was a great offensive line coach and responsible for much of our success on offense. He was also a great athletic director, overseeing all the school's sports and attending both boys' and girls' games. He had to verify every kid's grades every six weeks to make sure they were still eligible to play, as well as handle many other administrative duties. Being athletic director can be a thankless job because it requires wearing so many hats. He even led the team prayer before each game. One time, when he was running late, the team refused to take the field until after he arrived and they could have their prayer.

Jamie had made sure our buses were scheduled to arrive at six o'clock on that rainy day to take us to the game. But as six o'clock rolled around, where were the buses? Jamie called the bus barn and was told they were on the way. Everybody knows that I'm absolutely crazy about being on time—always have been—so I was getting very anxious. After the second call to the bus barn, we got the same response: We're on our way. But by 6:35, still no buses. At 6:45, Jamie asked me, "What are we going to do? The game starts at 7:30." I told him and the kids that if the buses didn't arrive in five minutes, they were to sprint to the locker room, grab their gear and car keys—whoever had a car or truck—and pile in as many kids as they could. Five minutes later and still no buses, I blew the whistle and the kids scattered for their vehicles, while the ones without vehicles, scrambled for a ride.

That's how in a driving rain, our players in helmets were riding in a caravan of cars and in the backs of pickup trucks, down Highway 192. People driving along the four-lane were blowing their horns and wondering what was going on. I knew that getting us to the game this way was a big risk, but I made the decision to just get there however we could, because a no-show would cost us a forfeit and maybe another State Championship, a risk that I was not willing to take.

When we arrived, the players took off running out of their cars and trucks toward Gateway's field that was covered in inches of water. As the kids hit the end zone at full speed, they proceeded to belly flop, sliding about 15 yards, and then jumped up covered in mud, yelling, "We're here!"

———

We won that game by 50 points, and afterwards, in the parking lot, waiting for us, were the two errant school buses. One of the drivers said, "We're here to take you back to the school," and I said, "To heck with y'all. We're going back the same way we came." And we did, yelling and screaming, back on a busy Highway 192, still in a driving rain. Another huge risk, but what choice did we have now? We had to get everybody's vehicles back.

First thing Saturday morning, the transportation people called me, apologizing profusely for their screw-up. I told them, "This could have been disastrous in so many ways. Don't let this happen ever again." I'd already told the good Lord, and whatever guardian angels, *Thanks for looking out for the Osceola Kowboys—and their coach.*

———

Coaching Point: **Whatever it takes, make a decision, but with faith and trust in God, who's always in control!**

———

After we won the last—and tenth—game, we'd finished the season undefeated, with a 15-game winning streak. The ironic thing was that, as coaches, we were not jumping up and down with joy. After every game in any season, Pat would come join me on the field and give me a hug, win or lose, usually a victory hug. This time, after our 15-game winning streak, she said, "Why the gloomy face?" I replied, "It was pitiful. Did you see how sloppy we just played?" Most of the staff felt the same way. It's really sad when you can't enjoy your success unless you have perfection every time. As I've said, getting there is a lot more fun than staying there.

Coaching Point: **Success breeds success, but not necessarily satisfaction.**

In my left pocket was the shiny nickel that I had found on the field during the pre-game warmups before our first playoff game the year before. I considered it my lucky charm, and our team's lucky charm, too. After all, it had taken us to a State Championship and now, our 15-game winning streak. During the week, I kept it in a place of prominence, taped in the left-hand corner of my desk blotter after each victory. Then before the next game, I'd put it in my left pocket for good luck. So far, so good. We were on to the playoffs—again!

Coaching Point: **Make no mistake about it, whether it's a great football team or a successful business, it's the players—or the workers—who make great things happen. Of course you need good coaches and good leadership, but if everybody is not pulling on the rope at the same time, in the same direction, excellence is rarely achieved.**

CHAPTER 39

18-game Winning Streak & Mother Nature

As we entered the playoffs in 1999, riding a 15-game winning streak, expectations were high that we would repeat as 5A State Champions, especially when we were still undefeated going into the third round of the playoffs. We were about to face off with Mainland High School, a powerhouse team that we had beaten on their turf in '97 and '98. This year they were coming to Osceola and were loaded with talent. For most of the first three quarters, they literally mauled us, and well into the fourth quarter, were leading by 17 points. Our fans got quiet, our players looked like they had given up, and I was thinking, *Is this the way it's going to end, with a loss on our own field?*

We had not stopped Mainland from running the ball all night. No doubt their coach, gloating at the likely prospect of beating the State Champs—who'd beat them two years in a row—decided to go for the jugular, to embarrass us further by running up the score. Up to that point, after running the ball on most plays, the coach started calling for their quarterback to throw the ball, to add more points even faster. But then, a tsunami hit Mainland, by the name of the Osceola Kowboys. In rapid succession, in three plays, we intercepted a pass for a touchdown; knocked the ball loose, scooped it up and ran for another touchdown; and then threw a 60-yard bomb for yet a third touchdown. The rout was on. From a turnaround standpoint, this was the wildest game in my entire career. Pat recalls it being the loudest. Our fans went from calm and quiet to loud and crazy. Our players became like sharks in a feeding frenzy. Within eight minutes, we had gone from 17 points down, to the lead. Then, on the final play of the game, we intercepted a desperation pass from Mainland and ran it back for one more touchdown. When the game ended, the score looked like we had beaten them soundly all night, but that was definitely not the case. If Mainland had just kept running the ball, they would have won that game and moved on to the semi-finals. But that wasn't meant to be, and it turned out to be our night.

The next week, we are playing the semi-final game at Rutherford High in Panama City, where two years earlier in the semi-finals, we had lost to them. To save money, we decided not to practice at FSU on the way as before, and instead of staying at a hotel on Panama City Beach as we did the last time, we stayed in Lake City on Thursday night after working out at Lake City's High School stadium on Thursday afternoon. The next day, we went straight on to Rutherford's Tommy Oliver stadium for the big game. The weather was cold, but not freezing as it had been two years earlier. The game was exciting and close the whole way, but in the end, we suffered a 20-21 loss. And I do mean suffered. I was so devastated that I took the lucky nickel that had been with me for 18 straight wins, out of my left pocket and threw it into the woods. Added to the embarrassment of losing, when I looked for Pat after the game, I saw her standing with her brother, David Parsons and his wife, Gayle, who had driven down from Dothan, Alabama, to surprise us. First time they'd ever seen me coach. I felt mortified. But ten minutes later I was brought back to reality when one of our big tackles came up and said, "Hey Coach, what are we eating for the post-game meal?" Kids keep things in perspective.

> *Coaching Point:* **Sometimes young people have a better knack than adults for accepting the losses in life and moving on. Listen to them.**

It was in 1999 that my mom started to have health problems which lingered and progressed during most of the next year. I loved my mom and dad so much, I was deeply pained as she got sicker and was in and out of the hospital several times. In October of 2000, the doctors told us that she would not live much longer. When I visited her one Friday afternoon, she held my hand and pulled my ear to her mouth, whispering, "I'll be fine, Son. Go win another football game tonight." On the way to the stadium, I sobbed uncontrollably. Two days later, Mom went to heaven. I thought about how my dad had done everything for her their whole life together. During 60 years of marriage, they were inseparable. And I remembered how just before she slipped into a coma, he painted her toenails pink, as he had done every week for years.

Coaching Point: Some losses you never get over…

———

With a heavy heart, the next Friday night, I celebrated my 200th win as a football coach, surrounded by players, coaches, friends, and family members. But the occasion was bittersweet as I had attended my mom's funeral just two days earlier.

Two hundred wins had placed me in the elite coaches category in the state of Florida. Pat had all the newspaper articles framed, including a gold plaque marking the date and time of this momentous win. That plaque still hangs in my office. I look at it often, and when I do, I think of the thousands of players and hundreds of coaches who were responsible for this achievement.

We had another very good season that year, but ended up getting beaten in the third round of the playoffs.

———

September 11, 2001, I was sitting in my classroom when a teacher ran in and screamed, "Turn on the TV!" She was crying and everybody wondered what was going on. What we saw on television that day changed all of our lives. Witnessing people leaping from the burning Twin Towers in New York City, then the collapse of those buildings as people ran screaming through the smoke and debris, brought tears to us all and a shared feeling of frightening chaos. That afternoon, we met with our players and prayed together, before sending them home to be with their families. The next day, we practiced, but no one, including myself, could get into it, as our entire thoughts were with all the people who had suffered from this despicable act. I remember that Pat and I decided to go to Disney's Epcot Park on Sunday afternoon, just to get our minds off of this terrible tragedy. The park was open but virtually empty. It was so eerie that we stayed for only a few minutes, then left and went back home.

Life did have to go on. We played the rest of the season, finishing undefeated, as we had in 1999. It was exciting, but in retrospect, felt hollow because of what had happened on September 11th.

On December 23rd , Pat said, "Let's go eat out at our favorite steak house." In the parking lot, before we walked in, we ran into our team doctor, Chris Chappell, and I said, "Fancy meeting you here." Turns out that was no coincidence because when I opened the door to go inside, everyone in the restaurant stood up and started singing, "Happy Birthday." I was shocked that Pat had rented out the restaurant for my 60th birthday surprise. I really appreciated everybody being there and thought, *Wow, I've actually lived six decades.* At the party, Pat made an announcement that she was going to have a palm tree planted in my honor behind the school scoreboard to commemorate this milestone. That tree has thrived and stands to this day.

The next two years as we continued to have good teams and entered the playoffs each year, I don't think our kids and fans really understood how significant it was to be in the playoffs every year.

Coaching Point: It's human nature to take things for granted.

Before we moved from Texas to Kissimmee, Pat had expressed her concern about Florida hurricanes, and I had assured her that there hadn't been a hurricane in the Orlando area for 50 years. But Mother Nature was about to make up for lost time. In August, 2004, Hurricane Charley was predicted to come into Florida's southwest coast and then move north to Tampa, nowhere near us. So we weren't concerned and made no preparations. All of a sudden, the storm changed course, bypassed Tampa, and made a beeline for Kissimmee, packing winds of 140 miles per hour. Watching the news, just before the power went out, we learned that Charley was in Lakeland, only 40 miles way, and the meteorologist urged everyone to take cover immediately. With no time to spare, Pat and I grabbed a mattress, rushed into the bathroom in the center of the house, climbed into the bathtub, and under the mattress, hunkered down. The next 45 minutes seemed like a lifetime as the house shook, we heard explosions, and thought our roof was coming off. After the 140-mile-per-hour winds finally passed, we heard only silence, so we fearfully crept out of the bathtub, found a flashlight, and saw that our entire swimming pool enclosure was gone. Vanished. Although our house suffered minimal damage, we were shaken emotionally. We felt fortunate, though, when we saw devastating damage throughout much of Kissimmee. Thousands of trees were down, power was out for two weeks in some neighborhoods, many roofs were blown off, and hundreds of houses were destroyed. School was out for a week, but to try to salvage our football season, we phoned as many players as we could reach in an effort to hold some sort of practice. Very few showed up though, as they were helping their families and friends dig out from the storm.

Two weeks later, having barely caught our breath, with school back in session and practices resumed, here came a second storm. Hurricane Frances. In between school and practices, Pat and I gathered up sand bags and boarded up our windows with plywood. Even though we were prepared this time, I decided we were not staying in our home for this storm.

Because the school's football locker room was located in a cinder block building with a steel reinforced roof, I told the principal that our coaching staff and families would stay there for the duration of Frances. So, hunkered down in that building were all the coaches, their families, several dogs and cats, a pet raccoon, lawn chairs to sleep on, and food and drink to sustain us. After buying provisions, Pat and I arrived later than everyone else and saw that most of the floor space was already occupied. There was no room for us or our two chaise lounges until one of the coaches said, "You and Pat can have the room with the ice machine." With the storm raging, Pat and I climbed onto our chaise lounges and settled in for the night. But every time we started to doze off, we were jolted awake by the intermittent "tink-tink" of ice falling in the machine. The ice noise stopped, though, when we lost power. Then all hell broke loose. Every fire alarm in the building went off, with strobe lights flashing and sounds blaring that almost burst our eardrums. Dogs were howling and people were yelling frantically, "Stop that noise!" With a hammer, we managed to knock a fire alarm off the wall, but that didn't stop the sound.

It was so deafening, we knew we couldn't stay in the building all night and we were getting desperate to escape. We looked outside and saw that every building on the campus was lit up with fire alarms, every building except one, in the distance. We made a battlefield decision to evacuate. In the dark of night, with winds blowing at a hundred miles an hour, we locked arms, ducked our heads, and moved all 25 people and animals to the quiet building 50 yards away. When we safely got inside, the defensive coordinator's wife, Team Mom Kathy yelled out to Alan, "Where's Sally?" Several asked, "Who the hell is Sally?" Alan said, "Where's Sally? Damned if I know." Sally was Kathy's pet raccoon who, in the haste and panic, had apparently been left in its cage back in the locker room. Kathy said, "Alan, you gotta go get Sally." "Hell no," he said, "not in hundred-mile-an-hour winds!" But Kathy insisted. Actually more than insisted, until Alan and another coach finally made their way back to the locker room building and managed to safely evacuate Sally.

The next day after the storm passed, everyone headed nervously home to assess whatever damage had been done overnight.

—-—

Two weeks later we were scheduled to play a game in Tampa. Another storm was coming by the name of Jeanne. The game was cancelled, then rescheduled as Jeanne headed out to sea.

We lost that game, had just finished our post-game meal and were headed east on I-4, when I got a call from Pat. She said, "You're not going to believe this, but Jeanne did a U-turn out at sea, and is scheduled to hit Melbourne around two o'clock tomorrow with a 30-foot storm surge." Melbourne is only 60 miles from Kissimmee, so when we got back, I told the kids to just throw their travel bags on the floor and head home. "Good luck," I said, "and we'll see you when we see you." The next morning, I called the principal and said that we're all heading back to the reinforced locker room and to please have the fire department turn off the fire alarms. They said that they couldn't do that, but would give us the key to turn them off if they activated again during the storm. They did go off that night and several coaches, again locked arm in arm through another hundred-mile-an-hour wind, found the main box and shut off that godawful sound. When we got home, we saw we had experienced *some* damage, but nothing horrible. However, for the next eight hours Pat and I watched TV as the weather reporters chronicled hundreds of tornadoes that were exploding all over central Florida. None of them, thank God, hit us.

———

The rest of the season was a disaster for us as we won only two games. And to add insult to injury, we got beat by St. Cloud for the first time in eight years. Also for the first time in eight years, we did not celebrate Thanksgiving morning with a short preparation practice for the next day's playoff game, because we weren't going to the playoffs. On those special mornings, before we would send the kids home for their holiday meal, we always had our players stand up and talk briefly about what Thanksgiving meant to them, about who they would celebrate the day with, and what were some of the special items on their family's menu. I missed our ritual this year and, of course, wasn't thankful for the reality that caused us to miss it.

———

Going into my ninth season at Osceola, I did something that I would regret terribly. Because our team was young and in a rebuilding mode, I changed my offensive philosophy. We had enjoyed skill players for eight years, including having a thousand-yard rusher, and sometimes two in the same year. Several years we enjoyed a back who gained over 2,000 yards. All those players were gone now and I was looking for a quick fix. I got enamored with passing the ball and running what's called the spread offense. As they say, I had drunk the Kool-Aid. Throughout my career, I had been very successful doing what I'd always done: run the ball, then play action pass, and play good defense. But when I changed my core philosophy, I was outside my comfort zone and it cost me dearly.

The tenth year was worse than the ninth season, and the principal and I were soon to have a talk.

CHAPTER 40

You Just Fired Me?

During my tenth year at Osceola, as things got even worse, the principal and I had many talks. He wanted to boost the team's morale by having the coaching staff go visit team members' parents at their homes. He also considered hiring a PR person to help alleviate what he feared was an increasing sour mood in the community. When I told the staff of the principal's ideas, they looked at me like, "Are you kidding?" In the past, I had always been a strong leader with no fear of changing jobs if I felt I wasn't on the same page with the principal. But now, being older and more settled in our comfortable life, I went along with the principal even though I didn't agree with him on some of these ideas. No doubt I had lost some of my characteristic spunk and hard-headedness.

At the end of my tenth season, after another loss to St. Cloud, for some reason—with all evidence to the contrary—my optimism about the next season kicked in. As I washed the car on Saturday morning, I felt reenergized and that the worst was behind us. I told Pat, "I'm going to get this thing turned around." She smiled and said she loved the return of my fiery attitude.

Monday morning, the principal walked in to my office, and just before I could talk about these positive feelings, he said, "You're getting ready to retire, right?" I replied, "No, as a matter of fact I'm jacked up about getting us back on track." Then the bombshell hit. He replied, "Well, I'm going in another direction." I said, "Looks like you're firing me." "Oh no," he said, "I just want you to head up this new community development program." I retorted, "I don't want any of this B.S. As I see it, if I want to coach and you don't want me to, looks like you're firing me." On that note, I walked out of my office and didn't come back until two weeks later to clean it out. The Scible reign at Osceola was officially over.

Later that day after I walked out, several newspapers called and wanted to know what was going on. I said, "I've been fired." Then they called the principal who told them he didn't fire me; he just wanted to go in the famous "another direction." Semantics be dammed!

On the morning I returned to school, I was met by the top assistant principal who told me that I had a teaching job for life if I wanted to stay. I thanked him, but said, "No thanks. I will keep teaching my two classes, but I'm outa here as soon as I get another job."

The hunt was on. Here I was 64-years-old, with 43 years of coaching experience, and a resume touting my 240 wins and a Florida State Championship. I applied and interviewed for several jobs in the state, and although they loved the resume, my age probably scared them a little. I think they were wondering, *How many more years is this guy going to coach before he retires?*

For two months, nobody hired me.

One day in January, I got a call from an assistant coach at Auburn University, Andy Lutz, who had been a dear friend for years working with us at the Glazier clinics. He asked me if I would be interested in a head coaching job that had just opened up in Dothan, Alabama. I was very familiar with Dothan. Pat and I had visited many times to see her mom and her brother who lived there. The wheels started turning. Pat was thrilled at the prospect of living near her mother and brother, and I started networking with every person I could think of to promote me for the job. This was not my first rodeo pulling out all the stops to make connections. I had done this to get that job in Texas. But this time was a different ballgame. A few major college coaches and Pat's brother, David Parsons, who owns a successful accounting firm, went to bat for me. He and other influential local businessmen began calling the Dothan City Schools superintendent on my behalf.

About three weeks later, I got a letter from the Dothan Schools human resources director informing me that I had to come take math and English proficiency tests before an interview could be set up. Math? I hadn't taken any math classes since 1961, and I wasn't very good at math then. So I called my son, Gregg, who was still teaching high school math at Osceola, and we began a two-week crash course. He would give me a basic problem to solve, and I would give him a blank stare. About a week later, I told him that if math kept me from getting this job, then to heck with it.

The day of the test, Gregg drove me the six hours from Kissimmee to Dothan, quizzing me with math problems the whole way. I was as nervous as if I were an astronaut getting ready to blast off to the moon. Turns out, the test wasn't that hard and before I left the room, I was told that I had passed with a good grade. An interview was scheduled for two weeks later. As we were leaving town headed back to Kissimmee, Gregg drove us by the football stadium and we were impressed with how big it was. I later found out the stadium seated 10,000.

I have always done well at job interviews. Lord knows, I've had a lot of practice. My presentation packet with full details on the running of a successful high school football program would be seen by each member of the school board, as well as by the superintendent and school principal. Thanks to David, all those packets were professionally bound. I nailed my interview with the superintendent and principal, and walking out, I felt confident.

———————

A week later I was standing by my truck in the Osceola school parking lot ready to leave for the day, when my cell phone rang. It was Dothan superintendent Sam Nichols offering me the job. I gladly accepted, and Pat and I celebrated that night by popping a bottle of champagne by the pool.

The next week, Pat and I went to Dothan and I signed the contract to be the athletic director/head football coach at Dothan High School. That night I attended the public school board meeting and was officially approved before being interviewed by some local TV reporters. David and his wife, Gayle, and Pat's mom, Annie Ruth, were happy that we would be moving to Dothan. My daughter Jennifer, and my dad, Walt, were also happy for us, but sad that we would be leaving Kissimmee. Pat's sister, Linda, was also sad that her sister and best friend would be moving away. My son, Gregg, was just happy to see his dad employed again.

———

Pat put our house on the market, and Gayle started looking in Dothan for a house for us. April in 2006 was a hot time in the Florida real estate market. It seemed everybody was buying and selling houses every other day, and housing prices were skyrocketing. So this was a great time to be a seller. Our Florida real estate lady was the wife of one of David's fishing partners. She knew the Kissimmee market well and we were pleasantly shocked at the price our house listed for. It was as if our house was the last available house on the market because people knocked on the front door every day wanting to look at it. But we had to turn them away because we had a contract with an agent. We sure didn't need to enlist St. Joseph's help in selling *this* house.

Our agent, Terri, called and said she had some concrete offers, and asked if she could come over and present them to us. When she showed us the first offer, it was higher than our listing price. I said, "Sold!" She asked, "Don't you want to see the other offers?" We were shocked when all the other offers were even several thousand dollars more. We had lived in that house for ten years, and we signed a contract that more than doubled our original price. Jokingly, I said to Pat, "I told you the move to Florida would be a good idea." She laughed and said, "Oh, shut up."

Six months later, at the start of the nationwide real estate crash which began in Florida, the price on that house plummeted. As the economic downturn took its toll, those poor people who were so excited when they bought our house had to foreclose and lost nearly everything.

If I hadn't lost that Kissimmee job when I did, our net worth would have plummeted, too, as did the net worth of millions of people around the globe. Wall Street, banking greed, and real estate corruption almost ruined our country and possibly the world. I thank God every day that Pat and I were a few of the lucky ones.

———

I went to Dothan and had a productive spring practice. Thanks to David's and Gayle's hospitality, I was able to stay with them for three weeks during those spring practice days, and enjoyed Gayle's delicious dinners that were usually preceded by fancy hors d'oeuvres.

Gayle continued her search for our new home, as did a local realtor, Jenny Holman. In May, Pat drove to Dothan and looked at many houses in what we'd said was our price range, but saw nothing suitable. After an exhausting day, Jenny said, "Let's look at one more. It may be a little more expensive than what you had in mind, but I think it's worth a look." The house was in a new neighborhood and not quite finished, but Pat fell in love with it, and the next day I did, too. For a little more money than we had budgeted, we had a brand new home and were thrilled.

For the next several weeks, Pat was again saddled with packing and sealing boxes. When I was home, I helped, but of course, after years of practice, she'd gotten real efficient handling these chores.

Before we left Kissimmee we had a huge garage sale. I would rather wrestle an alligator then go through a garage sale, but this one was a whopper. By the end of it, we let people into the house and sold just about everything that wasn't nailed down.

I hired one of my former coaches to help load and drive the U-Haul to Dothan. Hey, I was moving up in the world. I still used a U-Haul, but I didn't have to load or drive it this time.

The night before we left, I had many emotions in my head and heart. For one thing, I was very sad that I was leaving Kissimmee the way it ended. Also, my dad was old by now, and I hated the fact I wouldn't see him every day, but at least he was happy and healthy as he hugged me good-bye. I had left my daughter, Jennifer, in 1983, had returned in 1996, and now here I was in 2006, leaving her again. But this time, she was a grown woman with a family of her own. I had experienced the thrill of coaching with my son, Gregg, for eight wonderful years and we would miss each other, but it was time for me to start a new job. I knew that Linda was sad to be losing Pat, her sister and best friend, but I also knew she understood. And, again, as in Texas, Pat had to leave a really good job that she had grown to love. But we were happy to have another opportunity, and we sure were better off financially than when we'd arrived in '96.

When we got to Dothan, Pat had the chance to completely furnish a new house just the way she wanted it. She and Gayle were busy for weeks and the credit cards were on fire.

Several weeks later, Pat was offered and accepted a counseling position at Northview High School, Dothan High's dreaded rival.

And I worked in my new job as Dothan High's athletic director and head football coach.

Coaching Point: **What seems like devastation one day might turn out to be very positive in the not-too-distant future.**

CHAPTER 41

Hello Dothan – Goodbye Dothan

Whan a school hires a new football coach, they look at many factors in making their decision, and just to recap, here's what Dothan High School got with me: a coach with 43 years of experience, who had won 240 games in seven different states, in ten different jobs, who also had won a State Championship in Florida, and who had coached at every level of football—from freshman, JV, varsity, college, and semi-pro. I had started my career in 1963, and now, in 2006, was about to turn 65, with unlimited energy and no signs of stopping.

I realize all that may sound a bit braggadocious, but as Detective Joe Friday famously said for years on TV's *Dragnet*, "Just the facts, m'am. Just the facts." And as legendary Alabama coach Bear Bryant reportedly said, "It ain't braggin' if it's true."

———

Pat and I loved our new four-bedroom house which she and her sister-in-law Gayle had furnished just the way Pat wanted. Pat was loving her new job as a counselor at Northview High School, and I knew Northview was fortunate to have hired a person with her outstanding credentials and extensive experience.

In July, we were thrilled to welcome a new member to our family, our first granddaughter, born to Pat's son, David, and his wife, Tammy.

We were able to fly to Dallas for the weekend when Hannah was just one-week-old. I remember Pat holding Hannah for ten straight hours that Saturday.

———

The previous head coach who had been fired from the Dothan job was still on the teaching staff, and after several meetings with him, I decided he would be a great asset as my defensive coordinator, so I hired him. This turned many eyes, including the superintendent's. But I had hired many people during my career, always looking for a person who was a hard worker, loyal, and who possessed very good football coaching skills. So even though he hadn't made it as a head coach, I felt he would embody all of these desirable traits, and it turned out he did.

Summer practice went well, and I had installed the offensive system that won me hundreds of games over four decades.

The previous Dothan High principal who I first met during my job interview had been promoted to a district position, and I was now having to become acquainted with a new principal. She and I got along very well, but it seemed that the faculty wasn't enamored with her being hired. Sometimes people don't like change, especially if it involves a new or different way of doing things.

At the time I was hired, there were many problems in the athletic department. Certain situations existed before I got there, and I was charged with trying to right the ship. I believe that over the course of the first six months, I was able to make great progress in that regard. However, problems between the new principal and most of the faculty were growing, and I was caught in the middle. I've always been loyal to my bosses and I had no intention of changing my philosophy now. It was imperative that I remain neutral and avoid taking one side or the other. I felt a great need to heal any wounds between the athletic department and the teaching staff which had been festering long before I got there.

As athletic director, I was now an administrator as well as the head football coach. For the first time in my career, I would be tasked with more administrative responsibilities beyond just coaching football. These included management of the athletic department's annual budget and managing personnel of *all* the school sports—not just football, but also baseball, soccer, basketball, track, tennis, and golf. The *coup de gras* was when the new principal at one of our first meetings said, "Oh and by the way, you're also in charge of the cheerleaders and the cheerleader coach." When I responded that I thought the principal handled those duties, she replied, "Not anymore."

The cheerleader coach and I got along fine, but she was more than a little headstrong and quite a tough disciplinarian, so problems between her and the girls' parents were frequent. My phone would ring at least once a week with some conflict that put me in the position of having to mediate between the two. Oh boy! Talk about a no-win situation.

At our first football game, I got a pleasant surprise when my dad, my daughter, and my son showed up. The final score wasn't terrible, but we lost. After the game, Gregg said to me, "I knew you might have some problems, Dad. Your kids just didn't look quite as talented as your opponent."

On the football front for the rest of that first season, even the games that were close ultimately didn't go our way. In high school sports, talent runs in cycles. Some years you have great talent, and some years not so much. We were in the "about average" category, but for some reason, I was experiencing more problems than I was accustomed to. Poor attendance at practice due to some of the kids' personal problems and their issues off-the-field were almost daily occurrences.

Even so, we played some of our games very competitively, but others were Friday night blowouts. I have to say, though, on the kids' behalf, that our schedule included some of the toughest 5A opponents in the state of Alabama.

We did have some bright spots that first year. The first game we won was in Troy, against Charles Henderson High School. It was a glorious night and winning felt so good. We won one more game before the season ended, but a big loss to our rival Northview High in our last game left the locals not too happy with their new hotshot coach. You can imagine how tough all this was for Pat, who was a counselor at Northview.

In December, I went to see our superintendent, Dr. Sam Nichols, and expressed my concerns about the direction of our program. I told him that I thought it might be a good idea for us to part ways. I said to him that sometimes the problems were because of me, and sometimes because of the situation, and sometimes a little of both. He was surprised to hear me talk about "parting ways," and in reply, said that he was very pleased with the work I had done so far, particularly cleaning up some of the athletic department problems. He said he felt that the football problems would get better and that he didn't expect success would happen overnight. I left the meeting feeling better about things and was ready to start preparation for the next season.

———

For the first time in my 44-year career, I decided to turn over the entire offense to another coach who had convinced me that the spread offense would suit our kids best. The trend in Alabama high school football was to have offensive and defensive coordinators separate from the head coach, just as colleges do. Most of the big schools, like Dothan, operated this way which made the AD/head football coach like a CEO of the program and in charge of making the major decisions.

When summer started and we began installing the spread offense, the kids were excited. Practice attendance was at an all-time high. The kids arrived early and stayed late. Everyone lifted weights and then we hit the field. The linemen went their way and worked on strength and footwork drills, while the skill players began catching balls and learning pass routes. This would last about 45 minutes, and then we'd spend over an hour on what's called "7 on 7." It's skill players versus the linebackers and defensive backs, and is played at a fast pace with the no-huddle tempo and no tackling. It's like touch football or playing basketball on grass. The kids absolutely loved this, and wanted to stay all day playing "7 on 7."

My role now was to move around the various segments of the practice field and shout encouragement to the staff and kids. Everything was really looking great and optimism everywhere was high.

In early summer, I got a call from Hoover High School in Birmingham, asking me if we would be interested in playing a fall pre-season game. I said yes, and our Dothan fans were abuzz about this game. Hoover was a perennial State Champion in Alabama, and had obtained notoriety through being featured in a reality-type series on MTV.

I planned to follow the tradition in Alabama high school football by also taking the JV players to the Hoover game. This meant two big charter buses for 80 to 90 players, even though only about 30 kids would ever see the field. Along with the transportation costs, was the added expense of feeding almost 100 players plus 25 cheerleaders. When I first arrived at DHS, I had mentioned to the staff that I felt it would be wise to take around 40 players for each game because that's all who would even have a chance to play. But I was told that if we take only 40 and the other team has 100 on the sidelines, it would look like we're not even a 6A program. I relented and said, "Okay. In Alabama, we'll do as the Alabamians do."

So two buses headed for Hoover. This was a fun trip for the kids and they got a taste of what it was like playing a national high school football powerhouse. But it didn't taste good getting beaten so soundly.

For my second season, I don't think our offensive coaches did a bad job of coaching. It's just that our players were ill-suited for running this style of offense. When you go no-huddle, and throw three incomplete passes in a row, your defense is right back on the field—quickly getting exhausted and increasingly ineffective. Once you're into the season with a poor strategy though, it's too late to change because the kids and staff get confused. I had won in many high-powered football states including Texas and Florida doing what I do: multiple formations, sound running game, play action pass, and good defense. But once again, as in Kissimmee, I had let myself be persuaded to go in another direction. In retrospect, again, I should have stuck with my proven formula.

Coaching Point: **Experience is a wonderful thing. It enables you to recognize a mistake when you make it again.**

As the second-season losses piled up and the fans became more disgruntled, the fun and excitement of the summer were gone.

Around this time, a lot of negative media about me started showing up on a local internet site. The blogger repeatedly wrote that I had come to Dothan only for the money. Because I knew that wasn't true and I didn't even know who he was, I was unperturbed, but Pat was devastated by the blogger's relentless personal attacks against me. She kept saying, "We've never experienced anything like this *anywhere.*"

When I had turned 60, my goal was to coach until I was 70. I was never looking for anything other than to keep coaching football for as long as I could. I wasn't one of those wanting to retire so I could go hunting, fishing, or playing golf. I'd never had those hobbies and I wasn't interested in starting them. With a Master's degree in administration, I never wanted to be an administrator. To still earn a paycheck would be nice of course, but wasn't essential. When Pat and I arrived in Dothan, we were already receiving pensions from our jobs in Texas and Florida, and I was on the verge of receiving my first Social Security check. Since we had sold our house in Florida for more than double what we'd paid for it, we were ready to take some of that profit and establish a lifetime income annuity. I was proud that I'd come such a long way since 1983, when I was homeless and jobless. And I was proud that Pat and I together had attained relatively sound financial security for our future. So I wasn't looking to pad our finances by coming to Dothan. I just wanted to keep coaching football.

But midway into my second season at DHS, I knew once again that this wasn't a good fit. My history had always been having a strong start and a quick turnaround during my first and second seasons, but here in Dothan, nothing was coming together. By mid-season, I knew in my gut, *I'm outa here.* I was looking for an exit.

At our last home game, before taking the field, I told the kids that this would be my last game as their coach. Word spreads fast in a small town, and before the end of the first quarter, probably everyone in the stands knew that I was gone, including a reporter who approached me at halftime and said, "I heard you resigned." I said, "I'll talk to you after the game." My resignation was headline news in the *Dothan Eagle* Saturday morning. Maybe there was a collective sigh of relief all around, but no one was more relieved than I was.

Coaching Point: **Do what you do! If you have built a successful business using your business plan, don't change your methods of success. That rarely works out in the long run.**

CHAPTER 42

"We're Going to the Beach!"

The Dothan superintendent who hired me was a great man, and I felt I had let him down. But I knew that I did what was best for the Dothan Tigers—and myself—by leaving. Dr. Nichols had always treated Pat and me with great understanding and compassion, and now accepted that it was time to wish me well. As I left his office, I suggested that he hire a good young coach who would rebuild Dothan High School's football program from the ground up. Dr. Nichols later did this, and with good young talent that came along, the Dothan Tigers over the years have become a very respectable football program.

Knowing my contract would be up at the end of January, Pat asked me what I was going to do. I told her I wasn't sure yet, but I was going to take a few weeks to try to figure it out. I looked at a couple of other Alabama jobs, but didn't apply. I did apply for several Florida jobs and had several interviews, even though I was concerned there wouldn't be a big market for a coach who was 67-years-old.

One day in late February, I got a call from an old friend who had been an assistant principal at Osceola when I was there, and was now the principal at Terry Parker High School in Jacksonville, Florida. He said, "I hear your Alabama deal didn't work out and I was wondering if you're interested in one more rodeo? We have an opening for a head football coach and we would like to interview you." My reply was something like this, "As you know, I coached in Florida for almost 20 years, and as a matter of fact, Pat and I retired from Florida when we came to Alabama. I've been through Jax many times, but we've never really visited there." Jokingly, I said, "Isn't the ocean close to Jacksonville?" Laughing, he said, "Yes it is and you could probably live on the ocean and commute to school." Very quickly, my interest soared.

A day before the interview, I drove to Jacksonville to get a look at the school. Then following my GPS, I drove about 15 miles east and arrived at the Atlantic Ocean. Straight in front of me, right on the ocean, was a restaurant called the Crab Shack. With the temperature a balmy 78 degrees, I went to the deck where I would soon have dinner, ordered a drink, and couldn't believe my eyes. The sky was blue, sunlight was glistening off the water, sea gulls were flying overhead, and waves were crashing on the shore of a big white beach. It was one of the most beautiful sights I've ever seen. Then I noticed that two tables over, sat the coaching staff of the city's professional football team, the Jacksonville Jaguars.

I had a warm fuzzy feeling as I called Pat, and said, "This looks like paradise to me. If this job has any potential, and they offer it to me, I think we should accept." She readily agreed.

The interview went well and I liked everything I saw. They said that they would get back to me soon, and sure enough, a few days later, the Terry Parker High School principal, Scott Flowers, called me and offered me the job. I accepted, and immediately called Pat to tell her, "We're going to the beach!"

Coaching Point: **As the saying goes, "If you are made of the right stuff, a hard fall results in a high bounce."**

The date that they wanted me to start the job conflicted with a trip that Pat and I had already scheduled and paid for to Las Vegas during her spring break at Northview. So the principal said, "Go enjoy yourself and we'll see you the following week." While in Vegas, I got a call from my old Kissimmee defensive coordinator, Alan Baker, who congratulated me and said, "Looks like you landed a good 5A job. Good luck!"

I started my new job around the first of April, 2008. I lived in Jacksonville during the week and came home to Dothan on the weekend. Until Pat's counseling job at Northview High ended with the school year in June, we couldn't move to Jacksonville, so I lived for the next two months in an extended stay hotel called Value Place located about a mile from the school. It was a real dump but one I could afford.

My job as head football coach and P.E. teacher got even better when I discovered that my teaching responsibilities would involve only two weightlifting classes first thing in the morning, and would be comprised entirely of my football team. The field house—located about 300 yards from the school—was older than in any other place where I had coached, but it was the exclusive home for our Terry Parker Braves. I would stop by the school's front office every morning to sign in, then head over to my building for the rest of the day.

In the 1980s, Terry Parker was an elite school in Jacksonville. The student body was made up of upper-middle to upper-class students whose parents were doctors, lawyers, and such. By the time I arrived in 2008, the school's population had changed significantly, comprised mainly of urban kids and a high percentage of non-white students. For the first time in my career, my transition into this new job was enhanced by a mentor who knew the ropes. Greg Stanton had graduated from Terry Parker in the 1980s, and had returned to his alma mater three years prior. I was replacing him because he had been hired to coach at a brand new high school in nearby Ponte Vedra. But until that job started, he stayed on for two more weeks to help me with everything I would need to know about my new job. Greg and I had known each other five years earlier when he was an outstanding coach at Lake Mary High School in Orlando. We had competed many times while I was coaching in Osceola, and had great mutual respect for each other. Now, Greg told me that after my first phone conversation with Scott Flowers, the Terry Parker principal, Scott had come running over to the fieldhouse exclaiming, "Guess who I just talked to? Jim Scible!" and Greg immediately said to him, "You better hire his ass!"

While coaching at Terry Parker, Greg was innovative in many ways, both on the field with his style of offense and defense, and in the weight room where he had developed a great computerized weight lifting program which I copied with his encouragement. Plus, Greg also gave me the rundown on all the player personnel coming back that season.

I did have one major problem, though: none of the coaches, except one, was coming back. Greg was taking them with him to his new school. This put me in a horrible predicament! Back in Kissimmee, I had a staff of 20 coaches; in Dothan, about 15 coaches; and over 20 coaches in Texas. Coaching is not a one man show. You need a staff. And here in Jacksonville with only one assistant coach remaining, I was desperate. I put ads in the local newspaper and in the *Florida High School Coaching Journal*, and was relieved when I started getting a lot of calls from prospects. If they could fog a mirror and wanted to coach, I was interested. Divine intervention set in, because before the start of spring practice, I ended up with a great staff.

One of my coaches, Steve Castle, was living in Boston when I first saw his resume. I have to admit that I was suspicious of his being the real deal as a coach because as a young man, he had been a practicing attorney and successful entrepreneur in California. Not only that, he had earned several advanced degrees. But his resume indicated that more than anything, he'd always wanted to be a high school football coach, and he was coaching in Boston when he contacted me. More than eager to escape Boston's winter weather, he was thrilled to accept the job at Terry Parker High in early May, 2008.

Coach Brandon Higdon came on board as my defensive coordinator, commuting daily for practice from another school near Jacksonville where he taught during the day. Another coach, Rick Badger from somewhere in Alabama, took two weeks off from his school and lived in a rundown trailer at the back of the Terry Parker field house, while he coached the defensive backs and ran the equipment room.

Other coaches included Jim Zaborowski, who worked full-time painting big cranes at the ship channel and would leave his job every day in time for practice as our offensive line coach. Big Toby Bullock came on board in late May and coached our defensive line. Coach Larry Reed, the only holdover from the previous coaching regime—the one who I'd thought when heading into spring practice might be my *only* assistant, coached the receivers. Surrounding these coaches were many others who helped out for a short while, but at the top of my list was John Dunn.

John Dunn had been Terry Parker's wrestling coach for many years when he came to me and said, "If there's any way I can help, I'll be glad to." I told him how he could help would be to first head up our JV football team, and then to take on the most challenging and important task of all: to be in charge of our football team's academics. John agreed, and single-handedly was responsible for monitoring our players on a weekly basis to make sure they remained academically eligible to play. An arduous task, for sure. In 45 years throughout my career, I'd never had such a coach be so diligent, disciplined, and dedicated to the year-round oversight of these players, including during summer school. With a notebook three-inches thick, Coach Dunn kept track every week of over 100 players' transcripts, credits, grades, classroom behavior, and then, kept me apprised nearly every day. Coach Dunn was both the hammer and the nail, keeping our kids eligible to play.

So after four weeks of rebuilding the Terry Parker staff from the ground up, I was proud to have assembled such an outstanding group of coaches just in time to start spring practice in May.

For several reasons, spring practice went much better than I anticipated. First, very few kids missed practice. Then, they picked up my offensive system easily. They loved to compete and they loved football. Many of them had prior academic problems and family issues at home, but playing tough football was no issue for them at all.

We dressed over 70 kids for the spring game, which we won, and the kids were on fire. Even though Jacksonville is a big city, word about Terry Parker spread far, wide, and fast among other schools' football players. During the summer, when practice started in June, players started coming from everywhere to enroll at Terry Parker High and to join our football program. During one summer practice, Coach Reed asked me how I was recruiting all these kids, and I told him that I hadn't contacted anybody; they were just showing up. I remember when I asked one of the players who'd been on the team for three years, why all these new kids were coming. He said, "Well, everybody knows by now, Coach, that our new coach has won the Florida 5A Championship and over 240 games, so I guess they wanna be with a winner." It's true, many of the new students had grade problems which affected their eligibility, but with Coach Dunn working full-time that summer getting them in and out of summer school, those issues were effectively resolved, and our ranks swelled.

Coaching Point: **He who will not be denied, will find a way.**

———

Meanwhile, Pat was still back in Dothan, and bless her heart, having to pack up our house for yet another move. Fortunately, this time she decided to hire some people to help.

She came over to Jacksonville one weekend to find us a place to live, and by the end of day one, had found our new home: a brand-new $400,000 vacant condo located only three blocks from the beach. We got it for a very reasonable rent because in that 2008 economic downturn, the owners just wanted to get *some* money for a place that no one had ever lived in and which they hadn't been able to sell. Lucky for us that we found ourselves in one of the nicest places we'd ever lived. The complex was like a resort, complete with pool, hot tub, and fitness center. Our third-floor condo featured big living areas, dining room, and a kitchen fully-furnished with all new appliances. The view from the balcony was awesome. Later, when our kids were visiting, our daughter-in-law exclaimed, "You all have moved to an oasis!"

In early June, after nine weeks of living in a low-rent hotel room, I packed my pickup truck with my few belongings and felt ecstatic as I headed to our new condo. Even though it was without furniture, waiting on Pat's arrival, I slept soundly and peacefully on the floor that night on top of my blow-up mattress. I couldn't help but recall a similar bliss from 25 years earlier, when I'd moved from being homeless in my truck to getting my first apartment in Houston. This was even better because after nearly a lifetime, I was finally living at the beach.

Coaching Point: **Don't spend a lifetime letting your dreams just be dreams.**

CHAPTER 43

My Final Triumph

D othan had left me with an empty feeling. For some reason I never felt comfortable in that job, and was disappointed that I had let so many people down who had lobbied to help me get the job in the first place. Until Dothan, I almost took for granted all my years of success as a coach and winning so many games. But after Dothan, I wondered if I had lost my effectiveness. I often asked myself, *Is it even possible for a 67-year-old man to relate to 16-17-and 18-year-old kids?* I looked young, felt young, but maybe my message was falling at last on deaf ears. I couldn't help but wonder if I had come to the end of my road.

But after that first spring practice in Jacksonville, I thought, *I'm back!*

———————

Everything was finally coming together, except one. We couldn't find a renter for our Dothan house. We'd already decided we didn't want to sell it—as if we could have during that 2008 economy, but we surely hoped to rent it so we wouldn't be paying two house payments every month. With that in mind, we moved what we would need for our two-bedroom condo in Jacksonville and put the rest of our furnishings in storage.

Managing the move's transportation logistics, Pat made the four-hour drive to Jacksonville on one day, we left my truck at the condo, drove back to Dothan in her car, and prepared to move our stuff the next day. We hired professionals to load the big U-Haul for the trek to Jacksonville. How many U-Hauls had I driven from one job location to another in 45 years? Too many to count.

When we got to Jacksonville, I hired some helpers to unload the truck and move our furniture into the condo. Later that day, after we turned in the U-Haul and walked into our new home, I softly said to Pat, "How about this, Honey? We're living at the beach." And live we did.

After I worked summer conditioning with the team from 7AM until about noon, I headed home and Pat and I had fun every day. We'd drive the pickup three blocks to the beach, hang out there for a few hours, go back to the condo and swim in our new pool for a while, get cleaned up, then go to our choice of many fine restaurants within a four-to-five-mile radius. On weekends, we could drive half an hour down to St. Augustine for the day, or go shopping at a great mall about seven miles from the condo, and then maybe take in a play in downtown Jacksonville that evening. We were having a ball while awaiting the opening of our football season.

I did have some major problems surface at work in early June. When I was hired, I was told there was "plenty of money in the football account." I was soon to regret that I hadn't remembered then the wisdom of that old saying, "Inspect what you expect." When I finally walked into the bookkeeper's office to inquire as to the amount in the account, after checking the records, she replied, "Coach, there's no money in your account. As a matter you're about $3,000 in the hole." I was shocked, and said, "This can't be right. I was told there was over $10,000 in this account." I immediately ran to the athletic director's office, burst in the door, and said, "Did you guys lie to me about the money?" The AD, who happened to be the first in my career to be female, apologized about the misunderstanding and said, "It'll be okay because you'll make your money running the concession stands during the games and on ticket sales." I was stunned. "Run the concession stand?" She replied, "We've done it that way for years."

I'm thinking, *I've done just about everything in my 45 years, including cleaning toilets, but concession stand running ain't one of them.* After days of discussion, meeting with the AD and the former coach, it looked like the concession stand deal was our only option. I thought, *I can't coach a game and run a concession stand at the same time. I'm good, but I'm not Houdini!* The next day I told Pat that I was going to need her to help coordinate the concession stand during the games. Real quick I found out this didn't go over too well. Apparently she wasn't Houdini either. She said, "I can't watch you coach and sell hot dogs at the same time."

I had to find a solution. I spent the next couple of days working overtime on this problem, calling all my old contacts for advice. I talked with an assistant coach from Bethune Cookman College in Daytona Beach who was a Terry Parker graduate. He suggested I call a guy from New York City by the name of Rick Allen who owned a very successful security business there, and had been a renowned professional wrestler known by the name of Sunny Beach. He, too, was a Terry Parker graduate.

When I called Rick, AKA Sunny, he said he was glad that Terry Parker had hired a State Championship coach and asked what he could do for me. I told him about our money dilemma, and he promised to get back to me soon. About a week later, Sunny called and said he was going to run a golf tournament for us in Jacksonville and would pull together lots of the high school alumni from the 1980s, his heyday.

Several weeks later, he called and told me that he'd established a registered non-profit named the Terry Parker Alumni Fund and that the golf tournament would be held at a local country club on a Saturday in the second week of August. He asked me to specify some of our program's most pressing needs, and I replied that our uniforms were outdated, we needed some new equipment such as shoulder pads, helmets, and practice gear, and also that I was at a loss as to how we were going to feed these kids their pre-game meal on Fridays. As I'd told Pat, we sure missed our Kissimmee's Team Mom Kathy Baker who organized all the pre-game and post-game meals for ten years at no expense to the school.

The day of the Terry Parker Alumni Club Golf Tournament arrived and what a great day it was! All our coaches attended and we got to meet an exceptional group of alumni who couldn't have been more enthusiastic about our efforts. Not to mention the joy of what was really for them, a reunion of all their old buddies from their high school football-playing days. At a reception the night before, Pat and I were so impressed that this school, which had certainly seen better days, had inspired such a successful group of alumni to travel from all over the country to help their alma mater. I hoped the tournament might raise as much as $5,000 to $10,000 for us, and that certainly seemed doable with this crowd.

Nearly two weeks later, on a Friday night during our first inter-squad scrimmage, many of those alumni, including former football players and former coaches, showed up to watch the scrimmage. Afterwards, Sunny asked me if several of them could speak to the team. I said sure, and told the kids to "take a knee." For 30 minutes, while hot, sweaty, and exhausted after a two-hour scrimmage, they didn't budge as several former Terry Parker players and coaches spoke with heart and passion about what the school and Parker football had meant to them. For these young players to hear and feel what these successful men communicated from their souls moved us all. I was happy that Pat was also there to witness one of the most inspirational moments of my career.

As if anything could top that, Sunny then said, "We've got something for you guys." In front of the principal, Scott Flowers, and the AD, Janet Carpenter, with the team and all us coaches looking on, Sunny unveiled a cardboard check from the Terry Parker Alumni Fund in the amount of $43,000, and quickly added, "There's more to come." WOW! After the whoops and hollers, and many hugs among us, I said, "This is the most generous thing I've ever been a part of. Thank you so much for the way you care about our team and Terry Parker High School."

———◆———

We needed new uniforms. Now we could order them. We needed pre-game meals. Now on Fridays, we could have them catered in. And then, one of the player's moms, Lisa Walker, stepped up as our Team Mom, helping to serve all the meals. Helping right beside her was my life partner, Pat, who also took the lead in planning the end-of-season banquet, relying on Lisa to help her. I was more than grateful to these fine women for their dedicated labors of love that not only benefited our program, but also made our players' lives so much better.

———

When Sunny said there was "more to come," he wasn't kidding. In addition to the $43,000 raised for us by the Terry Parker High School Alumni Fund in 2008, an additional $19,000 was forthcoming that school year, making the total over the next three years, in excess of $272,000. To this day, this alumni organization is the fundraising model for all the schools in Duval County.

———

Back in Kissimmee, my dad had been very sick for months. He had contracted Hepatitis C in some way we never determined, and was suffering all throughout the late spring and into the summer. We went to visit him many times, and it broke my heart every time. Never in my life had I seen my dad sick, and before this illness, he was a vibrant 89-year-old. The last time I saw my dad, he was under hospice care, but at home. I knew that he was near the end, and it was agonizing to see him curled up in a fetal position and barely able to speak. I thank God for my son, Gregg, his wife, Lynette, and my daughter, Jennifer, who cared for him every day. Dad was fading fast and on August 13, 2008, on what would have been my mother's 88th birthday, he went to be with the Lord.

I remember getting the news. We were on the football field in the middle of practice when I saw an assistant principal walking towards me. I knew immediately what had happened. I broke down crying in front of the kids, then walked to my truck and went home. I spent most of that night on my knees in our small guest bathroom, crying my eyes out. Now both my beloved parents were gone.

———

I don't know if Pat and I had ever experienced a more emotional month, with more highs and lows, than we did during that August. In addition, Pat had been worried about not having a job when the school year started, which would have been the first time for her in 37 years. She had previously submitted her resume and application to the Duval school district for a counselor's position, but none was available. Finally, soon after school started, she got a call from Terry Parker's principal asking her to come in for an interview. Not sure what to expect, she said she felt nervous about what Scott might have in mind since she knew it wouldn't be something in counseling. When he offered her a job in what was called the Renaissance Program, teaching kids who were behind in their credits in a multitude of subjects, she was apprehensive at first, but Scott assured her that based on her prior experience and positive work ethic, she would be up to the challenge and he hired her that day. It didn't take long for her to absolutely love this job. She relished the opportunity to help students whose self-esteem had suffered from performing poorly academically, including many football players referred to the program by John Dunn, that coach I was so grateful to have working tirelessly for me who made sure our kids remained eligible to play. He and Pat made a great team and she enjoyed getting to know the football players by helping them grapple with and overcome their difficulties, not just academically but also personally. Her efforts as a counselor to those kids—and not just as a tutor in the school subjects where they needed help—greatly contributed to the improvement of their lives, their behaviors, and their grade-point averages. She's often said that she enjoyed that position at Terry Parker as much as any other job she ever had.

———

Starting *my* job back in April, another challenge—in addition to having no coaching staff to speak of—was having no returning running backs. Right away, I spotted one of our best players, a senior, Sam Barrington, who was on our defense as a 5-Star linebacker. I noticed he was tall, strong, fast, and athletic, so I asked if he'd ever run the ball. He said he had, once or twice, back in seventh grade. But if I wanted him to, he'd give it a shot. At the end of the season, Sam had not only been a key linebacker for us, he also rushed for over 1,200 yards. Imagine what he would have done if he had been an experienced running back! We had another kid, Antonio Baker, who'd never played football, show up and try out for running back. He rushed for over 1,000 yards that season. Having two 1,000-yard rushers on the same team in the same season is very rare, for any coach.

Sam Barrington was one of the greatest kids I ever coached, not just because of his football skills, but because of his total character. He was a good student, a great leader in all areas of life, a humble young man, and a friend to all. He went on to play for USF, University of South Florida in Tampa, and started for them for three years. He was incredibly focused on his dream to play pro football, and realized that dream when he was drafted in 2013, by the Green Bay Packers for a four-year multi-million dollar contract. He now proudly wears #58 as a starting linebacker for the Packers, and was nominated by the team in 2016, for the Walter Payton Man of the Year Award for his outstanding service to the community.

We had the best season Terry Parker had experienced in ten years. We upset some powerhouse teams and barely missed our goal of going to the playoffs. There were many great kids and players on that team, too numerous to mention. Many of them went on to college and earned their degrees. Our quarterback, Ellis McGhee, and one of our receivers, Paul Blair, as well as all three of our linebackers, Sam Barrington, Sed Chaney, and Mike Jeune, went to college on football scholarships and they, too, earned their degrees.

———— • ————

After the season ended, our family suffered another devastating loss. In December, just a week before Christmas, Pat's mom, Annie Ruth Parsons, who had been ill for several months, passed away. Now, having lost two of our parents within just four months of each other compounded our sorrow.

———— • ————

In January and February, our football team had some great off-season workouts. In March, during spring break, Pat and I took a week-long cruise to St.

Thomas, Virgin Islands. I told her that I felt so great I thought I could coach until I was 70.

A week after we returned home from the cruise, we received a shocking letter from Duval County Schools. The letter stated that due to severe budget restraints as a result of Florida's economic downturn, the contracts for all teachers who had previously retired from teaching in Florida and who had since been rehired, would not be renewed for the next school year. Pat and I both had retired from Florida teaching two years before we came to Jacksonville, after we'd left Kissimmee and moved to Dothan. At the time, Florida's long-standing policy was to rehire a retired teacher who wanted to keep working. So we moved to Jacksonville to work under this policy. As the news of this sudden change spread, there was a groundswell of support for us. Over 1,500 kids signed a petition and sent it to the County school board in support of what we both had done for Terry Parker. The Alumni contacted school board members on our behalf, stating how wrongfully this was being handled. TV stations called and asked me to do news interviews. The end result of all this, as stated by the school superintendent, "You can come back and coach at Terry Parker, but we can't pay you." I relayed this message to one of the TV interviewers, and then rhetorically asked the news reporter, "Would *you* work for no pay?" Of course his answer was predictable. As much as we loved our jobs, we just couldn't see at our ages, 67 and 64 respectively, going to work every day for no salary. Plus, it was a matter of pride. Pat and I were heartbroken, but soon we would be unemployed.

Coaching Point: **As the legendary actress, comedienne, and screenwriter, Mae West, said during her long and illustrious career, "Money is applause." When you're not getting applause, maybe it's time to leave the stage.**

———

After getting the news in mid-March that my contract would expire at the end of June, I applied for several school jobs around Florida, but each time, was met with the same response: "We'd love to hire you, but just like in Jacksonville, our budget won't let us hire any previously retired teachers."

One day in early May, 2009, I came home and told Pat, "It's over. I'm done looking for jobs for the rest of my life. I'm finished." After 46 years of blood, sweat, and tears, I knew that at age 67, my career was over and I felt at peace.

Pat and I talked for a long time about where we would live now. We both loved Jacksonville and especially the condo where we lived in Jacksonville Beach, our favorite of all the places we'd ever lived. But we both decided that since the beach was made up of lots of young single people with skateboards or bicycles, and young couples with kids of their own, we wondered if we would fit into this environment over the long haul.

Because I had moved all over the country working 11 jobs in seven different states, I had no hometown I called my own. Pat and I finally decided that since we already owned a nice home in Dothan, Alabama, we would just move back there and see what happened. Dothan has been home ever since, but who knows? If someone were to call and offer this now 73-year-old one more coaching job in a warm climate, I'd probably say, "Let's get packing and call U-Haul." But the phone hasn't rung yet, and quite frankly, neither one of us has any regrets about that.

———————

With school out and summer beginning, we were in no hurry to get back to Dothan. We decided to stay in our condo for another three months so that we could just get up, go to the beach, lie around the pool, go to movies, go out to eat, take some trips, and do whatever we wanted, with no worries. And that's exactly what we did.

In mid-August, before returning to Dothan in September, we decided to take a trip to Key West for a week because we'd never been. A couple of days after we got there, we were out walking, when my cell phone rang. It was a sports reporter from the *Orlando Sentinel*, wanting to do a story about how I was adjusting to not being on the football field for the first time in 46 years. He said, "Today is the first day of fall football practice and it's 96 degrees here in Orlando. What are *you* doing right now?"

I replied, "Well, I'm in Key West with my wife, Pat. We're walking down Duval Street, and I have on shorts and flip flops and I'm drinking a Budweiser." He replied, "Well, Coach, I guess you're doing just fine."

Coaching Point: **When your career is finally over, no reason not to just kick back and enjoy life. After all, it was a helluva ride!**

Epilogue

For 46 years, my passion, even my obsession, was coaching football. As a matter of fact, football also became my god, so to speak.

It's not like I wasn't raised by wonderful parents who instilled in their son from the day he was born their love of God and Jesus Christ. Walter and Ruby Scible made sure that church and Sunday school were a prominent part of my upbringing. But somewhere along the way, I put what my mom and dad had taught me on the backburner, although deep down I knew that I should have been praying daily and taking my family to church every Sunday. I still believed in God and Jesus Christ, but for years, I used the excuse of my coaching job to keep me from practicing my faith.

That changed in January, 2015, after I had eye surgery. During my brief recovery, I could not read or watch TV, and I think maybe God used that opportunity to speak to me. That's when I began listening to hours and hours of audio tapes by the famous pastor, Andy Stanley. His teachings filled a void that I realized had been in my life for decades. With that awakening, I rededicated my life to Jesus Christ.

I think Mom and Dad would be proud.

I know that I am eternally grateful.

Acknowledgements

s of 2016, my wife Pat and I have been married for 31 years. She's lived through most of the stories in my football coaching career, and she's heard about the good and bad times before 1985, when we married. Over the years, she asked me many times, "When are you going to write a book?" And my answer was always the same: "Never!"

In November of 2014, a friend of mine, Ross Callen, was writing a blog, and asked me to contribute some stories from my coaching career—sort of like a short memoir. For a couple of days, I went at it, and when Pat saw what I was doing, she said, "Well, if you're going to do that, you might as well write your book." The next morning, when she woke up, I said, "Guess what? I started the book. I've been writing for three hours."

For the next three-and-a-half months, I wrote incessantly—up to seven hours a day, seven days a week. I don't know how or why all the events of my 46-year career just flowed from my brain to the paper, but I have to thank Pat for loving me and for pushing me to start this labor of love.

———

After the intensity of writing that first draft, I was very fortunate to discover a professional editor who happened to live right here in Dothan, Alabama. Although we'd never met her, Pat and I felt we already knew Amanda Arnold. We'd enjoyed watching her on Houston television when she was a popular prime-time news anchor there, and it's one of life's great coincidences that Amanda has been the guiding light for bringing this project to fruition. I can never thank her enough for all the work she has done to help this old football coach actually write a book. I wrote the skeleton—the bones of the book, but it was Amanda who put meat on the bones with her unique combination of curiosity, attention to detail, and unfailing vision of the big picture. Pat, Amanda, and I spent several hours during each of many weeks for over a year, improving what I had written in those three-and-a-half months. Much love to Amanda and Pat.

———

Lastly, to all the players and coaches I have known and loved since 1963: Thank you for the opportunity to have been part of your life. Without you, I wouldn't have had the privilege to pursue my life's calling as a coach and to have learned so much from you.

Love you all and God Bless,

Coach Jim Scible

45123402R00163

Made in the USA
San Bernardino, CA
01 February 2017